Best Wishes
from

Peter Hayward.

For the Sake of the Children

Known locations to where the Medway Towns and North Kent evacuees were sent during World War II. It should be noted that South Wales was the destination for the majority of these evacuees.

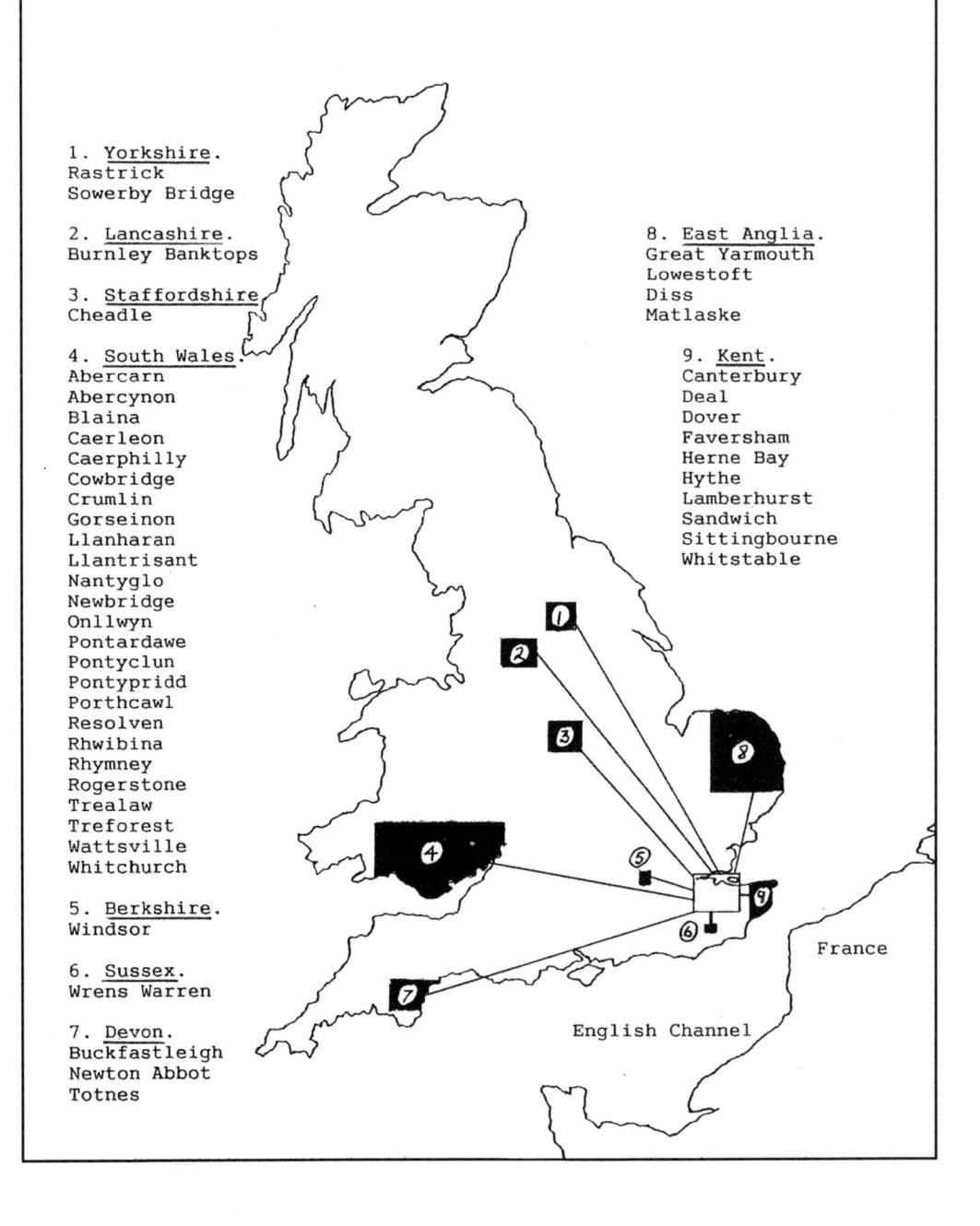

1. <u>Yorkshire</u>.
Rastrick
Sowerby Bridge

2. <u>Lancashire</u>.
Burnley Banktops

3. <u>Staffordshire</u>
Cheadle

4. <u>South Wales</u>.
Abercarn
Abercynon
Blaina
Caerleon
Caerphilly
Cowbridge
Crumlin
Gorseinon
Llanharan
Llantrisant
Nantyglo
Newbridge
Onllwyn
Pontardawe
Pontyclun
Pontypridd
Porthcawl
Resolven
Rhwibina
Rhymney
Rogerstone
Trealaw
Treforest
Wattsville
Whitchurch

5. <u>Berkshire</u>.
Windsor

6. <u>Sussex</u>.
Wrens Warren

7. <u>Devon</u>.
Buckfastleigh
Newton Abbot
Totnes

8. <u>East Anglia</u>.
Great Yarmouth
Lowestoft
Diss
Matlaske

9. <u>Kent</u>.
Canterbury
Deal
Dover
Faversham
Herne Bay
Hythe
Lamberhurst
Sandwich
Sittingbourne
Whitstable

France

English Channel

For the Sake of the Children

The story of the evacuation of school children
from the Medway towns and North-West Kent
during World War II

Compiled by Peter Hayward

Buckland Publications Ltd
Barwick Road
Dover CT17 0LG

This book is dedicated to my Children:

Elizabeth, Daniel,

Kingsley and Edward

This book is a companion volume to
Children into Exile – the story of the evacuation
of children from Hellfire Corner
in the Second World War

Copyright Peter Hayward 1999

Published in 1999 by Buckland Publications Ltd
Barwick Road, Dover, Kent CT17 0LG

ISBN 0 7212 0976 9

Printed in England by Buckland Press Ltd, Barwick Road, Dover CT17 0LG

CONTENTS

		Page
Introduction		9
Chapter		
1	The Preparation	11
2	Into Exile – But to Where?	22
3	Problems still remaining in the Evacuated Area	63
4	On the Move again – This time to South Wales	73
5	More Memories of Wales – The good and the bad	121
6	Private Evacuation	162
7	Gravesend to Where?	178
8	The National Camps Corporation	195
9	1944 Evacuation	200
10	The Schools' Perspective	213
11	Epilogue	231
	Acknowledgments	238
	Personal Name Index	240

Young Snodland children, complete with gas masks and labels, leave on their 'great adventure' in 1939
(Photo by courtesy of the Kent Messenger Group)

ILLUSTRATIONS

Map showing where Medway children were evacuated	Frontispiece
Young Snodland children	6
'Holcombe' (Chatham Grammar School for Boys)	10
Government leaflet – 'Evacuation Why and How'	11
Civil Defence poster	13
Government registration card	14
Evacuees wave goodbye	15
Chatham Town Hall in 1939	16
Byron Road Primary School	17
London evacuees in Maidstone	18
London evacuees arriving in Maidstone	19
Evacuation poster	20
Medway children leaving Gillingham Station	21
Winifred Bassett, 1939	27
Evacuees greetings postcard	29
'Maths' School boys leaving by train	32
Ordnance Road School children leaving	34
Chatham County School girls arriving in Faversham in 1939	42 and 43
Frank Turner's evacuation label	50
Special evacuee rail ticket from Rochester	51
The Queen's message	54
King's School boys at Scotney Castle and Bayham Abbey	57
Medway Education Board letter re Fred Silver	62
An Anderson shelter arrives in pieces	65
Mayor's letter concerning air-raid shelters	66
Balmoral Road, Gillingham	72
Calvary Chapel, Rhymney (The Tin Chapel)	76
Evacuee card	78
Children of St Michael's School Chatham	79
Roy and Derek Utteridge with foster sister	80
Don Phillips' class at Abercarn	82
Jack and Don Phillips with their foster father	83
Don Phillips' letter home	84
Don and Jack Phillips and others	85
Christmas greetings telegram	86
Don Phillips outside his old school	87
Red Cross sale card	88
Chatham children at Cardiff	90
Jack and Don Phillips on Mount Rhyswg	91
Leaflet explaining danger of invasion	94
Rochester Grammar School prefects	100

Chatham County School girls at Porthcawl	103
Short's flying boats on the Medway	104
'Spirit of Britain' postcard	108
Letter from Winnie Bassett's foster father	110
Contribution card	111
Warship Week programme	115
The Pavilion, Porthcawl	118
Roy Godden with his foster parents	120
Evacuees leaving by train, June 1940	124
Rochester Technical School in Caerphilly	135
Pupils of Holcombe on top of Pen-y-fan and a Chatham Grammar School reunion 1998	136
Village school at Ynysmeardy	139
Sheila Rusted with her foster father, Mr Smith	141 and 144
Sheila Rusted at Abercynon with local residents and evacuees	142 and 143
KCC contributions letter to Mr T. W. Shilling	146
Rosemary Macey and evacuees at Wattsville	147
Rosemary and Brian Macey with foster parents	148
Shirley and Patricia Nokes with their father	161
Hitler's 'last appeal to reason'	167
Joyce and Mildred Hallums with others	168
Letter from Miss Gruer of 10th November 1941	169
Joyce and Mildred Hallums with Jill Heaver	170
Christmas 1943 grocery bill	171
An example of 'welfare' correspondence	174
Joyce and Mildred Hallums with mother, 1944	175
Sketch of the *Medway Queen*	177
Gravesend children aboard the *Golden Eagle*	179
The *Medway Queen*	180
The *Golden Eagle*	181
The courtyard of Dartington Hall	188
The boot mending class at Dartington Hall	190
Evacuees at Wrens Warren Camp during the war	194
An extract from the brochure for Wrens Warren Camp	196
The woodwork hut at Wrens Warren Camp	197
Boot repairing at Wrens Warren Camp	198
Christmas party at Wrens Warren Camp, 1940	199
Diagram of a German 'Doodlebug'	210
Drawing by Ione Bates of 'Evacuation'	214
Chatham Grammar School for Girls, 1998	215
Cover of 'Maths' School magazine, 1940	221
Rochester Maths School boys at Pontypridd	224
Newspaper headlines for 8th May 1945	231
A street party in Chatham	232
Medway map showing where bombs and doodlebugs fell during the war	237
The King's message	239

INTRODUCTION

BY THE TIME WAR AGAINST GERMANY was declared on the 3rd September, 1939, the Government Evacuation Scheme was already into its third day. Almost 1,500,000 people had been evacuated from city centres and areas of special importance, such as the Medway towns, to reception areas of supposed safety.

The Government Evacuation Scheme was born out of the dread of immediate and widespread bombing of cities and towns once war became a reality. Of the 1,500,000 people evacuated during these first three days, 800,000 were unaccompanied school children and included those from in and around the Medway towns.

These children had been rehearsing at school the evacuation scenario until the time came when these rehearsals became the real thing and the children left as school units to unknown destinations.

Little thought can have been given by the authorities to the areas where some of these children were initially sent, because it soon became apparent that some of the first designated destinations proved unsuitable and, eventually, quite unsafe!

This book follows the journeys of these children into exile, firstly to other parts of Kent and then to locations much further afield in South Wales. It also includes some accounts of the school children from Gravesend and other areas surrounding the Medway Towns. There are small sections on the schools' perspective and on the little known National Camps Corporation. The bulk of the book consists of the personal accounts of evacuation from the evacuees themselves. It illustrates the disintegration of family life, the culture shocks and, in some instances, reasons why families left their home towns never to return.

But before we embark on our journey of evacuation, it is interesting to note the following article, written by Mr W. T. Killen, who was a teacher at Holcombe Technical School, Chatham, for 59 years. The article gives a clear insight into life in Germany in 1937, just two years before the outbreak of war:

In 1937 boys of Holcombe Technical School [now Chatham Grammar School for Boys] went on a school exchange to Bremen in North Germany. They sailed on the SS *Bremen* and were highly amused to learn that the captain's name was Ziegenbein (Goat's leg)!

For the teachers that time in Germany was a chilling revelation of what Nazidom really meant. People were terrified of making any political transgression. When we wished to discuss politics householders would talk in low tones and turn up the radio in case they were being bugged by neighbours or, taking us outside, they would choose a lonely place such as the local cemetery.

At one meal time I mentioned having seen some Storm Troopers rattling collection-boxes for the 'Help the Poor Fund'. The servant remarked with a smile, 'I wonder how much they put in their own pockets?' The householder, livid with rage, jumped up, bashed the table and shouted, 'You should not say such a thing!'

Surprised by his outburst, I remarked that obviously she was only joking. He glowered saying, 'Don't you realise that if my children had heard her saying that, and reported me, I would be gaoled?'

One morning, when I entered a class-room to take a lesson in English, the boys all stood rigidly to attention, gave the Hitler salute, and shouted, 'Heil Hitler.' 'Good morning boys,' I greeted them. There was dead silence. Then the captain said, 'In Germany we say "Heil Hitler."' I smiled and explained, 'I have come to teach you English, and some German. Now, in England we say, "Good morning boys," not "Heil Chamberlain." So you see we are exchanging our national customs.'

The old part of 'Holcombe', now the Chatham Grammar School for Boys (photo by the author in 1998)

After the lesson the headmaster, who was an ardent Nazi and a member of the 'Partei', sent for me and said he had received a complaint. Fortunately he had a good sense of humour so I was not reproved.

Sitting in on a lesson, I was embarrassed when the teacher stood two Jewish boys in front of the class and pointed out their racial characteristics: hooked noses, black hair and sallow skin, so different from the Aryan Germans!

Attending an art class, I was surprised to see various types of planes suspended from the ceiling. The lesson began with the teacher asking pupils to give details of the planes, such as their size, speed, bomb-load, etc. Then the art lesson followed, the lads being told to draw a picture of a bombing raid on an enemy town!

On a visit to Heligoland we were under constant surveillance by binocular-carrying guards. One stopped us and insisted that one of the lads kept his Brownie camera buttoned up under his macintosh. Later I heard this lad muttering numbers. When asked why, he explained that he was counting the steps between the gun emplacements, then writing them down.

On our return from Nazi Germany, as our ship approached the landing stage, we had seen a policeman slowly pacing the quay. It was a most reassuring sight.

Chapter One

THE PREPARATION

As the likelihood of another war with Germany grew in the 1930s the subject of civilian evacuation became an important topic and was discussed in the House of Commons. By the end of 1938, the responsibility for overseeing evacuation in the event of war was placed with the Ministry of Health under the direction of Sir John Anderson. Britain was then divided into three distinct zones – Evacuation (those areas considered to be the most vulnerable in the event of attack), Reception (those areas considered safe enough to receive evacuees), and Neutral (areas where no movement of civilians, either in or out, was considered necessary).

Because of the presence of Chatham Naval Dockyard and of the many other military installations in the immediate vicinity, the Medway Towns area was, in 1939, designated an evacuation zone. The following long range plan issued by Southern Railway gives numbers of Medway evacuees destined for other parts of Kent:

The government issued a range of public information leaflets leading up to and during the course of the war. Leaflet No. 3, issued in July 1939, dealt with evacuation.

EVACUATION WHY AND HOW?

PUBLIC INFORMATION LEAFLET   NO. 3

Read this and keep it carefully. **You may need it.**

Issued from the Lord Privy Seal's Office July, 1939

Evacuation – Long Range Plan – 1939 – Medway Towns

2nd July 1939 – Medway Evacuation (understood to take place on two days)

Railhead provisionally fixed   Canterbury East
  Numbers to be detrained   9,000
  Nos. allocated to District   Canterbury C B   2,500
                                     Bridge-Blean R D   3,500
                                     Elham R D   3,000

Railhead provisionally fixed   Dover Priory
  Number to be detrained   2,000
  Nos. allocated to District   Dover R D   2,000

Railhead provisionally fixed   Deal
  Number to be detrained   1,300
  Nos. allocated to District   Deal Borough   1,300

Railhead provisionally fixed   Sandwich
  Number to be detrained   5,300
  Nos. allocated to District   Sandwich Borough   1,300
                                     Eastry R D   4,000

Medway evacuation to take effect on and from 2nd July 1939.

Issued by: Southern Railway, Traffic Manager's Office, Operating Department, Waterloo Station, 26th June 1939. [In the event, of course, evacuation did not start until 1st September 1939.]

As local authorities drew up plans in mid-1939 for the possibility of evacuating school children should war become a reality, they found themselves faced with various problems from the parents themselves. The following article which appeared in the Chatham, Rochester and Gillingham News *on 18th July, 1939, highlighted the situation:*

GILLINGHAM'S EVACUATION SCHEME
Mayor appeals at Council Meeting for registration of parents and children.

Difficulties with regard to completing arrangements for the Town, in connection with the Government's evacuation scheme, were emphasised by the Mayor of Gillingham (Councillor I. J. Newnham) at a public meeting of Gillingham Town Council, at Gillingham Municipal Buildings, on Tuesday.

Arrangements as to the evacuation of school children were well in hand, but the attitude adopted by mothers with children in relation to evacuation, was one of apathy, the Mayor stated.

The Mayor attended, in company with the Deputy Town Clerk, a conference of local authorities at Tunbridge Wells on Wednesday in last week, which was addressed by Mr Walter Elliot, the Minister of Health. After the address, questions were invited, and it was apparent to him from those questions that the Reception Officers in the areas to which the mothers with younger children were to be evacuated were experiencing great difficulty in endeavouring to arrange billets. That was due to the fact that the Officers in the evacuating areas could not supply the particulars of the persons to be evacuated, because the persons concerned had given no indication as to their intentions with regard to evacuation.

In spite of the issue of circulars, advertisements in the local Press and public notices, and assistance given by the school teachers, who attended at the elementary schools on certain evenings during May last to register the names of persons who desired to be evacuated, only 103 mothers, 143 children of pre-school age, 12 expectant mothers, and 7 blind and 10 crippled had registered their names.

This Civil Defence poster reflects just one aspect of work that women were called upon to do during the war

That did not by any means represent the picture which would present itself if war, by any chance, broke out. The Government estimated that a very much larger percentage of the population would want to leave Gillingham if and when the need arose.

An Entirely Voluntary Scheme

The Mayor emphasised that he would like to make it quite clear that the evacuation scheme was an entirely voluntary one, and no compulsion in any form would be used. He said he would earnestly appeal, however, to all those classes of persons to whom the scheme applied to consider very carefully whether, in the event of an emergency, they would desire to evacuate from Gillingham. If so, they must register their names at once at the Municipal Buildings, either with the Deputy Town Clerk or the Education Secretary. By doing so they would be assisting both the Evacuation Officer and the Reception Officer to provide the necessary billets, and at the same time ensuring that proper accommodation would be provided for them in the area to which they would be transported.

He sincerely hoped that no emergency involving evacuation would occur, but they had to prepare to meet such an eventuality, and he wanted the public of Gillingham to respond to his appeal. Now was the time to register, and he wanted all mothers with younger children, expectant mothers and blind and crippled people, who wanted to be evacuated in the event of hostilities, to do so immediately.

Councillor Tye said that with regard to the statement made by the Mayor, he would like to point out that observations had reached him that mothers did not desire to be parted from their children. They had told him that they would much rather they and their families were killed altogether, rather than that the children should be separated from their parents and perhaps find themselves orphaned in another part of the country.

* * *

As September 1939 approached and the international situation rapidly deteriorated we see a notable change in the attitudes of parents. The following article appeared in the Chatham, Rochester and Gillingham News on 1st September, 1939:

THE WORLD CRISIS.
Children In A Danger Area.
Rehearsal of Evacuation Carried Out in Medway Towns' Schools.
Parents to play their part.

Rochester, Chatham and Gillingham were among the forty evacuating areas of Great Britain which carried out school evacuation rehearsals on Monday.

	E.D. LETTER CODE	SCHEDULE No.

To M ....
Parent or Guardian of

Child's Full Name *Frank George Victor Turner*

Parents will want to be able to keep in touch with their children if evacuation has to take place. This will normally be possible through the post; but it is hoped that children and their parents will always be able to be traced, wherever they may be, if this card is used.

WHAT YOU ARE ASKED TO DO

(i) Keep the card carefully; (ii) hand it to the enumerator who will visit the house where you are living when National Registration takes place; (iii) Write on it, when you hand it to him, your name, the address, and the name and address of a near relative or friend.

Name of Parent or ~~Guardian~~ } *George Ernest Turner*

Address *43 Edinburgh Rd Luton Chatham Kent*

Name of Near Relative or ~~Friend~~ } *W. Glover*

Address *13 Edinburgh Rd Luton Chatham Kent*

M40206 8/39 702

A good example of the type of registration card used for school children during the evacuation period. The front of the card was rubberstamped with the name of the school, 'official paid' postmark and addressed to the Town Clerk's Department

Evacuees wave goodbye
(Photo by courtesy of Imperial War Museum, London)

At the end of last week elementary school teachers were recalled from their holidays, and at the request of the Board of Education schools in the evacuating areas were re-opened.

The object of the exercise was to make certain that children and parents knew what would be expected of them in the event of the international position taking a turn for the worse.

Musters as large as possible were held in the Medway towns, some children away on holiday not being brought home in time for the exercise.

The children carried all necessary changes of clothing and other emergency kit, including their gas masks. They were not obliged to take food.

If the children are evacuated, the Government will pay a 10s. 6d. billeting allowance per week for each single child, and 8s. 6d. per child where more than one are billeted. This allowance will probably be obtainable by householders from the post office.

At Rochester.

The whole of the school evacuation arrangements at Rochester are directed by the City's Education Committee, following requests from the technical and secondary schools for the adoption of a uniform procedure.

The elementary schools of the City were re-opened on Monday morning and are now in session as during normal term time; the remaining fortnight's holiday has, in fact, been cancelled and all children should return to school as early as possible. If the crisis tension eases before September 11th, the date on which term was to have recommenced, it is likely that the holiday will be resumed. All the while there is a possibility of evacuation becoming necessary, however, the schools will be kept open.

As far as keeping the scholars at school is concerned, varying arrangements are being adopted by the secondary and technical schools.

All schools carried out full evacuation rehearsals on Monday morning, and in every instant it was confined to the school premises. Elementary schools mustered an average of 20 per cent of the total complement of scholars, and the authorities were well satisfied at the manner in which they were dealt with.

About two hundred scholars assembled at the Rochester Technical School, at Eastgate, at 9am, representing almost the whole of those resident in the Medway Towns. Scholars from Faversham and other outlying parts were, for the most part, unable to attend.

A full-dress parade took place on the school premises, the pupils being arranged in parties corresponding to the capacity of railway carriages, and a master took charge of each. The full complement of the staff was present and successfully superintended the exercise.

At the conclusion of the rehearsal, the pupils did not return to their homes, but remained on the premises – where they lunched – until the end of the normal school hours.

They will continue to attend school until the beginning of the autumn term, or alternatively until evacuation becomes imperative. An attractive schedule is being arranged for them, including games, lectures and discussions, the programme in respect of each group being arranged under the supervision of the master who would be in control in the event of evacuation.

Chatham Town Hall in 1939

At Chatham.

At Chatham the evacuation rehearsal was taken one step further, the children marching school by school to the station yard to catch imaginary trains to their various reception centres.

In an actual emergency, evacuation would begin in the early morning and continue on until later in the afternoon, the schools in groups of three assembling two hours before the time to catch their appointed train.

For the purposes of the rehearsal an imaginary timetable was set up with 'trains' leaving Chatham station every quarter of an hour from 11am to 12.30pm. The schools assembled about 9am when inspections of kit were carried out by the teachers and each child issued with a label with its name and school number and a card with the school number and the child's group number in the school.

Promptly at the time assigned, schools set off for the station in procession, each led by a scholar carrying a banner bearing the name and number of the school. Such was the effectiveness and completeness of the rehearsal that many residents thought that the children were actually being evacuated, as the rather pathetic lines of children, many barely more than toddlers, marched by, carrying rucksacks and gas masks.

In all about 1,300 children took part, representing about a fifth of the total for the Borough.

Mr Taylor (Chatham Education Secretary) said that, although only 20 per cent of the children had taken part, the Education Department was prepared to evacuate 100 per cent, but that, if parents did not notify the authorities beforehand, and sent their children at the last minute, the work of the evacuators would be made doubly hard and there might follow a shortage of helpers.

In the event of war, Mr Taylor concluded, parents and children under school age who wished to take part in the scheme would be evacuated on the second day, after the school children had been settled in the reception areas.

At Gillingham.

'Everything went off like clockwork – without a hitch,' said Mr Andrew Johns, Education Secretary of the Borough, when speaking to a *Chatham News* representative about Monday's evacuation rehearsal by Schools at Gillingham.

The children went to their own schools, according to a pre-arranged plan, at various times during the day, in readiness to march to Gillingham Railway Station. They were all prepared to leave for their various destinations in the reception areas by 13 trains, the first train leaving at 9am and the last at 5pm. All scholars and the teachers, and voluntary helpers in charge of them, assembled at the schools fully two hours before their trains were due to leave.

Byron Road Primary School, Gillingham Established 1898

Gas masks were inspected, and it was ascertained that the luggage each child carried, mostly in rucksacks and satchels, were securely packed so as to avoid any halts and delay en route. The children, who could be readily identified by names and numbers on lapels which they wore, walked to the railway station in groups under the watchful eye of the police and special constables under Mr F. G. Shellock, Inspector of Special Constabulary at Gillingham.

At both stations there were first-aid posts staffed by lady health visitors ready to deal with minor casualties.

About 260 scholars of the County School for Boys, Gillingham, also took part in the evacuation rehearsal, on Monday, according to schedule. This school, together with other schools in the Borough, remained open during the weekend, including Sunday, in order that parents could seek the advice of teachers in regard to evacuation matters.

*   *   *

Just one week later the rehearsals turned into reality as the Government evacuation scheme got under way and thousands of Medway children boarded trains for unknown destinations.

The following article appeared in the Chatham, Rochester & Gillingham News *on the 8th September, 1939, which gives a graphic account of the departure:*

A GOOD JOB WELL DONE.
Large numbers of schoolchildren and mothers evacuated from Medway Towns.

Nearly 6,000 children from schools in the Medway Towns, together with about 3,000 infants, mothers and blind and crippled persons left their homes on Friday and Saturday, and were evacuated to areas of safety under the Government's scheme.

At the time of the evacuation it was described as 'a purely precautionary measure'. From the events which have followed, the wisdom and foresight of the authorities has been fully realised, and hundreds of parents must be thankful that their children are evacuated.

Early on Friday morning trains began to depart for rural areas in East and South-East Kent,

Evacuees, having arrived in Maidstone, go by bus from St Michael's School to their billets in September 1939 (Photo by courtesy of the Kent Messenger Group)

and the evacuation was continued on Saturday. Other people have been leaving this week, and facilities still exist for those who wish to go elsewhere.In each town of evacuation and reception the arrangements were carried through with efficiency, and characteristic of the scenes at the stations was the cheerfulness of the children.

London evacuees arriving in Maidstone in September 1939 pictured in the Agricultural Hall – where they seemed to be roped off like cattle!

On arrival at their destination the children were marched to centres where they were allocated to their billets. From reports already received from the reception areas the evacuees show that they are settling down in their new homes and are happy and comfortable. Boys of the Rochester Mathematical School began to make themselves useful soon after their arrival by filling sandbags for the protection of the Hospital.

Almost without exception people in the reception areas are doing almost everything they can for the comfort and happiness of their visitors. Many of the temporary foster parents are providing clothes and toys for the less fortunate children. Some generous farmers in the Canterbury area have allowed the youngsters to help themselves to the fruit in their orchards where there are abundant crops.

Many kindnesses, too, were shown the children before they left, and at Borstal a group of residents made a collection of £4, which was to be spent on the children's comfort. In addition to the Government scheme carried out by local authorities, hundreds of Medway Towns people have made their own evacuation arrangements and left the district for all parts of the country.

Rochester.

Two youngsters waiting their turn to board a train during the evacuation at Rochester Station, were given helpful advice by a friendly police-sergeant.

'. . . don't forget to wash your face every morning,' he told them.

The youngsters looked glum for a moment and then one turned to the other and said with conviction, 'And don't you forget to wash behind your ears!'

This was just one of the human little scenes that characterised Rochester's evacuation. If one had not known otherwise, the whole affair might have been mistaken for a huge Sunday-school treat. None of the children were worrying. For the first part they did not realise the seriousness of the situation. To them it was an unexpected holiday, and not unwelcome freedom from school.

As they waited for their trains, they passed the time eating apples or chocolate, reading comics or eagerly discussing what it would be like at their new home.

'Coo, I hope I live in a sweet shop,' a bright little one was heard to remark.

Many children, loaded down as they were with packages, cases, gas-masks and other paraphernalia, had found it possible to take away something to amuse themselves with. One boy was carefully holding a cricket bat and another a football. A few girls carried their favourite dolls, but most had their playthings hidden away from prying eyes.

Children began leaving the station shortly after 8am, and many hundreds of them were got away safely. Schoolmasters and mistresses, the Police, and others who had volunteered their services helped to ensure that all arrangements went off smoothly.

Parents' response to the evacuation scheme was not so satisfactory as was hoped, however, and there was only about 50 per cent of the number of boys and girls expected to turn up.

On the day, the number of children, teachers and adults evacuated was 2,461, not including those at the King's School, who made their own arrangements. The blind and crippled persons, mothers and children under school age, and expectant mothers went on Saturday, numbering 688. Others went on Sunday and Monday, bringing the total evacuees up to 3,260.

Chatham.

Starting early in the morning on Friday, over 2,000 children, teachers and helpers were evacuated from Chatham into their prepared reception areas. Such was the value of the previous rehearsal that the evacuation proceeded 'swimmingly', to quote one official.

One of the boys summed up the attitude of most of the children when he said in a secretive whisper: '. . . we'll have some fun – mother isn't coming and teacher'll be too busy to notice us. I hope mum and dad will be all right,' he added thoughtfully. In all 1,827 children were evacuated to the Sittingbourne, Faversham and Swale Rural areas, together with 184 teachers and 68 voluntary helpers, some of them mothers.

The first train left Chatham Station at

EVACUATION
OF
WOMEN AND CHILDREN
FROM LONDON, Etc.

FRIDAY, 1st SEPTEMBER.

Up and Down business trains as usual, with few exceptions.

Main Line and Suburban services will be curtailed while evacuation is in progress during the day.

SATURDAY & SUNDAY, SEPTEMBER 2nd & 3rd.

The train service will be exactly the same as on Friday.

Remember that there will be very few Down Mid-day business trains on Saturday.

SOUTHERN RAILWAY

An evacuation poster issued by Southern Railway just two days before the outbreak of war about 8am and seven hours later the last train steamed out. On Saturday the process was repeated when nearly 500 mothers, children under school-age, expectant mothers and a few school children were evacuated to the same areas. Again evacuation was expeditiously completed. Blind and crippled people of the town were evacuated by motor-coaches to places of safety.

Gillingham.

'Everything went off quite smoothly and without any trouble whatever,' said Mr Andrew Johns, the Gillingham Education Secretary, when speaking to our representative on the evacuation of over 2,000 school children between the age of five and fifteen years from Gillingham on Saturday. In all 2,698 children left Gillingham Station, representing about a third of the total for the Borough. The first train left soon after 9am, and parties of children left approximately twice every hour until 5pm.

The boys' and girls' departments of Barnsole Road School were the first party to leave, and as early as 7am the children started to assemble. The kiddies, some little more than toddlers, provided studies of both humour and pathos as they marched to the station, laden with packages and bundles of a vast number of shapes and sizes.

The whole evacuation, however, was carried out in a light-hearted manner of an outing, and the children appeared to welcome the evacuation as a holiday, hardly realising the significance of it all.

Other schools evacuated were Woodlands, Napier Road, Barnsole Infants, St Aloysius Roman Catholic, Richmond Road, Byron Road, James Street, St Mark's Girls, Brompton Church of England, Arden Street, College of Commerce, Richmond Road (Girls' and Infants'), Skinner Street, St Mary's Roman Catholic School and the Garrison School. The children have gone to the Canterbury, Herne Bay, Sandwich, Deal and Dover Priory areas.

Two trains from Rainham evacuated the pupils of Rainham Senior, Junior and Infants' School. About 185 scholars left on the first train at nine o'clock, and a party of 72 boys and girls followed on a later train. On Saturday over a thousand mothers with children under school age and expectant mothers were evacuated. The Town Clerk of Gillingham (Mr Robert Booth) was in charge of the evacuation, and Mr Baldock and Mr Smith were at the station.

Medway children being evacuated from Gillingham Railway Station (Photo by courtesy of the Kent Messenger Group)

Chapter Two

INTO EXILE – BUT TO WHERE?

MEDWAY CHILDREN WERE UNIQUE *in that most of them were evacuated twice under the Government Evacuation Scheme. Some were even evacuated a third time as late as 1944. The first evacuation, to other locations in Kent, seems, in retrospect, to have been ill-conceived and badly thought out. Here we have comments from some of those evacuees who took part in the first evacuation with some supporting newspaper articles. The first article from the* Chatham, Rochester & Gillingham News *of 8th September 1939 recognises the heavy responsibilities the teachers undertook during the whole evacuation process:*

THANKS TO TEACHERS

W. Rolfe Nottidge, Chairman of the Kent Education Committee, has expressed his Committee's thanks to the teachers for their ready response to the demands made on their time, energy and patience during the past critical period. He writes:

'Most teachers have had their holidays interrupted, some having been recalled from a distance, so that they can report daily in anticipation of a state of emergency. Those in evacuation areas have particularly heavy duties to face. Everywhere these requirements are being met with quiet assurance. The President of the Board of Education has expressed his keen appreciation of the spirit of help and service shown by teachers and I agree with him that it augurs well for the successful carrying out of the actual process of evacuation.

'The brunt of the work must now fall upon those in the reception areas. I am confident that all engaged in education will accept new responsibilities with cheerfulness and courage, and that the evacuated population will find everywhere a cordial welcome. I feel confident that we can succeed in keeping the children happy.'

* * *

Joan Quarrington *(now Mrs Poynter) shares her memories of those early days:*

When Hitler began his stranglehold on Europe in the 1930s, plans for the evacuation of children from densely populated areas were discussed. The Munich crisis of 1938 brought the evacuation scheme to the forefront and parents were asked for their consent to send their children from vulnerable areas to places of safety. My father agreed and, as my older sister was still at school, it was arranged that we should travel together. However, as we all know, Neville Chamberlain, our Prime Minister, returned from a meeting with Hitler, waving a piece of paper and declaring 'peace in our time'. We all heaved sighs of relief and returned to our normal routines – and the idea of evacuation receded from our minds.

Not for long though! The summer of 1939 saw Hitler ignoring his promises and, by August of that year, the onset of war seemed inevitable, and the evacuation scheme again swung into action. Teachers and children were requested to return to school on the 1st of September. By this time my sister had left school and therefore I would be going alone.

There arose another dilemma; during the summer I had gained a scholarship to a grammar school, where I was due to start the following week. To which school should I report? After some consideration my mother decided the primary school, because I knew everyone including the teachers, and a familiar face might be more reassuring in unfamiliar surroundings.

After eating a hearty meal, I found myself standing in the playground, holding a small suitcase and gas mask, and my dress bedecked with a label announcing who I was. It was a very hot day and the walk to the station seemed endless. However, reach it we did, and after many headcounts we boarded the train. I can't remember any tearful goodbyes – I think we left our mums at the school gates!

The train started with the usual jerk and grinding sound and, when the platform slowly disappeared, the younger ones began to look glum. This was soon counterbalanced by the excitement for some children of their first train journey.

After a short while the trained pulled into a station, and we all piled out. Imagine our surprise when we discovered we were at Sittingbourne – only ten miles or so from home and familiar to many. We boarded buses and were taken to the main hall of the boys' grammar school, where we were lined up in front of a row of pleasant ladies who gave each of us a bag containing a bar of chocolate, an apple, some biscuits and, I believe, soap and a flannel. We were delighted and decided the 'evacuation' was a good thing.

We trooped back to the buses, this time accompanied by a billeting officer complete with clipboard, and headed for a small village. When we got there we formed a 'crocodile' and walked behind the 'clip board' man, pausing now and then to deposit a child or two in a house. We came into Coldharbour Lane and halted while our guide carefully studied his list and then said to my partner and myself, 'You two will do, you are two strapping girls who should be able to cope with four fierce dogs!' On saying this, he knocked on the door and pushed us inside. I stood with my back to the door, petrified. A nasty incident a few years previously had left me with a deep distrust of our canine friends. The barks and growls coming from the rear of the house did nothing to change my mind. The barks however, were definitely worse than the bites and the dogs proved friendly, and did much to allay my fears.

After unpacking, we were soon out in the streets again finding old friends and discovering new ones. The local children were extremely welcoming and I revelled in the freedom and independence that we now enjoyed. During those days I learnt to walk on stilts and to roller skate. We were also initiated into the noble art of 'scrumping'!

Sunday, September 3rd 1939, was another glorious day and after breakfast Doris (a fellow evacuee) and I decided to explore the surrounding area and we walked to the next village. Suddenly a woman rushed up to us yelling, 'Run, kids, run. War's been declared and we shall be bombed in a few minutes!'

We obeyed and ran and ran until, on hearing a 'plane, we dived through the gate of the nearest cottage and banged on the door, pleading to be let in. A man answered our thumpings and invited us in, then he saw the state of our shoes and ordered us round to the back door, but then he said, 'There's a war on. I think we might use the front door for once!' We flew inside and came to a halt when confronted by the whole family standing around a table hovering over their open gas mask boxes. When the wife discovered we were minus ours, she sent us on our way with orders to hurry.

Hurry we did, and it was two panting, frightened girls who almost fell through the door of our foster home. We soon calmed down however, when we saw our sensible hosts conducting mundane Sunday chores – feeding and walking the dogs and cooking the Sunday dinner.

As the days shortened and golden September turned into grey October, boredom set in, relieved only by endless games of Monopoly – and one morning a fortnight attendance at a school in Sittingbourne. This still left us with plenty of time to fill and, as the feared air raids failed to materialise, I went home, at first for weekends until Christmas when I was allowed to stay for good. Others had decided on the same course, and our grammar school reopened, albeit for only part time. Five half days a week gave me a routine and a purpose, and I enjoyed this regime. I was quite prepared to continue like this for the foreseeable future but, by early summer 1940, the retreat from Dunkirk and the threat of imminent invasion made another exodus of children inevitable.

Mr E. Towlson, an ex-Chatham Grammar School boy, remembers his evacuation days. His first move was to Herne Bay and then to Faversham:

I never attended Holcombe, my only recollection is of attending a selection interview which must have been in early 1939. By September '39 with thousands of others I was evacuated to, of all places, Herne Bay. After a couple of months I joined the Chatham Grammar School which by then was established in Faversham.

I was lodged with some dozen or so other lads in Barrack House opposite the Shepherd Neame Brewery. We attended lessons in the local Grammar School as I remember.

Quite how long we stayed in Faversham I'm not sure but I do remember a very hard winter spent in that old Dickensian house.

Albert John Smoker recalls his first evacuation:

I was attending Rochester Technical School, and in August I was on holiday having completed my second year. 1938 had brought us to the brink of war over the Nazi invasion of Czechoslovakia, and now the same thing was happening as Hitler invaded Poland, and war seemed most likely. Towards the end of August wartime preparations were in full swing, including plans for evacuating school children from inner cities and large towns to safer places in the country.

As the Medway towns contained the Chatham Royal Naval Dockyard and the barracks HMS *Pembroke*, the RM Barracks, the RE School of Military Engineering and other military installations, the area was certain to be a target for German bombers. My school was therefore among those to be evacuated.

We were still on summer holiday when we were ordered to report to school with a small suitcase containing a change of clothing and night clothes, washing items, toothbrush etc., ready for evacuation. We were assembled into our classes, issued with name labels and lined up ready to be bussed to Chatham Railway Station. When we got to the station we joined hundreds of other children. Everything seemed chaotic, but eventually we boarded a train not knowing where we were going.

We travelled for about 30 minutes and then pulled into a station which proved to be the town of Sittingbourne. We all burst out laughing at this because we were only 12 miles from home! We were then given some refreshments while a group of people organised us into parties. I was taken by car, with a lad called Roy Scudder, to Glovers Crescent to live with the Hughes family.

We stayed at this address for about two months then Mrs Hughes became ill and we were moved to other homes. I went to the other side of Sittingbourne, to Barrow Grove to live with a lady and her young son. Her husband was away in the Forces.

We had no schooling to start with, but were directed to local farms to help with the harvesting such as fruit picking and hop picking. We were promised that we would be paid for our efforts, but in the event we never received a penny – a very sore point!

Every household at that time was being encouraged to have an allotment for the purpose of growing vegetables, and at the rear of the house a recreation ground was divided up into plots, one of which became ours. I well remember working hard in digging up the turf to allow for planting.

In the Spring of 1940 we were again ordered to be moved, this time a little further afield – to South Wales!

The Herne Bay Press *for 9th September, 1939, reported the arrival of evacuees from the Medway Towns:*

ARRIVAL OF EVACUEES
Children Happy On Beach

'I only wish I always lived here,' was the happy shout of one of a number of school children who had arrived at Herne Bay on Friday as evacuees from Gillingham and who were enjoying themselves on the beach on Saturday. The boy's circle of young friends all seemed of the same opinion.

It was a glorious day of 'real summer', and it was a pleasure to see these children had so quickly and happily settled down in our midst.

Three special trains had brought the children and teachers and other adult helpers to Herne Bay on Friday, and they were met at the railway station by many local helpers who had volunteered for duty in connection with the evacuation services, and marshalled to the Grand Pier Pavilion.

There was a fleet of East Kent buses and many private cars in the vicinity of the Pier entrance in readiness to convey the children to their new homes.

In the Pavilion, Mr J. W. Alexander, honorary Evacuation Organiser, was at the 'mike' and gave intructions to helpers and children.

On a series of long tables there were set out the provisions which were to be served out to the children as 48 hours' food supply - each receiving a 14 ounce tin of corned beef, tin of condensed milk, tin of dried milk, pound of biscuits, and half a pound of chocolate. Each child was given a large paper carrier, and then at various points around the tables received different articles of the allotted provisions.

For the purpose of the billeting, the children were sorted out into parties for the various districts where householders had consented to receive them, and then were marched to buses or private cars to be driven to their destinations. Many of the school children were billeted in Herne and the neighbourhood.

The evacuees on Saturday were all mothers and babies ('babies' including children under five years old). Similar procedure was followed to that in the case of the school children on the previous day, and provision for a mother, or a Medway town helper, was in the same scale as for the school children. But the provision for the babies did not include the meat ration.

Gladys Austin (now Mrs Gladys Hamer) recalls her first evacuation, to Herne Bay, in 1939:

In 1939 I was ten years old and attending St Mark's School in Gillingham. On the 1st of September, two days before war was declared, my brother Norman and I were evacuated to Herne Bay. At the same time my father was called up for the Army, leaving my mother and my baby sister Freda at home.

When we left we had to have our hands free so my Grandmother made us haversacks to carry our essentials in. We also had our gas masks, and we had labels attached to us saying who we were. When we arrived in Herne Bay we were billeted in a boarding house on the seafront named 'Docklands'. There were twenty of us evacuees there, plus two or three mothers with young babies. The mothers also helped to look after the rest of us.

It was at 'Docklands' where I learned not to take sugar in my tea! We stayed at 'Docklands' until January 1940 and then we moved to a smaller boarding house in order to make room for soldiers who had been rescued from Dunkirk.

We didn't attend a proper school while we were in Herne Bay, instead we were taught in rooms over some shops, and I am sure our education suffered because of this. Often we couldn't go to lessons at all, but we didn't run wild in the streets. We were found other things to do, such as visiting Canterbury Cathedral and other interesting places. However, in May 1940 it was decided by the authorities that we were to leave Herne Bay and go to South Wales.

Winnie Bassett (now Mrs Winnie Rolfe) was a Medway girl whose first experience of evacuation was to Sittingbourne:

We were in the process of changing schools in 1939 having passed the scholarship for the Chatham County School. Because we lived on the doorstep of our Primary School, when the time came to go, our parents decided we were better off with teachers and pupils we knew. So, at Sittingbourne we began the rounds of a few lessons half a day a fortnight with the Sittingbourne County School for Girls latest entry, in an old school by the railway station. Every time a train went by we watched the teachers' mouths moving, but no words were audible. I was living with relatives so I stayed for almost a year. My friend returned home and went to school in the Medway Towns until the second upheaval in June 1940. I returned home at the end of the Summer term. Sittingbourne had no Anderson air raid shelters at that time, so it seemed safer to be in Chatham. Later events proved the assumption was correct; the original choices of Reception areas were somewhat naive.

Winifred Bassett, aged 11 years from a photo taken in November 1939

As I told my son when he wanted to see the film *The Battle of Britain*, I had no intention of paying to see something I had watched the first time round for nothing, and with a grandstand view from the top of our shelter!

At the beginning of September 1940, my father became so worried about the situation that he persuaded my mother to make arrangements for me to join our school in Pontypridd. She was to take me and two younger girls who had passed the scholarship that summer. It was years later that I found out that my father was so convinced that the invasion was imminent that he reasoned it was the only way to get my mother to leave him to fend for himself, and get out of the danger area. It was just as well she did not know his thoughts or she would never have left him. We travelled to Wales on Friday 13th September – the day that Buckingham Palace was bombed.

Don Phillips *and his brother were another two school children destined to spend a short while in Sittingbourne:*

My brother Jack and I were evacuated to Sittingbourne on the 1st September 1939. We stayed with Mr and Mrs Fullagar at 61 Chalkwell Road. They had no children of their own and they probably found it difficult dealing with two mischievious boys. I was just seven years old and my brother was almost three years older.

We went to Sittingbourne by train, and the school we went to was somewhere near the High Street. I had just moved up into the Junior School and my teacher's name was Mr Lowden.

Our parents used to visit us at weekends and we would wait for them at the end of the road by the Coniston Hotel. If they could not make it on the Saturday they would come on Sunday. One weekend they couldn't come at all because our dad was on essential war work (laying telephone cables). Mum and Dad sent us a postcard explaining why, but it was very disappointing for us.

One incident I remember quite well was when my brother went out for a walk with his friend Brian Charlesworth. They eventually walked all the way home from

Sittingbourne to Connaught Road, Luton (Medway). Our father had to get his car out and use his valuable petrol to bring them back to Sittingbourne, which did not amuse him at all!

We only stayed in Sittingbourne until Christmas 1939; then Mum and Dad decided we should come home.

Don's older brother, **John (Jack) Phillips,** *now gives his account of their stay in Sittingbourne:*

When the war began I was still two and a half months short of my tenth birthday. Although we children were quite oblivious to what was going on in Europe in 1938 and 1939, the inevitability of war was fairly well recognised by all but the most naive optimists. Hitler's enormous war machine was many times larger than he needed to occupy a compliant Austria and conquer the ethnic German Sudetenland. Hindsight has always persuaded me that Chamberlain was not as gullible as history draws him, for he did achieve some few months of breathing space and frantic preparation by his delaying tactics at Munich.

We were virtually on a war footing long before September 1939. Ration books were printed and distributed; gas masks were manufactured in their millions; identity cards were issued. Anderson shelters were offered to all family units considered to be at risk – and indeed, two days before war was officially declared, we, the children, were already on the move.

On Friday, 1st September, in the middle of the morning, a line of Chatham & District double-decker buses was strung out in Pheasant Road, just outside the school railings. Teachers were frenziedly trying to hold groups together, class by class, against tears from the children and more tears from distracted mothers in pinafores, tormented by belated second thoughts.

Our names were written on luggage labels pinned to our coats, and we all had our boxed gas masks strung around our necks. Donald and I both had light, canvas haversacks and in addition I had a small attache case. The haversacks contained sandwiches and the attache case clothes. Donald was wearing glasses with one eye-piece papered over. (He had a lazy eye and the technique was to cover the good eye and force the lazy one to work. It was clearly effective, because after a few months he was able to do away with glasses and his eyesight was quite normal.)

We were all smartly turned out in grey suits and caps, and polished black shoes with socks pulled right up for a change. Lots of onlookers stood around, curious to see this strange exodus – including our school friends who were not being evacuated. They were in their old play clothes and I think most of them were envious of our 'big adventure'. In the preceding weeks the non-evacuees had taunted the prospective evacuees with much name-calling: 'Cowards!', 'running away', 'afraid of old Hitler', and so on. We responded of course, with taunts of our own: 'Cowards yourselves! – afraid to leave your Mummy's pinny-strings!'

But on that Friday morning there were no taunts. The teachers, harassed and worried, checked our names against lists on tally-cards as we boarded the buses, where we seemed to sit for ages. Finally we moved off, bus by bus, faces pressed against the glass, waving at our parents, and drove in convoy along the Luton Road, beneath Luton

Arches and on up to Chatham Station where a special train was waiting to take us to a place of safety – Sittingbourne!

When we arrived at Chatham Station the train was already partly filled with children from other schools, some destined for Sittingbourne, some for Faversham and some, I think, for Canterbury. The train moved out almost at once and immediately Donald and I started into our sandwiches and apples and bars of chocolate. I don't believe we stopped eating until we reached Sittingbourne. All our teachers travelled with us, even the half who would return to Luton to teach the residue who were not to be evacuated.

At Sittingbourne we were trailed into more buses and taken to a local school in Milton Regis where we met our foster parents. Ours were Mr and Mrs Fullager. The first thing I had to do when we got there was to write a letter to my parents telling of our safe arrival and giving our address.

Sittingbourne was an odd choice for a 'safe' location – a scant eight or nine miles from Chatham. It had no major industry save Bowater's Paper Mills, but it was too close for real safety, and on the direct flight path from Germany to the Medway Towns. Whoever chose Sittingbourne as a haven for evacuees clearly gave the Luftwaffe too much credit for bombing accuracy, for the first bombs to fall in Kent fell near Sittingbourne, killing a cow.

Most of my time at Milton Regis is vague and unmemorable. I cannot recall the school at all after our first arrival. I remember a derelict windmill in the fields to the west of the village, and a red-bricked walled meadow near the railway lines, where I found my first mulberry trees. What a thrill that was! No-one else would eat the luscious fruit but me. The anonymous other children backed away staring, expecting me to drop dead at any moment. The two mulberry trees were probably centuries old, and were very likely in the precincts of some ancient monastic foundation.

The weather in September and October 1939 was glorious, and at weekends I went exploring the local lanes. During that period which came to be known as the Phoney War, all the signposts were still in place. They were only removed after the debacle of Dunkirk the following summer when the fear of invasion was at its height.

One Saturday, a friend and I were wandering about the lanes near Borden,

A postcard designed specifically for parents to send to their evacuated children – in this case to Don Phillips long before another meaning for 'gay' crept in

Bredgar and Oad Street when we came across a signpost to Stockbury and Bredhurst. So we followed the finger-post and soon found ourselves crossing the Maidstone-Sittingbourne road. Stockbury church sat atop the hill, and we clambered up the hillside and found a new signpost to Bredhurst, a mere two and a half miles away. In truth it seemed much further, for there are several narrow, steep-sided valleys to negotiate, including the Queendown Warren Bank. Another hour or so later we stumbled up the village street of Bredhurst, with three and a half miles still to trudge to Luton. All we had had to eat since breakfast were apples and plums stolen from convenient orchards. We had no money for bus fares, but I knew the way to Luton from Bredhurst. I had walked the route many times before, but always with my father.

With blistered feet we tottered down to the big elm trees at Ham Lane and along the winding Capstone Road, arriving more dead than alive at the back gate as my mother was taking washing off the line in the late afternoon. We must have covered some 13 or 14 miles altogether. My mother did not know what emotion to express, but we were tired, footsore and hungry, and at least she could ensure that we didn't remain hungry. We were tucking into jelly and fruit and custard when a policeman came to the front door with Brian's father. My mother's reaction to what the policeman had to say regarding two missing children was unexpected to say the least – if not downright unseemly. She burst out laughing!

In the middle of the ensuing uproar, my father arrived home from work, oblivious of the drama that had been unfolding in the kitchen. When all had been explained to him, he was predictably more cross than anyone else, for he had to get out his car, a little Morris 8, which was kept in a lock-up garage near the Hen & Chicks public house, and use up a gallon or so of his precious petrol ration to drive the pair of us back to Sittingbourne!

Few other memories remain for me of Milton and Chalkwell Road – the air raid warning on the Sunday morning a few minutes after the formal declaration of war; the big red and green meccano set belonging to the older boy next door, but above all the glorious late summer weather. Golden, sunny, hot days with the meadow grass long and yellow; catching red- and yellow-bellied newts in an abandoned sheep-wash pit; and blue, blue skies with scarcely a cloud to be seen. If it rained at all, I didn't notice it.

We were back in Chatham by Christmas 1939.

John Clark *remembers with some detail his evacuee time in Shepherdswell near Dover:*

I remember leading the procession of evacuees, carrying a banner, from Richmond Road Elementary School to Gillingham Railway Station in September 1939. After our journey to Shepherdswell we were taken from the station to a large hall near the church. We were lined up and various villagers walked down the line choosing whom they wished to have billeted with them.

I can remember having a name and address label tied to my lapel, and being given a bag of sweets at some point. The kind people who finally picked me were a Mr and Mrs Ousley of Le Chalet, Westcourt Lane in Shepherdswell. Mr Ousley had been a purser on what was known as packet boats in those days, and Mrs Ousley had once taught English in France. There was definitely a French ambience to their home, with delicious meals, always finishing with a demi-tasse of black coffee.

Le Chalet was constructed of asbestos panelling, and inside the floors were red tile. The rooms were full of objects like ormolu clocks, large paintings of Hussars in battle situations, shark's teeth, a stuffed swordfish, a ticking grandfather clock and in the hall stood a large copper and brass model steam engine in a glass case. This was made by the Ousley's son, Jack, and is now, I understand, in Dover Museum. The Ousleys were almost self-supporting, having a quantity of chickens and growing all manner of fruit and vegetables in their huge garden which backed on to thick woods. There was a large lawn at the front, with many trees and bushes, and I have been told since that this front garden, which was in a dip, had originally been a swimming hole for the village children.

The Ousleys were very kind to me in so many ways. I still have a bound copy of Strand magazine from the First World War, given to me by Mr Ousley, which I used to spend hours poring over in his office. He taught me a smattering of French and gave me a French dictionary which I still use on occasions. He would pay me for helping him in the garden, but I must admit I couldn't wait to get out in the woods. Mr Ousley would invariably wear a collarless shirt with a front stud in it, and a black waistcoat with watch chain, but when he got dressed up he wore a stock with a stickpin and homburg hat, and looked very French with his waxed moustache.

I can remember my brother Charlie coming down to visit me at the village school during the winter of 1939/40, when the snow was thick on the ground. He had recently returned from France and was dressed in peaked cap, jodhpur-type pants and puttees and he wore a holstered revolver, which fascinated me. Charlie was not an officer at that time, but something to do with ordnance survey in the Royal Engineers.

Other memories of those days include marching with my friends along West Court Downs, with various sticks and rifles at the slope, and when a plane came over, throwing ourselves on to the side of the road and 'firing' at it in the approved fashion; a Lysander aircraft crashing just up the road from Le Chalet, near Grabham's Farm; going to a party at the local squire's house right by the railway station; and the local butcher's boy threatening me with violence if I didn't bring him some comics, which I inevitably forgot!

I stayed in Shepherdswell for about six months, and there were emotional scenes at the railway station when I left. I went back home to Gillingham when the Germans started shelling Dover and the risk of invasion seemed imminent. I kept in touch with Mr and Mrs Ousley and spent holidays with them after the war until 1947. My six months spent in Shepherdswell were a happy time for me. Living with the Ousleys gave me a certain taste for the better things in life. I did visit Le Chalet again in 1992 with my wife. It is now number 71, and the owner kindly let us look around the house and it proved a very emotional and tearful occasion for me. The widow of my old playmate from the war years and after, the late Herbert Adams, lives next door in his parents' old house. I met her and was able to find for her a picture of her husband taken by me in 1947.

I was only home in Gillingham for a short time before being evacuated again, this time to the village of Onllwyn in South Wales, but that's another story!

The following article appeared in the Chatham, Rochester and Gillingham News *for the 8th September, 1939, and gives a good indication as to how some of the school children were received when they finally arrived at their various destinations. It also gives good details of numbers and how they were distributed in and around the Canterbury and Whitstable areas:*

IN THE RECEPTION AREAS.

The evacuated school children and mothers and young children from the Medway Towns received a warm, sympathetic, and friendly welcome when they arrived at their new homes in Canterbury and the surrounding villages and in the Whitstable district. The organisation for their reception was in each case remarkably efficient.

On Friday a fleet of over 20 motor coaches was parked in the station yard ready to convey children allocated to the villages.

Punctually at 9.58am the first train steamed in, and from each compartment hands waved a greeting. Doors were quickly unlocked, and the children from Troy Town and St Peter's Infant Schools, Rochester, detrained on to the platform, and within a few minutes marshalled by their teachers, were marching in an orderly fashion into the road outside. Rations in carrier bags were issued from a long line of tables by volunteers, and with a minimum of delay the children were got into the coaches and set off for their new homes, 86 to Saltwood, 102 to Sellindge, and 40 to Elham. At the villages they were met by billeting officers, who took charge of parties, and took them to their new homes.

Boys from Rochester Mathematical School wave goodbye in September 1939 (Photo by courtesy of the Kent Messenger Group)

Fifteen minutes later the second train arrived, bearing the children from Napier Road Senior School. The same efficient process of distribution took place, and, carrying their rations, the children promptly went off to Bekesbourne (16), Bishopsbourne (15), Harbledown (23), Hollow Lane, Canterbury (67), Bridge (49), and Sturry (103).

The third train arrived at 11.30, bringing 374 pupils of the Rochester Mathematical School, University School, and St Peter's School. These were destined to find homes in the city. Cars driven by volunteers, took the children where there was any distance to be covered.

The afternoon contingents began to arrive at 3pm, the first train bringing the children of Woodlands School, who went off by coaches to Barham (72), Blean (100),

Chislet (39), Lyminge (57), and Stanford (32).

The next train brought 159 pupils from Rochester Girls' Grammar School, 20 from Borstal Infants, all of whom were distributed, in the same way as in the morning, in the City of Canterbury. The last train of the day brought 219 children from Skinner Street, St Mary's Roman Catholic, and the R.E. Garrison Schools, Gillingham. The children of the first and third schools went by coach to Littlebourne (36) and Sellindge (58), and the St Mary's children remained in Canterbury.

Cheerful And Composed.

As far as the helpers were concerned, nothing was too much for them to do. As small children trooped out of the station, some carrying luggage almost as big as themselves, they were relieved of their burdens. Everybody, with kindly words and jokes, left the children in good spirits, and the smiling faces of the kiddies was a tribute to the success of their efforts. Tribute must also be paid to the Medway teachers in charge of the parties.

A considerably less number of children arrived than was expected, only about a third being received out of the total planned for.

The Medway children arrived at Whitstable by three special trains, the total number being 652 of the 2,000 expected.

Councillor H. Collar, assisted by Mr G. W. Sheard and Mr D. Ibbotson, was in charge of the reception arrangements, assisted by teachers, S.J.A.B., Police, and Specials and a large number of volunteers.

The whole operation was directed by means of a loud speaker van. A fleet of cars, in charge of voluntary drivers, conveyed the children to reception depots at Swalecliffe School, All Saints' Hall, St Mary's, Westmeads, Oxford Street, and the Girls' Endowed Schools and the Shaftsbury Camp, Seasalter.

At the depots the children were divided into small parties, and taken to their wartime homes. Needless to add, as in Canterbury, they received kindly welcomes from the householders, by whom they will be cared for in the days to come.

Fewer Evacuees than Expected.

The second day of evacuation brought to Canterbury and Whitstable the mothers and little ones, aged, infirm, blind, and cripples. Again the numbers were considerably below expectations. The total from Gillingham, Strood, and Rochester, was just under 700. Of these, about 300 were billeted in Canterbury and the remainder distributed as follows: Bekesbourne (15), Bishopsbourne (16), Harbledown (18), Elham (22), Barham (64), Blean (37), Lyminge (27), Stanford (43), Chartham (10), Hythe (2), Bridge (22), Wickhambreaux (26), Lower Hardres (17), Sellindge (44).

All the evacuees were grateful for the kindness shown them and the excellence of the organisation. The Mayor (Councillor Mrs Williamson) was present for long periods, and provided the arrivals with tea.

The Youth Hostel has been placed at the disposal of elderly evacuees and domestic science teachers are in charge of the cooking. There is a very happy party there.

An enquiry bureau has been established at the Simon Langton Schools, and all addresses are indexed.

Sunday was spent adjusting billets, and offers to take evacuated people and children were being received all day. The demand exceeded the supply.

As the trains arrived at Canterbury East, helpers were ready to take luggage, prams – of which there were hundreds – and babies. Indeed, one of the sights of the evacuation was that of senior Langton boys acting as nursemaids. S.J.A.B. men handed round cups of tea, and, after drawing rations, those destined for the villages departed in the motor

Pupils from Ordnance Road School, Chatham, leave for the railway station in September 1939, destined for other parts of Kent
(Photo by courtesy of the Kent Messenger Group)

coaches. Those from the City were taken to the Simon Langton Schools in a fleet of private cars, and there drew rations before, in charge of billeting officers, they once more set out in cars for their billets. One of the volunteer drivers was the Bishop of Dover.

Some of the Arrivals.

Among the arrivals in Canterbury were two elderly twins, a man of 93, a woman of 94 and about fifty expectant mothers. All these, especially the last-mentioned, received special care and were taken to suitable accommodation. Unfortunately, one mother with five young children who arrived by one of the later trains, could not be found accommodation, as she declined to have the family broken up, and she and the children had to be taken back to Rochester by car.

A kindly act on the part of a Canterbury resident may be quoted as typical of many others. A billeting officer was having difficulty in securing proper quarters for an expectant mother who arrived during the afternoon. The resident, hearing of this, asked the officer to wait, went to the telephone, came back, and said, 'I have arranged accommodation for the lady. Will you take her to the . . . Nursing Home as my guest?'

At Whitstable the evacuees were also taken to the reception depots by volunteer car drivers, and then to their new homes. Blind folk were taken to Radley St Peter's, in Queen's Road, Tankerton. The helpers here were no less assiduous in their kindness and help to their emergency guests.

There arrived at Whitstable 228 mothers, children and others, but the third special train contained only five adults and five children. Again the procedure was the same as on the previous day, and the arrivals were soon happily settling down. One of the instructions on the papers given to billeting officers was 'To establish cordial relations between householders and evacuees', and right well they did they job.

The children at Whitstable came from Temple, Station Road, St Peter's, and Balfour Road Schools, and from the Cottage Homes. Many parents visited their children on Sunday in the Canterbury and Whitstable areas.

Two further small parties arrived in the Canterbury district on Monday, including a helpless cripple and four expectant mothers, and a number of secondary school children. Of these, 17, including one of the mothers, were sent to Barham, nine to Hartington, and the remainder were billeted in the City.

* * *

Another article appearing in the same copy of the newspaper gives an indication of how the Troy Town Boys' School was received in Saltwood, near Hythe:

A WONDERFUL RECEPTION.

In a letter to the Editor, Mr J. E. Marchant, an assistant master at Troy Town Boys' School, who was among those who accompanied the children, writes:

The Troy Town Boys' School evacuated last Friday is billeted in or around this beautiful village of Saltwood, three quarters of a mile from the ancient Cinque Port of Hythe.

We are a party of 74 children and 12 helpers. Our reception here was wonderful; kindness has been showered upon us. Our billets are most comfortable.

Some 15 boys are billeted at Sandling Park, which is a large mansion, and reminiscent of Cobham Hall; another 7 are together in what was formerly the manor house of the district. The others are mostly in large houses.

Twenty-five minutes quick walking is required to cover the distance between our most distant houses. In very few cases are children housed in adjoining buildings, so that in the event of aerial bombardment, we should be very safe.

Our present programme consists of walks and games. The 'Locals' have challenged us to a cricket match, which is to take place on Tuesday.

Most of us have visited Hythe, but sea-bathing is 'taboo' on account of jelly-fish and dragging under-currents. Saltwood Castle has also been visited. This is noted as the place where the Knights, who murdered Thomas à Becket, slept the night before the tragic event. On Sunday we all attended the 800 years old Saltwood Church.

Would you please convey to the parents and friends of all the children that there is no need to worry.

*   *   *

Pamela Costen (*now Mrs Chew*) *has vivid memories of September 1939:*

I well remember the week preceding the 3rd September 1939. We had had rehearsals, packing our cases and then proceeding to our school (Fort Pitt Grammar School, Chatham), so that when we were told yet again to report, we hoped it would never really happen – and yet each evening that week we had heard the telegraph boys knocking on doors all along the road, calling the men to their various services. My father's turn came on the Wednesday as we were evacuated on the Friday. He was to go into the Royal Air Force – he had been a flyer in the First World War.

My mother was left alone and I was so worried about her. My sister was five years younger than me and so my mother told me never to be parted from her. I think children grew closer to each other because of the situation. I know Jean and I never lost this feeling for each other up until she sadly died. As my father left, I heard him say to my mother, 'Get the children away from here as soon as possible,' as they expected the whole area to be laid to waste.

On that Friday we were all apprehensive and yet there was a certain amount of excitement in the air. We boarded the train at Chatham – and in no time were alighting in Sittingbourne. I suppose the idea was to spread the children out away from the naval and military establishments in the Medway Towns.

It was a warm day, we had been handed a carrier bag full of essential foodstuffs, and then began the humiliating experience of being chosen by folk who were kind enough to open their hearts and homes to us. We were billeted with a very old couple who were so friendly and warm. My mother told me I had to help them as much as possible, which of course I did. My sister was so homesick and would say, 'When are we going home to Mummy?' I just cuddled her as, of course, I wanted that too, but I had to stay strong for her sake.

We stayed with this old couple until after Christmas when Mrs Maxted fell and broke her arm. We were sad at leaving there but it had to be. Our next billet was with a young couple who had a baby. We were happy there too, but it was only to be for a short time. France had capitulated and in no time we were packing our cases once more and on a train to Wales . . .

The following poem was written by **Pamela Chew** *and describes that first day of evacuation back in September 1939:*

> A Day In My Life.
> (1st September 1939)
>
> 'Report to your schools,' the radio said
> – at the break of day we were out of bed.

Our cases packed, a hug from our Mum,
my sister and I – we just felt numb.
Away from our safe and happy life,
to an unknown place, our feelings were rife.
Our father had gone just the day before
– a memory of sobs as they kissed at the door.
Now she stood bravely, waving her hand,
our beloved mother, how could she stand
to watch all her family leave one by one,
how could she manage when we were all gone?
Up to the school at the top of the hill,
unusually quiet, a feeling of chill –
Where were we going, with whom would we live,
perhaps it's a dream and soon they would give
Reasons why we should all in the main,
return to our homes and be normal again.
To the station we walked, sisters and brothers,
'stay together' had been the request of our mothers.

On to the train, and we'd hardly sat down
when the mistress informed us 'this is the town.'
No names on the station, as you might guess,
but the place was familiar, it couldn't be less
than half an hour's journey from all we held dear
– it won't be so bad, there's no need to fear.
Whom were we fooling, not ourselves that's for sure,
just nervously hoping we'd have strength to endure.
The day was so warm, we were starting to flag,
would we walk far and carry our bag
of food we were given in order to share,
with the folk who were willing and ready to care –
for children confused and unable to see
that this new way of life was going to be –
a happy experience as well as the sad
and that life would be fuller and we would be glad
to look back with nostalgia at new found friends
– when the five years had passed and my story ends.

Pamela Chew

Pamela Austen *recalls her evacuation to Herne Bay:*

Although only five years old, I shall never forget my first year of being evacuated. My two cousins and I left Chatham railway station with our gas masks over our shoulders and a name tag on our clothes. My mother was not even there to say goodbye. She worked in Chatham Dockyard and probably couldn't get the time off.

My cousins and I wanted to be billeted together, but when we got to Herne Bay they went to one house and I went with another girl and two boys to another house. We all slept together in an attic-type room. When we got home from school we would be given a very frugal meal and then sent to our room; sometimes this would be as early as 4.30pm. We were given two chamber pots to take with us, and after a while we found out that both boys had worms, so four five-year olds would spend some evenings watching worms in a pot!

Some time later we all started scratching our heads and were told by the lady of the house that we had unwelcome visitors. In the summer holidays I caught whooping cough. The next thing I knew, my uncle, who was home on leave, took me to an aunt who had a public house just outside Chatham. I scratched my head all the way home telling my uncle it was alright, I've just got visitors! I had long curly hair at the time, most of which had to be shaved off to get rid of the head lice.

Eventually, most of the evacuees that went to Herne Bay, went on to Wales, but our mums would not let us go. I was sent back to Herne Bay when I was better, and went to a different billet. I also found out at school that the other two children we shared the first billet with had also been re-billeted. My new billet was run by two elderly spinsters who looked after me and another girl very well until the end of the war.

One incident I remember quite well is when my uncle, home on leave from the Royal Navy, came down to Herne Bay, collected his two sons and then me and took us all for a walk along the sea front. We stopped and sat on a seat. He then produced three bars of chocolate from his pocket and gave us one each. We sat there looking at the chocolate, and Uncle said, 'Eat it before it melts.'

We all said together, 'We are not allowed.' He asked us why not and we told him that the chocolate must go into the sweet tins back at the billets. We pointed out that it was not part of our sweet coupon allowance. Uncle could not persuade us to eat the chocolate so he took it back and gave it to our hosts at the billet. We were allowed one sweet or piece of chocolate before going to school, and one when we came home. It is hard to believe that three children, two six and one seven years old would refuse to eat a bar of chocolate!

My two cousins lived two doors away, and for the rest of the war they were made to wash at a table outside the backdoor, no matter what the weather was like. When one of the ladies I was with asked their host why they had to do this, she replied that it would make men out of them!

Janice Prentice was only four years old when she was first evacuated from Gillingham to Herne Bay in 1939:

Herne Bay was not successful, but 56 years on there are still a few memories. In the late summer of 1939, our two families – my mother, brother Billy, baby sister Brenda, my mother's good friend Ada Halsey with Betty and Derek were sent to Herne Bay on the Kent coast to be safe from Hitler's bombs. But I think he knew where we had gone because I have a memory of being whisked back into the bottom of Brenda's Tan Sad pram and my mother and all running up a road, the air raid siren speeding us on – back to the safety of our landlady's (Mrs Cookson) kitchen and the smell of Bovril.

We weren't in Herne Bay very long, but the photograph of us all on the beach is a very happy one, in spite of Derek throwing a stone and cutting my head! I don't remember how we travelled to and from Gillingham, but I think we had returned home by Christmas 1939.

Dorothy Shilling *(now Mrs Dorothy Lower) recalls her first evacuation – to Canterbury:*

I was due to start at Rochester Grammar School for Girls in September 1939, but at the very end of August that year we were called to school to prepare for a 'trial run' at evacuation.

On 1st September we were transported by train to Canterbury and billeted with local families. I was fortunate and was well looked after by my foster parents, Mr and Mrs Castle. In fact, I remained in contact with the family until both my foster parents passed away. The school too was very caring and our early days in Canterbury were filled with historical visits, lessons in church halls – even hop-picking somewhere up near the Kent Cricket Ground! I remember on 3rd September 1939, we met with teachers in the precincts of Canterbury Cathedral and attended morning service. It was a beautiful sunny day. During the service the air raid warning sounded and everyone filed into the Crypt where the Dean informed us that war had been declared. The 'all clear' sounded shortly afterwards and we dispersed to our foster homes. By the time I reached mine, they were busy putting up sticky paper 'criss-crosses' on the windows and fixing blackout curtains.

Very soon we were able to attend for regular lessons; the old hospital in Longport provided the accommodation, and at all times we kept our own identity, Rochester Grammar School, with our own teachers.

The winter of 1939/40 was very cold and Canterbury was snowed in for quite some time, but it was great fun trudging through the moat alongside the Dane John Park. In fact the war seemed very remote.

My mother used to come down to visit me from time to time, and there were always regular letters from her.

At Easter 1940, many of us returned home to the Medway Towns for the holidays – fortunately before the bombing of Canterbury had started. I didn't go back to Canterbury after the Easter break, but stayed at home in the Medway. By May 1940 things in France were looking bad, and our second evacuation, this time to South Wales, was being arranged!

Appearing in the Chatham, Rochester & Gillingham News *for 8th September 1939 was the following announcement about two of the youngest evacuees on record:*

Two Happy Events.

Two babies have been born to evacuated Gillingham mothers – both bonny infants. The first was on Saturday night, shortly after arrival, Mrs Lester being the mother and the child a girl. The second was on Sunday morning, after the sirens had sounded for the air raid. This time a boy was born to Mrs Lane. Both mothers are in the Dane John Maternity Hostel (Canterbury), and are being given every possible care by the Matron

(Miss Maycock), and her staff. Mothers and infants are doing well.

* * *

Arthur Johnson and his brother Kenneth were evacuated to Sandwich in September 1939:

I still have clear memories of becoming an evacuee; I suppose it was the first major event in my life!

I was born in Rainham, Kent, in April 1930, and lived in a small cottage near the 'Man of Kent' public house. We lived there until 1937, when my father, who was a hammerman in Chatham Dockyard, moved us to Gillingham, mainly I believe out of consideration for my ailing Grandmother, who came to live with us in the new house near the naval (now Medway) hospital.

I attended Byron Road Council School with my brother, who was two years younger than me. It was a strict but caring school, and I shall always be grateful to two staff members who encouraged my musical activities, which were to become a major part of my life: Oliver Glynn Roberts, and Mr Perris, a younger teacher.

News of our evacuation came at the end of August 1939. We were told to attend the school as usual, but to bring the necessary suitcase of clothes, and food for our journey. This whole exercise took place twice I seem to remember; there was a trial run on the first day, and then the real thing the next day.

Mothers came to see their children off, and were kept outside the gate of the school (this same gate, incidentally, is still there in Chaucer Road!). We were quite used to being taken in a crocodile formation to the local park for games, and so the idea of marching off to Gillingham Railway Station was not very unusual. Again, trips by train to the Kent coast were not unusual, so when we were lined up on the 'down' platform we didn't find it too unfamiliar, although we did not know where we were going.

Our destination turned out to be Sandwich. On our arrival we were assembled in the Salvation Army Citadel, and then taken in groups by our teachers to be billeted on the unsuspecting Sandwich households.

We were in the charge of Mr Perris; he made sure we were taken into a house with a piano, for which I was most grateful. Our hosts were a Mr and Mrs Hedgecock, with their teenage son Dick. The house was number 60 Woodnesborough Road, and Mr Hedgecock was an ex-naval rating who now looked after the engine and boilers of the local laundry. Our hosts had a most entertaining African grey parrot named Joey, who gave us endless amusement. Joey would cause confusion by imitating the Greenwich time signal, which of course heralded the radio news broadcasts.

Sandwich, as I remember it, was a low-lying area, criss-crossed with drainage dykes, where baskets would be left in the water to trap eels. I once saw a large eel swimming along a dyke in the town centre!

The local chimney sweep would travel around on an ancient tricycle, with his brushes tied to the back. He could clear the pavement of pedestrians very quickly when he ventured near the kerb. There was a network of railway lines in the area; some belonged to the Kent coalfield, and some to the East Kent Light Railway. I remember seeing men riding along some of these lines on hand driven trolley cars. Most lines were unfenced and crossings unguarded in those days.

I remember we went to the cinema in Deal and saw Deanna Durbin in *Two Smart Girls Grow Up*, and also a newsreel showing the sinking of the German battleship *Graf Spee*. That was a real treat.

Gillingham County Grammar School for Boys had also been sent to Sandwich, and both we and they would meet in the evenings in a damp field opposite the Woodnesborough Road houses. Many of us had harmonicas and playing these was a major activity.

We had lessons both in the local church school and in the Salvation Army Citadel, where our own teachers from Byron Road taught us and made us carry out air-raid drills which consisted of standing against the inside walls of the building. There were several lengthy air-raid alerts while I was at Sandwich, but most were false alarms, I believe.

Our stay at Sandwich was not a long one. News got around that the children of Ramsgate, only a few miles away, were being evacuated to escape possible shelling, so our parents fetched us back to Gillingham. I have good memories of my time at Sandwich, and of the kind family who took us in.

We were to be evacuated again, a private arrangement this time, but that's another story!

Derek Utteridge *was in the process of changing schools when evacuation was first thrust upon him:*

I was born in June 1928 and was thus just over eleven years old at the outbreak of the war. Immediately prior to the war I attended St Paul's Boys' Junior School in Chatham, living in Union Street in a house now long since demolished.

I had passed the scholarship exam earlier in the year of 1939 and expected to start at Gillingham County School in early September, together with Geoff Coomber and Dickie Abrahams. Incidentally, it was the first time that St Paul's had had three successful candidates in the same year.

With the commencement of the war on the 3rd of September, we were in limbo. We had never attended the school in Gillingham as pupils, and I don't know where that school went at the time, nor where St Paul's School went either. [Author's note: Gillingham County School for Boys was evacuated to Sandwich in East Kent.]

The day that war was declared, 3rd September 1939, I was with my younger brother at a relative's in Gillingham, and we spent the first half hour in their air raid shelter after that famous first false alarm. Our widowed mother was frantic with worry about us, not knowing quite where we were. Anyway, shortly afterwards arrangements were made for my evacuation.

Sittingbourne was a reception area for evacuees, and Mr Pocknell, the Headmaster of St Paul's, arranged for us to go to Borden Grammar School there. I believe that he and the Head of Borden Grammar School were acquainted. In the event, only Geoff Coomber went with me, he to a family in Upton Lane, and I to a Mr and Mrs Jopson in Park Road.

I returned from Sittingbourne in about February 1940, to the Gillingham County School, sharing the Chatham Girls' Grammar School building opposite St Augustine's church on the Rainham road. In June 1940 the Gillingham County Boy's School was evacuated for the second time, this time to Rhymney in the Welsh valleys.

Molly Batey *(now Mrs Molly Hurford-Jones) remembers her experiences of her first evacuation:*

In 1939 I was a pupil in the prep department of Chatham County School. Schooldays progressed normally throughout the year until the end of the August holiday when we who were to be evacuated attended school for informal lessons and to practise the procedure for evacuation. This included instructions on the amount of luggage we could take (I carried a large rucksack because this was as much as I could manage), suitable clothing to wear, including the obligatory gas mask and a packet of sandwiches (and of course my beloved teddy bear) for the journey to . . . Well, we had no idea where and neither did our parents for that matter!

At last the day came. It was Friday, September 1st, 1939 (two days before the outbreak of war) that our mothers had to take us to the school where we said goodbye to them, formed a long crocodile of 198 children from my school, and with children and teachers from other schools, we marched to Chatham Station with the leaders carrying a banner (I presume showing the name of the school). It was an extremely hot September day. We felt the heat more probably because we were wearing our winter gym slips, macks and velour hats ready for the coming of winter.

On arrival at Chatham Railway Station we boarded the train which took us to Faversham, Kent. We were marched once again, this time to a church hall where local people were waiting for us with tea and lemonade. Afterwards we were allocated to the people who were willing to take us into their homes. I believe the authorities tried to keep brothers and sisters together; as I was an only child I was rather apprehensive to say the least.

Chatham County School for Girls arriving at Faversham, Kent, on 1st September 1939
(This photo and that on page 43 were taken by Miss Tudman)

The lady with whom I was billeted was very kind, a widow with one daughter. Saturday, September 2nd was another beautiful sunny day and we had tea in the garden. Sunday, September 3rd I went to chapel with my houselady who sang in the choir. I sat in the congregation with instructions from her to wait at the end of the service, on the pavement outside. Unfortunately, at 11am, just as the service was finishing, the syren sounded. I didn't wait for anyone and scooted up the road to the house, rushed down to the cellar (where I'd previously been told to go should we have an air raid warning) and sat down among her pots of jams and chutneys, waiting for the bombs to drop at any moment – such was my fear . . .

I later moved to another household; another widow and her three daughters, where I must say I was very happy, going with the youngest to Girl Guides and Sunday mornings to the parish church. I believe this widow had lost her husband in an explosion at a gunpowder factory on the outskirts of Faversham in January 1926.

During our time in Faversham the majority of the Chatham County School girls shared the William Gibbs School, using it on Tuesdays, Thursdays and Saturdays with the playing fields available on other days. But because I was in the prep department (the youngest children) we were allowed to attend classes in a large house called 'Cratloe' (now known as Preston Court), the home of Jasper Neame and his family, of Shepherd Neame the brewers. We were allowed to use the domestic staff bedroom in the attic where we sat around a large table for our lessons. We loved it there, exploring the grounds at playtime and entering the house through the tradesmen's entrance. I can still recall the lovely smell in the little apple store in one corner of the garden.

My time in Faversham was contented on the whole although of course I missed my home and my mother and father very much. By Easter 1940, children, including myself, were beginning to drift back to their homes and to half-time schooling at Chatham County School, eventually joining the remnants of Rochester Grammar School at Fort Pitt School.

Nora Ticker-Fry remembers with clarity her first evacuation to Canterbury:

I sat with my parents and younger sister on the banks of the Royal Military Canal at Hythe and watched, entranced, as the annual Venetian Boat procession glided slowly by. It was a warm and sunny evening and the boats were all beautifully decorated with flowers, streamers and lights. It seemed even more special as it was my birthday, Wednesday, 30th August 1939. I was 14 years old. It was to be the last truly happy day we were to have as a family for almost six long years.

The next day all had changed, and now my father was telephoning home to see if the children from Rochester Grammar School were to be evacuated that weekend. The answer was 'yes' so sadly we packed up our things and got the bus back to Maidstone. Going back on that sunny day, we saw many other children getting off other buses, clutching cases, gas masks, labels hung around their necks, and with sinking hearts we knew that was how we would look the following day.

We had to be at Rochester Station early in the morning, ready to take the train to Canterbury. The main party from the school had gone on the day before, so we were 'tail end Charlies' and travelled with expectant mums and disabled people. My eight year old sister and I found the journey quite exciting. We rarely travelled by train so it did seem rather an adventure. Many years later we discovered that on the day we left, Mother had written in her diary, 'This is the worst day of my life!' – and we had thought it was an adventure!

The next day, Sunday morning, 3rd September 1939, we went to Canterbury Cathedral. We walked in a school group through a side door and saw to our astonishhment, horses and carts in the Nave, emptying earth along the floor to protect it for when the bombers came. Down in the Crypt we were told that war had been declared, then the sirens sounded. After the 'all clear' we came back out into the sunshine and found that nothing had changed – and nothing much did change for the next ten months.

We went home several times to see our family, and we changed billets. Our school was in the Old Hospital and we shared that with several other schools. Life settled into a rather ordinary routine and I suppose I felt this was all it would be and that the war would soon be over. Arrangements were made for us to go home for the Whitsun holidays and then everything changed abruptly.

In May 1940, the Germans began their advance into Belgium and Holland and were soon to reach the channel ports. A few days later the epic evacuation of British and Allied forces from Dunkirk took place – and we were not allowed to go home! Canterbury had suddenly become an evacuation area (I often wondered why it was thought to be safe in the first place). We were told that we were all going down to South Wales. Our parents must have been told because mine came down the next day. I suppose it was to say goodbye to us, but my mother was asked if she would travel with the school and act as a helper. I expect it was my father who made the decision and so, when he went home that evening, Mother stayed and we hurriedly packed all our things. The next morning we marched up to Canterbury Railway Station and boarded a train for South Wales.

Jean Lyons (now Mrs Jean Spashett) remembers her first experience of evacuation:

In 1939 I was a pupil at Napier Road School, Gillingham; an excellent school which I still think of with fondness. Just before the outbreak of war, when evacuation was advised, the school arranged for some mothers to accompany their children as helpers.

Along with my best friend Ella, my mother and I were evacuated to the village of Thanington, near Canterbury. I believe the boys from Napier Road School were sent to the village of Bridge. We stayed with the Croucher family who were very kind to us and made us feel at home. Mr Croucher was a chief warden and on Sunday 3rd

September 1939, Ella and I had gone to the local sweet shop for our weekly comic and sweets. We were met on the way back by a completely unrecognisable Mr Croucher, clad in military style gas mask and full warden's uniform. He shouted and hurried us into the house as, unknown to us, the air raid siren had sounded. We were hurried into the gas-proof room where the rest of the family were gathered. We had all been pressed into filling every crack between the floorboards and around the windows with wet newspaper as advised by the authorities! Here we stood and listened to the declaration of war made by Mr Chamberlain.

We were initially given lessons in a building immediately next to St Mildred's Church in Canterbury. This made an extremely interesting place to be, because the other half of the building was an organ repair shop, where we were treated to scales at all hours of the day, plus the occasional bursts of beautiful music! All this was accompanied by the unique smell of the local tannery!! This old building still stands next to the church today.

Later we were transferred to Payne Smith's School in Canterbury. Here lessons began to return to normal. Cookery lessons were held in an adjacent building and I recall having to leap into a doorway, clutching my biscuit tin of cookery items to avoid being trampled by cattle being driven to the market nearby. While at Payne Smith's, a Shakespeare group of players performed for us. I was to meet them again during the course of the war.

The walk from Thanington to school every day was quite arduous but, then, children in those days were expected to walk, no matter how far!

My mother and I went home for Christmas 1939 and returned to Canterbury for a few months afterwards. However, most pupils were brought back to Gillingham during what is now called the Phoney War. By 1940, things had begun to hot up, and Napier Road School advised its pupils that they were to be evacuated again, this time to South Wales. I begged my parents to let me go, as I was keen to travel to far-distant places. My mother was determined to stay put in the Medway this time, but I was to go and I was to be accompanied by my cousin, Barbara.

__Joan Prosser's__ first evacuation coincided with her changing schools, which in turn highlighted one or two problems for her:

When war was declared in September 1939, it corresponded with the first term that our little group from Luton Council School were due to start at what was then called Chatham County School for Girls. I lived on the Darland Banks which, apart from a bisecting country lane, was a continuation of the same chalk ridge of the school's playing fields.

When the Government decided that the children should be evacuated from the Medway Towns my parents decided that I ought to go with my older sister. Iris was with the Chatham Technical School and so we both ended up in the same billet in Sittingbourne. This proved to be a very miserable time for me. I hated leaving home, especially leaving my mother. In my eyes the billet was awful. Mrs . . . had no understanding of a little girl not quite eleven years old. I had to go to bed by candlelight and the shadows on the stairs were frightening. I was not allowed to touch the wooden stair banister because she polished it daily.

School was a problem because the girls were several years older than I was. My sister was due to leave school and enter the Civil Service, so the 'grown ups' decided I may be happier at Kemsley (Sittingbourne) to where Luton School had been evacuated. I had a nice billet, probably helped by Miss Stubbs, a teacher from Luton School, who also lived there. My old teachers from Luton were very understanding and I was fairly happy. Eventually though, we were all sent home, much to my delight. But it wasn't long before I was off again, this time much further afield!

Patricia Hughes (now Mrs Patricia Kay) *was another young evacuee who went to Kemsley:*

I was first evacuated in September 1939 to Kemsley, near Sittingbourne, a lovely village built by Bowater Lloyd, a big paper manufacturer, for its employees. We all left with our gas masks and haversacks containing food and a few belongings. We were received in the village hall where I remember we had to sit on tiny chairs at tiny tables.

My sister and I managed to stay together and our first billet was with Mr and Mrs Kirkham and their daughter Barbara. Mr Kirkham was a big man with a shaven head. The thing I remember most about this billet was that every evening Barbara was given half a bar of chocolate, but not my sister or me!

It was not long before we moved, this time to Mr and Mrs Boorman and their son Alan. We were not told the reason for the move. Mr and Mrs Boorman were very kind to us, but their son was horrible! I remember once he waited for me after school with a frozen snowball. He threw it at me and it hit me in the face.

I remember being very protective towards my sister, and getting very upset if she was told off. I was a terrible tomboy and probably drove my foster parents mad. We only went to school one morning a fortnight and were supposed to spend the rest of the time doing homework – which of course we never did.

After about a year, and probably because Sittingbourne was a possible bombing target on the flight path to London, we were moved to South Wales.

Daphne Bradley (now Mrs Daphne Hawes) *and her younger sister Joyce were evacuated in 1939 to Faversham with Chatham County School:*

When we first arrived in Faversham we were billeted with a Mrs Smith in Roman Road. Her husband was a submariner and tragically went down with his submarine a few weeks later. We then went to Orchard Place, but our hostess became pregnant and could not cope so we ended up with a delightful family whose name was Dann and they had three children, Keith, Daphne and Adrian who were roughly our own age. Although the house was bursting at the seams with so many of us, we were made very welcome.

I remember having to go to about six different locations for lessons, and a lot of time was spent walking back and forth between them. And the snow that winter! We had so much that it was right up to the bedroom windows. In fact we had to climb out of the upstairs windows because we couldn't open the front and back doors!

Our parents came down every weekend so we didn't feel too badly about missing them. We used to go swimming in the creek, though having seen it recently it must have been a lot cleaner then! While we were in Faversham I remember a house just three doors away being bombed. It wasn't too long after that, in May or June 1940, that we were all packing our bags for our second evacuation, this time to South Wales.

Ione Bates, *another Chatham County School girl recalls her time in Faversham:*

As the threat of war loomed in 1939, most of our school, then the Chatham County School for Girls, was evacuated on Friday 1st September to Faversham, about 17 miles from the Medway Towns. I remember that day well, being ready for departure with name pinned to label and armed with gasmask, enamel plate and mug, knife, fork and spoon – none of which we ever used in fact!

We arrived at Faversham by train, assembled in a hall to be allocated billets in alphabetical order. I recall arriving at the billet with another girl, Joyce Boorman, and was surprised to find our householder ready to put us straight into the bath. It was a pleasant surprise for her to discover her two evacuees did not need decontaminating and a relief to me not to have two baths in one morning!

We received the news that war had been declared on Sunday 3rd September at 11 o'clock from the pulpit in Faversham Parish Church. At this point the service was halted and, as the air raid warning sounded from the nearby police station, we were hurriedly escorted by our staff to an underground shelter in the centre of the town. We remained there until the all clear sounded and with much relief came out into the sunshine again. As history now records, a lone aeroplane had caused sirens to sound in many areas. Perhaps this helped to make us realise that the war had begun.

As young teenagers we accepted our situation and at that time did not fully appreciate what an enormous task the staff took on in every way. They coped with the upheaval from their own homes and took on the extra responsibility of their pupils in the role of house staff, each teacher being in charge of a set number of pupils and caring for their welfare. We had a curfew – no pupil was allowed out after blackout time unless with her householder or another adult. Everyone in Britain was issued with an identity card which we carried with us at all times, as well as our gas masks.

Meanwhile education continued and the staff deserve an accolade for handling this task so well. Our lessons took place in various places – much of it at the William Gibbs School for Girls where each school worked its independent timetable taught by its own staff. Lesson times were very varied as were the several other places where we were taught around the town – even in the house where one of our staff was billeted. Somehow we did domestic science and I remember being so proud of a batch of raspberry buns that I posted them home to my parents. Just imagine – a food parcel from an evacuee!

As evacuees we were allowed to write home to our parents at half the postal rate by putting the word 'EVACUEE' across the left hand corner of the envelope. Many years later when recalling this historical fact with my old school friend, I was pulled up with a halt realising that we must have lived in the Penny Post era, for we were putting a green halfpenny stamp on our letters! Shades of Sir Rowland Hill!

As we were not far from home we were able to make use of a service provided by the green double decker Maidstone and District buses whereby parents could send a parcel from Gillingham Bus Station. This was put under the stairs of the bus and then transferred to the bus office in Court Street in Faversham where we could collect the parcel. We were able to use this service in reverse. What a very civilised method of despatching parcels and perfectly safe too!

Obviously we all missed our families and homes very much, but we made the best of the situation and coped. Experiences varied for everyone regarding their billets, some being luckier than others. On the whole I was lucky. With my 'alphabetical friend' we stayed in our billet for about three months but moved temporarily for three weeks at Christmas as it was not convenient to our householder for us to be there then. Afterwards I returned to the billet but Joyce was happy to stay where she was. I was relegated to a less pleasant room and had my meals with the maid in the kitchen where I mainly lived. My friend Daphne Hawkins was billeted across the road and was allowed over on some evenings when we did homework and generally amused ourselves – in the kitchen!

The maid of the house was a very kind person and I am still in touch with her, now in her nineties. I remained there for a few months by which time my householder found having an evacuee an inconvenience. She arranged for me to go with Daphne to be billeted at a doctor's house. Here we were made very welcome and were part of the happy household. Daphne and I had the responsibility of doing the blackout every day in the house with the exception, quite rightly, of the surgery, dispensary and the waiting room.

Faversham was an interesting town historically and we enjoyed pleasant walks around the countryside, notably Ospringe, Bising Woods and the Creek, even in the heavy snows of that winter. The doctor used to take us out on his country rounds by car on occasions. We would sit in his car while he saw his patients. Our school timetable was so flexible we were able to do this. When possible, the doctor would spend half an hour before evening surgery playing the piano beautifully and we enjoyed listening to the music very much.

I remember the often pervading smell of malt that came from Shepherd Neame's Brewery. One place that fascinated me was Davington Priory and its history. Its more recent history is now, I believe, notable for being the home of Bob Geldof!

As the months went by, this stage of the war became known as the phoney war, but by May 1940 when France was being invaded by Germany thus posing a threat to Britain, we were re-evacuated, this time to South Wales.

Pat Mortley (now Mrs Pat Blackie) *recalls her first evacuation:*

On Friday 1st September 1939 pupils of Rochester Grammar School for Girls travelled by a special train to Canterbury. It was the day the great evacuation plan swung into action, to remove school children from the Medway Towns to places less vulnerable to air attacks. On arrival at Canterbury we gathered in a hall where we waited to be chosen by the local people, who were to be our host families. 'Chosen' is not quite the correct description, in some cases, for the way in which we were looked over and picked out.

I was billeted in a small terraced house in Nunnery Fields, a house with no bathroom. Once lessons were organised we spent the morning sessions at the old Nunnery Fields Hospital.

The most outstanding memory for me is of being confirmed at Canterbury Cathedral on the 14th December 1939. As the expected bombings did not materialise immediately, I was thankful to return home to Rochester in the spring of 1940.

Helen Cross *was approaching her thirteenth birthday when she experienced her first evacuation:*

I was attending Napier Road Girls' School, Gillingham in 1939, and in the September I remember being taken to Sandwich in Kent, together with many others including my younger brother and sister. During our stay in Sandwich my sister and I had three different billets. The first was with a very old fashioned couple and their daughter whose house was next to the golf course. Our schooling, if you can call it that, was held in the Salvation Army Hall, where we mostly did reading, huddled part of the time round an old iron stove. The rest of the time we all had to troop over the golf course to Sandwich Bay and collect drift wood for the stove!

My sister and I were not happy at our first billet, and our second billet wasn't much better. It was not a 'home from home'. Our hostess made it very plain that she didn't want any evacuees, and made our lives very uncomfortable. By this time we were actually attending school though I have to admit I was no scholar! I was good at cookery and needlework classes and was therefore destined to do domestic chores at the billet. I saw little of my brother or my sister except perhaps after school.

Finally I asked the education officer for a move, hoping for a more caring and welcoming family. My sister and I were re-housed and the new hosts were not unkind, but when my mother, who was by now in the WRENS, came to visit us she was very, very shocked. The reason being that we had not only been welcomed to our new home by the people, but also by their obviously permanent lodgers – fleas and head lice in abundance! My mother had brought up eight children which could not have been easy, but we had never had anything like this. I was at an age where fleas and lice brought dreadful humiliation – as well as my mother's wrath! Shortly after this incident we were on the move again, this time to Wales.

Frank Turner *talks of his time spent in Canterbury in 1939:*

I was a pupil at the Sir Joseph Williamson Mathematical School in Rochester. On Friday the 1st September 1939 I boarded the train with the other boys and set off for an unknown destination, which turned out to be Canterbury. We were taken to the Simon Langton School where we waited in the quadrangle for people to pick us out. An elderly gentleman chose me and enquired if I would like to go and stay with him. I was taken home by car and that is how I came to live with Mr and Mrs Ware at 14 Cherry Drive, Canterbury. It was a wonderful billet in a middle class environment. I learned to appreciate a way of living completely unknown to a teenager coming from a working class home. Peter Thomas from Upper Luton Road was also chosen to live at the same billet.

Mr Ware was a schoolmaster and was evidently a member of a committee at Canterbury Cathedral. He took me by car to the Cathedral, where I was introduced to a number of people and found myself seconded to the sandbagging gang. From that time on, filling sandbags occupied practically all my spare time, weekends included.

I needed more advanced tuition than Simon Langton School could provide for me, so I went part time to the King's School to study Maths and Science subjects. We Math School boys fitted in quite well at the King's School because we already played rugby at the Math. That lessened any problems between the two groups of students from such differing backgrounds.

Frank Turner's evacuation label issued to him on his first evacuation, to Canterbury, in 1939

During the time I was at Canterbury, the Kent Schoolboy Championships took place and I won the javelin throwing, which I had learned to do at the Math School. Mum and Dad sent me my bicycle by train, so I was then able to cycle to and from school. I stayed with Mr and Mrs Ware until we moved to Wales in May 1940.

An example of interaction between evacuating and reception areas is recorded here in an article which appeared in the Chatham, Rochester & Gillingham News *for 15th September 1939:*

EVACUEES' HOSTS.

Mayors' Thanks for Canterbury's Reception.

The following letter of thanks for the reception of evacuees has been sent by the Mayor of Rochester (Councillor C. S. Knight), to the Mayor of Canterbury:

An example of the special tickets issued to some of the evacuees in 1939. This one was Frank Turner's for his journey to Canterbury

'May I convey to you, personally, and on behalf of the Corporation of Rochester our very grateful thanks to all those associated with the arrangements made for the reception of the evacuees from this City. I know that it has entailed an enormous amount of work, and that the task has been one of the most difficult undertakings you have had to handle; and this Corporation feel deeply indebted to you.

'I should be glad if you will convey to all the members of the Council, the Corporation staff, voluntary workers, and particularly to those who have given a home and a warm welcome to women and children who have had to leave their own homes in this time of national emergency, our deep gratitude and heart-felt thanks.'

There have been similar acknowledgements by the Mayor of Gillingham (Councillor L. J. Newnham) and the Mayor of Chatham (Councillor J. T. Hawes).

* * *

Peter Hoad, another Old Williamsonian, now gives his account of the evacuation of Sir Joseph Williamson Mathematical School to Canterbury:

The last week of August, 1939, would normally have been part of the school summer holiday, but war seemed inevitable, and instead we were asked to report daily to school while awaiting the order to travel to an evacuation area. This finally came on Friday, 1st September, when pupils and staff travelled to Canterbury by train. Not that we knew it at the time, but our school was just one of thousands evacuated on that day. Canterbury alone received over 9,000 evacuees, mostly from the Medway Towns, for billeting in the city and surrounding area. With the numbers involved there was an element of luck in the type of home you ended up in, and I was fortunate in that I was placed in a nice home with a charming family. Later I was joined by Denis from the same form as myself. I was about to enter the Upper 5th and due to take the school certificate examination the following year. There was a feeling among those in our year that we were rather too old to be evacuated, as most boys and girls aged 14 then would have already left school and started work. Evacuation was voluntary but there was no guarantee of schooling for those who stayed in Rochester, and my parents had decided that it was in my interest that I should go

On Sunday the 3rd of September Mr Chamberlain made his broadcast that we were now at war with Germany. Before he had finished speaking, the air raid warning sounded, but this turned out to be a false alarm. The first few days of the war were busy ones as, along with other boys from the Math, I helped fill sandbags and pile them against the Kent and Canterbury Hospital and also to assist in the construction of an air raid shelter in the back garden of my Canterbury home. There was a lot of rushing around visiting relatives and friends reassuring each other and making contingency plans for the future. One visit was to a farmer with the object of cultivating a possible food source in case of a future shortage. It was all something of an anticlimax after this, as everything went on more or less as normal, with no air raids, no food shortages and little activity between the opposing armies.

With the huge influx of pupils into Canterbury, there was obviously a shortage of school premises, and it was well into October before school started in an old building which had once been a hospital. It had been hastily converted for school use and facilities for laboratory work, assembly and PE were limited, although we did have the use of a sports field. Before the start of the war each school year had three separate forms, but now in Canterbury the Upper 5th had just two, and in my estimation about two thirds of our year had elected for evacuation. Mr Clark, the Headmaster, was with us in Canterbury, as was his deputy Mr Pattenden who also taught physics. Mr Meade our form master took us for mathematics and other subject teachers included Mr Rigg (English), Mr Taylor (French), Mr Thornhill (History), Mr Jenkinson (Chemistry), and Mr Fearnley (Art).

Because of the delay in starting schooling we were virtually on an extended holiday and it is this that I remember most about those first few months in Canterbury. Many of us had our cycles sent down and we must have explored much of East Kent and the nearby coast. It was all the more enjoyable because the fine weather went on for weeks, even though we did not arrive in Canterbury until September. In fact the weather that first autumn and winter of the war was remarkable for the fine spell followed by the severest winter for a number of years. The snow hung around for weeks and it gave us the chance to enjoy some winter sports. We had no difficulty in occupying ourselves in the evenings and spent many happy hours playing chess and Monopoly.

This was a pleasant period as far as I was concerned, but things changed in the Easter term and I attribute this partly to what has become known as the phoney war, when there were no air raids and very little activity at the 'Front'. Along with all my friends in Canterbury, I returned home for a few days at Christmas, and in the Easter term it became the custom to spend some weekends back in Rochester. Quite a number would take their suitcases to school on Friday mornings ready for a quick dash to the station after school to catch the train home. The return journey would be made early on Monday morning, just in time to start school. We were becoming part time evacuees and this is not what some of our Canterbury hosts, including my own, had in mind when they took us in. My guardians decided they had had enough by Easter. I could have looked for another home in Canterbury, but so many had drifted back home the the school had opened up again in Rochester, and I made a new start there at the beginning of the summer term. We shared the premises with girls from the Rochester Grammar; though classes were separate, we were taught by teachers from both schools.

Very soon after the start of the new term, the Germans invaded France through the Low Countries, and things went so badly for the Allies that Canterbury itself became an area to be evacuated from, and our school there moved to Pontypridd in South Wales. Two weeks later on Sunday, 2nd June, those of us in Rochester were evacuated to Porthcawl, a seaside town on the South Wales coast about thirty miles from Pontypridd.

Mrs E. Whale's first evacuation to Herne Bay was not successful:

In September 1939 my two sisters and I were evacuated to Herne Bay from Brompton in Gillingham. We were very unhappy there. My father received a dirty little note written in a churchyard, telling him why we were so unhappy. Soon after we had written the note, he collected us and brought us home to Middle Street in Brompton. We had been away about six months.

An urgent need was identified, early into the evacuation, for those children evacuated from Gillingham to Herne Bay, as detailed in an article from the Chatham, Rochester & Gillingham News *dated 15th September, 1939:*

GILLINGHAM'S EVACUATED CHILDREN.
Clothing needed for those accommodated at Herne Bay.

The Mayor of Gillingham (Councillor L. J. Newnham, JP) is appealing for clothing and shoes for Gillingham children who have been evacuated to various parts of East Kent. He writes: 'I am pleased to state that, from information that has reached me from the receiving areas, the children are being well cared for, and are very happy in their new surroundings, but, unfortunately, I learn that a number of the children are in urgent need of clothing and shoes. I therefore earnestly appeal to the citizens of Gillingham to assist in this matter by forwarding to me any spare clothing in serviceable condition. Parcels should be addressed to The Mayor of Gillingham (Clothing for Evacuated Children), Municipal Buildings, Gillingham. Any cash contributions would be gladly received and applied for the assistance of the children.

The Mayor has received appreciative letters from the civic heads of the towns and areas to which the children from Gillingham have been sent.

The Mayor of Canterbury (Mrs Catherine E. Williamson) and the Mayor of Sandwich (Major V. Prescott-Westcar) have both written in this strain, and the latter stated, 'Your school children are universally popular here and will form friendships that will last for life.'

I WISH TO MARK, BY THIS PERSONAL MESSAGE, my appreciation of the service you have rendered to your Country in 1939.

In the early days of the War you opened your door to strangers who were in need of shelter, & offered to share your home with them.

I know that to this unselfish task you have sacrificed much of your own comfort, & that it could not have been achieved without the loyal co-operation of all in your household.

By your sympathy you have earned the gratitude of those to whom you have shown hospitality, & by your readiness to serve you have helped the State in a work of great value.

Elizabeth R

Bill Churchman *of Holcombe Technical School (now Chatham Grammar School for Boys) recounts his evacuations with some clarity. First, he recalls his time in Faversham, Kent:*

Probably the earliest recollections are of Atherston Road School, which was a sort of clearing house from where we were despatched in the care of 'minders' to billets in the neighbourhood. The Fright family, consisting of Mr and Mrs Fright and their infant daughter Rosemary, took in Jack Cook and me and we were given a bedroom with a shared bed. The date was 1st September 1939, two days before war was declared. We were both 14 years old.

Sunday 3rd September I attended morning service at Faversham Parish Church. The vicar ascended the pulpit and read an announcement which told us that as from 11am that morning, England was in a state of war with Germany. Almost at once the air raid sirens sounded and the congregation dispersed.

At my billet I helped to dig and construct an air raid shelter in the garden. On another occasion I helped to fill sand bags at Civil Defence Headquarters in London Road. In the ensuing weeks we took refuge two or three times in the middle of the night in response to air raid warnings, but I do not recall any enemy activity. It was cold and damp in the shelter, and there was no sense of excitement or even of impending danger.

Schooling was supervised by our own teachers wherever a vacant school room or suitably equipped hall could be found. Teachers had the unenviable responsibility of following up complaints about billets. Their own domestic and family life was disrupted as much as ours was, and they were *in loco parentis.*

Some of our lessons were conducted at the Wraight School, but the science laboratory was a bit dated. Claud (Fatty) Wright, our maths teacher with a sharp wit, surveyed the room and asked, 'Where are the frogs legs?' – a reference to an experiment by a medieval Italian scientist. Of course, we all laughed like hyenas. Metalwork instruction was carried out weekly at the King's School at Canterbury, where lathes originally from Holcombe were installed.

Holcombe third year stream were studying for the Dockyard Apprentices' entrance examination – a critical year for us and, considering the adverse circumstances, most of us achieved fairly good results.

If a suitable venue for classes was not available and perhaps to get us out of our billets, we were taken for rambles in the lovely Kentish countryside, or visits to local places of interest. On one such occasion a group of us took a train to Selling and walked through the Blean Woods to Canterbury. On the way back we became lost, eventually finding ourselves at a farm gate. The farmer was not amused to see us all clambering over his gate and minced no words in telling us so!

We attended the broadside launch of a small ship, probably a coastal vessel, into Faversham Creek. There were also visits to a foundry at the Brents, to Shepherd Neame Brewery, the local diesel power station and to Davington Priory which I

Opposite – 'The Queen's Message' issued to foster parents after a period of qualification in looking after an evacuee

remember particularly well.

Our host, Mr Fright, was a lorry driver and I sometimes accompanied him on his round delivering crates of milk. For some reason my stay with the Fright family was short and I was moved to the Epps family, older people with a son about my age and two daughters, one working away from home, and the other, a younger girl, who was still at school. Both the Fright and Epps families were unfailingly kind to me.

Although we came from Chatham only 17 miles away, the local Kentish burr afforded us endless amusement – lads of that age are quick to pick up differences to use as the butt for wit.

A group of us were doing nothing in particular one day in the local park, when we were approached by police who asked us to participate in an identity parade. All kinds of thoughts entered our minds. We were lined up at the police station and three or four youths, the suspects, were mixed with us. An older lady, the victim, immediately identified the suspects, and I seem to remember we were given sixpence each for our trouble.

There was a well stocked public library at Faversham which many of us used. Travel was, and still is, an interest of mine and I well remember reading an account of road construction by a New Zealand civil engineer in a particularly wild area of the Middle East. It was called *Road Through Kurdistan*. Little did I think I would one day know that road quite well, but that is another story, another time, another place.

The winter of 1939-40 was particularly severe. I remember the curious sensation of frozen nasal hair on a day of 29 degrees of frost! A number of us budding ornithologists were crawling along banks and dykes, observing the suffering birdlife trying to find enough to eat. We must have been the despair of our host families when we returned to our billets soaked and half frozen.

The venue for the Dockyard Apprentices' examination in 1940 was the Star Hotel in Maidstone. This seemed to us to be the culmination of our studies and we took school life rather lightly thereafter!

The phoney war came to an end when Germany invaded the Low Countries and Northern France. Faversham as a reception area for evacuees was re-assessed. The Medway Towns schools which had gone to Faversham, among them the Chatham County School for Girls where my sister was a pupil, were suddenly relocated to Pontypridd in Glamorganshire. So off we all went, this time on a much longer journey.

George Prager *reflects on his evacuation to the East Kent town of Sandwich:*

During the tense days of August 1939 I was enjoying the summer holidays expecting to return to the Gillingham County School for Boys to commence my second year, having obtained a scholarship to attend there from Richmond Road Boys' School. I had lived with my grandparents from the age of six months although my mother and stepfather still lived in the Medway Towns. My grandfather was employed as a shipwright in Chatham Dockyard.

On Friday 1st September 1939, with school cap, blazer and school tie, a label with my name, school and form number tied to the lapel, a cardboard box containing a gas mask and a postcard to send home on arrival at my new home – and a suitcase containing a few essential clothes, I arrived at Gillingham Railway Station together

King's School, Rochester, transferred to Bayham Abbey, Scotney Castle and other places in Lamberhurst in September 1939. In 1940 the school moved to Taunton in Somerset where it stayed for the rest of the war
(Photos by courtesy of the Kent Messenger Group)

The younger boys from King's School were evacuated to Scotney Castle, Lamberhurst, in 1939. They are pictured here with Mr and Mrs Hussey

Older boys from King's School, Rochester, were sent to Bayham Abbey in 1939

with over 200 fellow schoolboys shepherded by staff of the school, to be evacuated we knew not where!

After a relatively short journey we arrived at Sandwich on the Kent coast, to be met by local dignitaries and townspeople. They served us with light refreshments after which the task of billeting us out was undertaken. Norman, a fellow evacuee and I were chosen by a very attractive lady and we were transported in a very large car owned by a retired army officer, to a large house very close to St George's Golf Course. Our hostess turned out to be a film actress named Judy Gunn. Her married name was Mrs Hue-Williams. Norman and I were very fortunate to be billeted there since we were cared for by the lady of the house, together with a cook and maid. A young baby and a Pekingese dog completed the household.

I vividly remember two incidents which happened on our first day at our new billet. Firstly, after dinner, we were served coffee in tiny cups, very strong, black and syrupy, with a slice of lemon. What luxury! Secondly, after the meal the young maid dropped an empty milk bottle on to the red tiled floor of the kitchen – and it bounced straight back into her hands!

War was declared on 3rd September at 11am. I can remember us all assembled in the lounge to listen to Prime Minister Neville Chamberlain broadcast to the nation on the radio. Immediately the air raid warning siren was sounded and very shortly afterward, the all clear.

School attendance started immediately on the Monday at Sir Roger Manwood's School, with various church halls, a Scout Hut, the Fascist H.Q. and The Ramparts providing the extra accommodation to satisfy both schools. Priority was given to fifth and sixth forms of both schools who were due to take exams in the current year.

Memories of my stay in Sandwich include playing rugby and cross country running – even in the snow, and of walking across the golf course in the snow and disappearing into a bunker, much to the delight of my companion. I also remember the Cattle Market, the Quay, the Toll Bridge and the Barbican.

By May 1940 the war was going badly. The Dunkirk evacuation started and arrangements were made for my school to be relocated, this time to South Wales.

The following article which appeared in the Chatham, Rochester & Gillingham News *for 15th September 1939 gives a very 'rosy' picture of how children from the Medway Towns were received in the ancient town of Sandwich:*

WITH THE EVACUEES.
Medway Towns' Children Happy In New Surroundings.
Kind Foster Parents.

The happiest people in Sandwich at the present time are 400 boys and girls evacuated from the Medway Towns. They are revelling in the novelty of their surroundings, bathing, rambling, playing cricket, and trying to forget that war or no war, home or no home, they must soon go to school and work.

Almost as happy are the kindly Sandwich folk who have made them so welcome. In bigger towns billeting has not been without its troubles. Householders faced with the necessity of 'adopting' a family of young children have protested against the billeting arrangements and are appealing to the billeting tribunals set up to judge whether hardship has been caused to them. But Sandwich has heard nothing and cares less about tribunals. Everywhere the children have been warmly received and mothered, and the few complaints that have so far been lodged have not come from the hosts but from their guests. As was inevitable, some of the helpers accompanying the children found the accommodation provisionally given to them unsuitable, and have changed their lodgings.

All Together.

'I took the entire family of five because I thought it would be a tragedy to break them up,' Mrs Cloke said. 'The youngest, Mickle, worships his brother Charles, who is nearly fourteen, and they would not be happy apart.'

'I have just brought in the third plate of bread and butter,' said Violet, the maid, who was serving tea in the garden, and Mrs Cloke laughingly agreed that there had been no fear of food wastage since her new family arrived.

Three children are billeted with the Deputy Mayor, (Councillor W. M. K. Marshall), and Lady Hambro has four.

Praise For The Railway.

'If anyone deserves honours it is the Southern Railway Company,' Mr W. W. Johnson, one of the masters who brought 250 boys from Gillingham County School, told the Press representatives. 'The transport arrangements went without a hitch, and the arrangements at this end were just as complete. Our train left at 3.05pm and some of our boys were in their billets by five o'clock. Buses were waiting at the railway station to take us to the Central School where area billeting officers were waiting to receive.'

Mothers with children under school age arrived next day. At present ninety-five per cent of the children are billeted on families, but arrangements are being made for some of the boys to enter buildings adapted as hostels.

Plenty of Recreation.

While the holidays are on the older children are assembling for bathing at Sandwich Bay, country rambles and organised games on the sports fields of Sir Roger Manwood's School.

A shift system will have to be introduced when the new school term begins, and it is proposed that from September 19th local secondary school boys and the boys from Gillingham County School shall each have instruction at Sir Roger Manwood's School. The local boys will attend in the morning and the Gillingham boys in the afternoon.

A similar system for elementary school children was introduced when the schools re-opened this week.

Chislet received 39 children from Woodlands School, Gillingham, under the evacuation scheme from the Medway Towns. The children arrived by special train at Canterbury East and, marshalled by teachers, were issued with carrier bags of rations by voluntary helpers and loaded into East Kent coaches and conveyed to Chislet, where billeting officers were waiting to conduct them to their temporary 'mothers', who had undertaken to take charge of them. There they received a kindly and sympathetic welcome and were soon made to feel at home.

Roy Townsend *remembers with detail his evacuation from Rochester to Whitstable:*

In September 1939 I was living at 11 Beresford Avenue, Rochester, and attending Balfour Road School. We were evacuated to Whitstable just before the outbreak of the war by a special train which kept stopping. The journey took a very long time.

We were with two older girls who were looking after us. Before we left my mother converted a pillowcase into a rucksack for my few belongings, and I can still feel the straps cutting into my shoulders. It was an extremely hot day and when we finally arrived in Whitstable we were taken from the railway station to a corner opposite what is now a bowling alley, where we just milled around in a crowd. Adults started arriving and choosing evacuees – just like picking a dog at Battersea Dogs' Home! Pretty girls with blond curls and blue eyes were the first to be chosen. The scruffy ones with the runny noses were the last to go.

Our little group managed to keep together and the ten of us were taken to a very large house with a big bedroom, just like a dormitory. I don't know what this house had been used for, but it was not like a normal household.

I never had a meal with a knife and fork in that house. They used to put a large container of really tasty thick soup or stew on the table, with large chunks of crusty bread, and we all sat round and helped ourselves. For breakfast it was a similar arrangement, but with cereals. For tea it was always caraway seed cake and bread and jam, and there was always a large box of apples where we would help ourselves. During the evenings the older children would toast bread on toasting forks in front of the fire. I was very fussy about food, but that diet suited me fine.

Four adults lived in that house, presumably to look after the children. Apart from cooking and washing clothes, the older children had to do most of the child care. That first winter of the war came in very cold. My mother had brought a hot-water bottle down for me. I remember her having a big row when she found out I had not been given this bottle, but that it was being used by one of the adults.

And for the only time in my life I had fleas while in that house, so I was moved to a 'one man dairy' in a small parade of shops. The man used to deliver milk on a large bicycle with a huge rack on the front. There were four of us evacuees at this billet and we used to sleep in the attic. Early morning we could watch the fishing boats sail out. The food in this house was 'knife and fork' food – meat and vegetables, porridge for breakfast. I hated meat and greens and I used to sneak some of it into my trouser pockets. I was a mess! The milk was fantastic, though, and with the cold winter it was very often frozen.

I can remember some of the evacuees running riot at school. We were evacuated with children from what was known as the Balfour Cottage Homes. Some of these children were orphans, or from broken homes, or 'in care'. And some of these boys were wild! I can remember some of them fighting with the teachers.

We used to spend a lot of time hanging around the harbour where the old red sail barges used to come in. I must admit that we were all pretty wild during those days, but then we were for most of the war with our fathers away. We were probably evil vandals, and I think we used to cause more damage than the the bomb blasts.

When it was decided to move our school from Whitstable to Wales, my mother returned me to Rochester, so in total I was evacuated for less than a year.

Fred Silver recalls his evacuation to Sittingbourne:

As early as February 1939 circulars were being sent to households concerning the possible evacuation of school children in the event of hostilities with Germany.

In July I was informed that I had passed the entrance examination for Rochester Junior Technical School. I was due to attend on 14th September 1939 to commence the autumn term. Towards the end of August, as the crisis loomed, we were instructed to gather at the Rochester Technical School gymnasium building each morning, equipped with certain articles of clothing, food for one day and a gas mask. All parcels had to be labelled with our name and school.

The scheme provided for brothers and sisters to accompany their older Technical School brothers. My brother and two sisters came with me. I was nearly 13 years old, my sister Olive just over 11 years, my sister Peggy nearly 9 years and my younger brother was David, only 4 years old. On the 31st August our parents were told that we would be sent away the next morning, Friday 1st September.

The following morning with our bags, cases, gas masks etc., we went with our parents to Rochester Railway Station. At this stage we did not know where we were going. After many tears and upsets we boarded the train. I remember my mother was interviewed by the local press and a family photograph was taken.

We eventually arrived at Sittingbourne – only 11 miles away! From there we were taken to the Borden Grammar School for distribution to our new homes. It was agreed that my brother and I would stay together, and that my two sisters would also stay together. They were billeted with a young couple in Ruins Barn Road, and David and I went to live with the young couple's parents a few doors away.

As a matter of interest (and great upset to my mother), my father, a reserve from the First World War, was sent to France on the 3rd of September, the day war was declared. This left my mother by herself to look after the family home.

In Sittingbourne my sisters had a reasonable family life and were fairly happy. My young brother and myself plus two other boys, David Mead and S. Salter, were with an older couple, who were both retired. Although we were well looked after, we had a more restricted life. We were never taken on outings etc., but all four of us made the best of things. Friday nights were bath night. This consisted of having a bath in an old fashioned bath tub in front of the living room fire. The lady would bath us one at a time, the youngest first. As soon as we were bathed we went to bed. The old gent, who had a large white beard, would sit in his armchair and watch the proceedings.

My two sisters were easily accommodated at a school in the village of Tunstall, so they had full time schooling. With us boys things were a lot different. David of course was too young to go to school and had to remain at our billet.

There were about 65 of us boys evacuated with the Technical School, and seven teachers came with us. We couldn't get full time education due to lack of facilities and a lot of our time was spent in going on rambles, fruit picking, sports and working on a couple of allotments allocated to us.

One treat that we as a family did have during our time in Sittingbourne, was that we were allowed to travel home for the weekend on a couple of occasions.

In May 1940 as the war deteriorated, we were told that we would be moving on. This time we were bound for South Wales.

In July 1939 **Fred Silver's** *parents received a letter from Mr J. E. Phillips, principal of the Technical Institute which included the following paragraphs:*

> You have received during the last six months circulars in connection with the arrangements for evacuation of school children if at any time such a step were necessary. Copies of the circular and form are enclosed which should be read carefully.
>
> In the event of a crisis all schools in the Medway towns would be closed and there is no doubt that they would not re-open during the period of hostilities.
>
> Arrangements are being made for the continuance of the education of the boys from this school in the district to which the school would be evacuated and it should be realised that if you desire your boy to have the benefit of the education provided at this school, he should be evacuated with the school if such a step became necessary. If you wish your son to be included in the evacuation organisation of this school, it is essential that you complete the evacuation form enclosed.
>
> It is essential that the total numbers for whom transport, educational and billeting arrangements have to be organised should be known beforehand, and therefore if you wish your son to be included in the evacuation organisation of this school, I should be glad if you would complete the evacuation form enclosed.
>
> It should be clearly understood that this is only a measure of organisation and it is hoped that the need for carrying out these evacuation plans may never arise, but it is essential that the arrangements be worked out beforehand to avoid confusion if the need for putting them into action did arise.
>
> The school closes for the summer holidays on Wednesday, July 26th, and does not re-open till Thursday, September 14th and this seven weeks break necessitates that all information be obtained now to avoid delay in bringing the organisation up-to-date when the new term starts in September.

Chapter Three

THE PROBLEMS STILL REMAINING IN THE EVACUATED AREAS

Soon after the first official evacuation *took place at the beginning of September 1939, many of the evacuated areas found various problems starting to manifest themselves. The Medway Towns were no exception.*

Almost immediately some of the evacuees had started returning home as the following newspaper article for 15th September 1939 reveals:

Evacuated Children.
Parents strongly advised against bringing them back.
Government Warning.

The Board of Education has issued a notice to follow up the Minister of Health's recent broadcast in which he warned persons who have left evacuation areas not to return to them. The Board, after referring to instances of parents bringing home school children who were evacuated with them to reception areas, continues:

'Parents are strongly advised against doing this. They ought to remember that an air raid on an evacuation area might make them very anxious to send their children away again, and should this happen it would not be possible to evacuate them anything like as quickly or as safely as was the case with the evacuation at the beginning of this month. Further, since schools in evacuation areas are remaining closed until further notice, to bring back the children would deprive them of all the benefits of education so long as the schools remain closed. This would be bound to handicap them in after life.'

The Government view is expressed not only in official warnings, but in the re-opening this week of schools in evacuation areas throughout the country, in order to give a further opportunity for children to be registered by their parents for evacuation, 'in case it should prove possible to carry out a further evacuation of school children.' Those last words express a warning in themselves.

The existence of a tendency to drift back to the danger zones, and isolated criticisms and complaints from reception areas, point to the importance of doing everything possible to smooth out local or individual difficulties. Later on there will be camps for some evacuated children, but those at present under construction will hardly touch the fringe of the problem. The National Camps Corporation, established under the Camps Act, is building 30 camps, the first of which should be ready for occupation about the end of this month. Each camp will house 350 children, making a total provision for 10,500, but the camps have been so planned that they could be doubled in size.

Local committees are being formed in many places to help in coping with billeting problems, and established voluntary organisations are also turning their attention to them. Women's voluntary services are encouraging the setting up of informal committees of a few local residents, who will work in consultation with the billeting officer and, as one of their tasks, will try to transfer refugees who have not settled down happily to more suitable quarters. The same organisation has already sent out a first handful of experienced social workers into districts that have asked for help in removing causes of friction; and it has now notified other areas that application may be made for such aid.

* * *

Just weeks after the initial evacuation took place, local authorities had the task of trying to decide how to deal with those children who did not go.

Local newspaper articles gave an excellent insight to the problems and to the decisions made. The following article appeared in the Chatham, Rochester and Gillingham News *for 13th October 1939:*

EDUCATION IN THE MEDWAY TOWNS.
Plans of Local Authorities for Unevacuated Children.
Limited Tuition.

At last week's meeting of Rochester Education Committee, further consideration was given to the question of making temporary arrangements for the education of the children who did not take advantage of the facilities for evacuation from the City.

Various proposals were brought forward for discussion including one which provided for the establishing of temporary schools in safety zones at some distance from this area, the children to be accommodated in holiday hotels or in large country mansions.

It was eventually decided, however, to experiment with the Education Secretary's scheme for meeting the problem of the education of children remaining in the City area. The experiment is being commenced at one school department in the City and, if it proves successful, the scheme will be adopted in respect of other school departments. In operating the scheme, small groups of scholars, not more than ten in each group, will attend at given centres once a week to receive text books, exercise books, etc., and instructions concerning the course of study to be pursued during the ensuing week.

The work will be done in the children's homes and will be confined to the mornings; in the afternoons, it is hoped that under the direction of the teachers, organised games for small parties, and rambles of educational value may be arranged. During the week, teachers will visit the homes of the children to give assistance and advice with problems encountered by the children.

The successful operation of the scheme will be dependent to a large extent upon the co-operation of the parents, who will be required to provide facilities for the children to study at home.

The meeting was presided over by Alderman F. C. A. Matthews, JP (Vice-Chairman), and others present were Councillors A. Fray, A. C. Lyle, P. B. Phillips and W. Edmonds, the Revd Canon W. J. Gray, RD., Mrs J. M. Browne, and Mr W. Cobbet Barker, together with the Education Secretary (Mr Edward H. Webb, FCIS).

The experiment is to be started at Troy Town Girls' School. Parents were instructed by letter to register their girls at the school last Monday, whether or not they desired them to take part in the suggested scheme of study.

The *News* was told yesterday that there was a good response, and just over a hundred children were registered.

The study scheme in connection with the school begins today (Friday).

Chatham's Scheme.

A scheme whereby children in Chatham will receive a certain amount of training in small groups will be put into operation on Monday and it is hoped that the plan will gradually enlarge in scope to include more and more scholars.

In a number of cases school buildings will be used for approximately 20 children at a time to receive instruction for not more than two hours at a time. Later it is hoped to extend the scheme by arranging for small groups of children to be educated in a similar way in halls and private houses.

At the moment the scheme only includes three groups for each of the schools where such training is possible, and preference is being given to children preparing for scholarship examinations, and scholars who have not much longer at school.

It is emphasised that the schools are not re-opening in the ordinary sense and only children who have been so informed may attend.

Children should not be brought back from reception areas under the

Anderson shelters were issued to householders in vulnerable areas – but it was up to the householders to erect them

impression that they will be allowed to go to school in this area. The facilities in Chatham are strictly limited and can in no way replace the training that scholars can receive in the reception areas.

The scheme is based on the fact that, if the number of children on the premises at a time is limited to 20 or less, they will be as safe as in their own homes and certainly

As the threat of enemy bombing grew, authorities began supplying households with air-raid shelters, known as Anderson Shelters. The following letter from the Mayor of Chatham gives advice about handling such shelters

Mayor's Parlour,
Town Hall,
Chatham.

J. T. HAWES, J.P.
MAYOR

DEAR SIR, OR MADAM,

You have been supplied with an air-raid shelter for the protection of your household in time of any enemy attack on this district.

Until such time as the shelter is erected in position, I do hope you will take every care to see that all the many parts are carefully stored and everything done to prevent the parts from being damaged or lost.

Such neglect may result in difficulty being experienced when the shelter is being erected and the shelter may lose much of its efficiency, with unfortunate consequences.

In particular, care must be taken during the time the parts are stored in the open, to see that the sheets are stood on end in such a way as to permit rain water to run off them.

Yours faithfully,

John T. Hawes.

Mayor.

safer than running about in the streets. Teachers have been instructed with regard to precautions that may be taken.

Classes will start at the following schools on Monday: New Road Council, Glencoe Road Girls' and Boys', Ordnance Street Boys' and Girls', Walderslade, Christchurch Senior Girls', St Paul's, All Saints, Luton Junior and Senior Boys' and Junior Girls'.

* * *

As the weeks went by, certain sections of the community continued questioning the success of the Government's Evacuation Scheme. The following article appeared in the Chatham, Rochester & Gillingham News *for 20th October 1939:*

EVACUATION 'FAILURES'.
Architects' Remedy for Alleged Defects in Government Scheme.
Large-Scale Building.

Grave charges that the Government's evacuation scheme has failed in several aspects are made in a report which has been submitted by the Association of Architects, Surveyors and Technical Assistants to the Minister of Health and the President of the Board of Education.

To rectify the alleged defects in the Government's scheme, the association states that a large-scale building programme should be undertaken for the evacuees.

After stating that large numbers of mothers and children have streamed back to the towns, the report adds:

'There are many instances of towns which have received evacuees, although they themselves are so indisputably exposed to attack that the evacuees should be removed at all costs.'

Teachers' Action.

There are numerous examples of teachers taking over halls and condemned school buildings on their own initiative and without authority, and commencing education without books and writing materials, without desks, and in buildings where heating is impossible in winter, and where the sanitary arrangements are inadequate.

In many towns there is not a single hall available. All have been taken over as A.R.P. centres, first-aid stations, or by the military.

The association's recommendations for rectifying the alleged defects are:

Further evacuation from the evacuation areas after the first air raids must be expected and prepared for. Every effort must be made to evacuate more people now.

Accommodation already exists for these people owing to the fact that only half the number for which preparations were made actually evacuated. Redistribution of those already in the evacuation areas, must begin so that additional people can be removed safely.

Dangerous towns which now have evacuees should immediately be cleared.

Powers for Local Authorities.

Local authorities in reception areas should be given not merely powers of billeting, but powers over all existing buildings in their area so that they can formulate long-term plans. The key to the success of evacuation for school children lies in providing facilities for full education. Education for both the local and evacuated children is at present hopelessly dislocated. This must be put right by taking over halls and big houses, and by building new schools.

Evacuated mothers at present tending to flock home must be provided with 'somewhere where they can feed cheaply, spend the day, do some useful work together, and leave their children on occasions'.

Finally, the association recommends that residential nursery schools must be formed for young children who are not accompanied by their mothers.

* * *

Dissatisfaction with the Government evacuation scheme continued to be shown in some quarters, as the following article from the Chatham, Rochester and Gillingham News *for 27th October 1939 clearly shows:*

UPS AND DOWNS OF EVACUATION.
*Dissatisfaction Expressed At Local And County Meetings.
But Approval For Scheme As A Whole.*

Dissatisfaction over various aspects of the evacuation of Kentish school children was expressed this week, both at the quarterly meeting of the Kent Education Committee, at Maidstone, and at the monthly meeting of the Medway Education Board at Fort Pitt House, Rochester.

General approval was expressed at Maidstone by the Chairman (Mr W. Rolfe Nottidge), but there was a number of criticisms by the Revd J. T. Wilkinson, with regard to the difficulties of mothers in evacuated areas getting out to see their children in reception areas.

The Revd Stanley Morgan asked whether evacuated teachers were being expected to work seven days a week; and an adverse comment on another aspect of the scheme was passed by Councillor W. J. Hedge at the Rochester meeting, when he described the Government's restrictions on the reopening of schools in evacuated areas as 'all Mickey Mouse'.

At the meeting of the Kent Education Committee on Monday, Mr Nottidge said that some districts in Kent had been affected by the Government's evacuation scheme, some were neutral areas, and others were reception areas. 'I think we may say we were fortunate, and we were able to make a good number of careful plans in advance – in the hope that they would never be needed – and that enabled us to cope on the whole satisfactorily with the situation.'

Mr Nottidge went on to say that it was decided at the commencement that elementary schools in the evacuated areas should remain closed. The tutorial system was now in operation, however, with the school as the headquarters on the work. The Committee had decided to provide trenches in the schools in these areas, and the number of children using them would increase as the work proceeded. In order to enable schools in reception areas to make provision for the large number of evacuated children, a large number of halls were being used for recreation and education.

Mr Nottidge added that similar arrangements were being made in respect of secondary and junior technical schools, which would begin operating the tutorial system on October 30th. The various heads were now working out the details.

'I can only say I was astonished to find the kind of work and the kind of co-operation that was going on under the extraordinary conditions I found in some places. There was one school, very little better than a barn, housing two schools, and you simply could not tell which lot of teachers or which lot of children belonged to which. They just fused, there was complete co-operation, and they were doing their utmost to overcome the difficulties and get on with the work. And that sort of thing is going on all over the County.'

The Chairman paid a particular tribute to the office staff, 'from the Director downwards'. The work has only been made possible, he declared, by the devoted work of everybody concerned, and he would like to include in that the London County Council staff, 'who are now working with us'.

Moving the adoption of the report of the Elementary Education Sub-Committee, Lord Northbourne also referred to evacuation. He had visited a few places, he said, and had been astonished to find not only the inevitable inconvenience being cheerfully coped with, but also the creation in the most unexpected places of situations of real happiness. 'It is quite a delight,' he told the Committee, 'in many rural schools, in some cases in buildings which have been discarded, and are now being reopened, and in all sorts of buildings which would normally be regarded as unsuitable, to find groups of children thoroughly enjoying themselves and as happy a little community as you could wish to see.'

Thronging Premises.

The Revd J. T. Wilkinson told the members that people were 'thronging the premises of the Erith Town Council morning and afternoon on problems of evacuation, and someone has got to answer them'. Mr Wilkinson spoke of a letter he had sent to H.M. the Queen, saying, 'It is pleasant to read that Your Majesty has been to visit your daughters at Balmoral. I petition Your Majesty to do whatever you can to make it possible for mothers in evacuated areas to travel into rural areas into which their children have been billeted.'

The reply received was: 'While deeply sympathetic with all mothers who have been separated from their children, the Queen much regrets that it is not possible for her to interfere.'

The Chairman interrupted to tell Mr Wilkinson he was out of order.

Resuming, Mr Wilkinson said there were in addition the expenses of the dispatch of clothing for mending and postage for correspondence. 'If you had these people in all day as we are having, putting their pitiful tales before us, you would understand,' he said.

'We are all in complete sympathy with you in regard to everything you have said,' interposed the Chairman, 'but these matters are the concern of the Government, and not ours.'

The Revd Wilkinson was finally ruled out of order, and the next business proceeded with.

'The matters which Mr Wilkinson has raised,' commented the Chairman, 'as far as I can see, fall outside the work of this Committee. I am sure we all realise the difficulties and many problems which evacuation has presented. I have spent a long time in the reception areas myself, and I do appreciate the tremendous efforts which have been made, and I have also come into touch with some of the difficulties. I am perfectly sure the Committee will not be backward in doing anything in their power to help, but they should not make it more difficult for others in these times by discussing matters which other authorities are trying to cope with.'

Mr Wilkinson asked to what authorities he could bring these complaints, and the Chairman replied: 'Evacuation: the Erith Borough Council. Reception: the County District Councils. Contributions: the County Council through its Public Assistance Committee.'

Weekends Off.

In answer to a question by the Revd Stanley Morgan, Lord Northbourne said that teachers who had been evacuated were not working seven days a week, nor was it generally impossible for them to get away for the weekend.

'But while evacuation is still fairly new, I should very much dislike to attempt to give any general ruling as to what it is desirable to ask teachers to do,' he added.

Mr Morgan said he had been approached by teachers and informed that some sort of instruction or hint or suggestion had been conveyed by letter, expressing the wish that teachers should not take the weekends off, and that they were expected to remain with the children. 'I have been asked if it is the wish of the Kent Education Committee that they should work seven days a week,' he said.

Lord Northbourne said he was unable to give a detailed answer, notice of the question not having been given, and the Chairman gave an undertaking that the whole matter of voluntary and compulsory work would be investigated and a reply given as soon as possible.

Mr B. T. Ellis pointed out that these were days of extreme difficulty, and teachers in the County were doing what they considered – and what the Kent Education Committee considered – to be voluntary work; and they were doing it in a manner which they hoped to be smooth and of goodwill between themselves and the Committee.

Collection Of Fees.

The procedure as regards the collection of fees of Kent pupils provided that the ordinary fee payable should be collected in respect of all children who had joined the evacuation party; the normal fee should be collected in respect of each child on the roll of Kent schools in neutral and reception areas as opportunities could be offered for his or her attendance at school. Parents of evacuated children from outside Kent should continue to pay the fee of the school formerly attended. Any fees tendered in respect of evacuated children to schools in the Committee's area were being received by the Committee as agents for the Authority of the evacuation area.

The Sub-Committee recommended that as soon as the arrangements are completed for the regular attendance of Kent pupils at school, although only for part-time education, the full-time tuition fee should become payable, and that pupils whose parents or guardians accept this arrangement be allowed to remain in attendance.

For the current term, pending the completion of shelters, many children had been unable to resume attendance and others were attending only at irregular times or receiving instruction away from the school premises. Representations had been made that there should be a reduction of fees for such children in respect of the current term. These representations were receiving the consideration of the Sub-Committee.

It was suggested that there were many parents who thought that if their children only attended once or twice a week, the fees should be reduced.

In answer, Mr Nottidge emphasised that parents who paid full fees only paid about one third of the cost of the facilities, and that considerably less than half the children of the secondary schools were full fee payers. The Committee had already decided, he said, not to reduce the value of scholarships.

'The whole question of fees is to be considered,' he said, 'and with the rising cost of living must be considered from all points of view, in order to do justice to the whole body of ratepayers.'

Delayed Schemes.

The Secondary and University Education Sub-Committee reported the receipt of a Board of Education circular, drawing attention to the need for the restriction of capital expenditure within the narrowest limits, and pointing out that it will be difficult to obtain materials or labour for any new building on account of the demands for the Services programme, and that although there is no general embargo on school building there must inevitably be a postponement of most of the building projects.

The Board would be prepared to consider proposals for the provision of new secondary schools, or extension or alteration of existing schools, only in the most exceptional circumstances. The Board will make every effort to facilitate the execution of works in progress, especially in reception areas where the buildings are likely to facilitate the education of an increased number of children. The Board point out, however, that the question of priority represents special difficulties at the present time.

The Treasury have intimated that consent to the exercise of borrowing powers will not be given unless the project is of pressing necessity, either for reasons of public need, or on account of war requirements.

In view of these considerations, the Board decided not to proceed with, inter alia, the provision of a new gymnasium and adaptation of existing gymnasium for a library at the Chatham County School for Girls. Plans will however, be completed, in order that the work may proceed as soon as circumstances permit. The same decisions were made in respect of new buildings at Fort Pitt for the Medway Technical College.

Medway Board Decision.

At the meeting of the Medway Education Board, Councillor Hedge said it seemed to him that the Board of Education was prepared to smile on small classes of about 20 children taught in private houses, but in schools that had been built for the job the children could attend to receive tasks but not to have instruction.

The discussion followed a statement by the District Education Officer (Mr P. S. Taylor) on the return to the Towns of evacuated children.

He said that in the first two weeks of the war numbers of children had returned home. There had then been a lull, but now the drift back had increased following the Government announcement regarding parents contributions to the upkeep of the evacuated children.

He added that there was little tendency to return among secondary and technical school students, and what little there was, had been made up by an increase in evacuation.

In reply to a question by Councillor Hedge, Mr Taylor said that in certain schools teachers were in contact with scholars for the purpose of giving them homework and guidance. Ordinary classes had not been started.

The heads of secondary schools had consulted as to what could be done for the children left behind. Certain small groups were being gathered together and told what they could do. 'The Board of Education,' the Education Officer continued, 'will not allow ordinary instruction to be given. They will allow you to run classes in private houses, but not in school buildings.'

The scene in Balmoral Road, Gillingham, as school children assemble for evacuation to South Wales in June 1940
(Photo by courtesy of the Kent Messenger Group)

Chapter Four

ON THE MOVE AGAIN – THIS TIME TO SOUTH WALES

With the end to the period known as the phoney war, with the defeat of the allied forces at Dunkirk, and with the distinct possibility of imminent invasion of this country by German forces, urgent action was taken in May and June 1940 to evacuate thousands of school children from the immediate danger area. This time they were to leave Kent entirely, with the bulk of them travelling the long distance to South Wales, to a different country, a different culture, a completely different way of life. Again, those children who left as part of the official Government evacuation scheme, left as school units. The following article appeared in the Chatham, Rochester & Gillingham News *on 24th May, 1940, reporting on the first of the Medway children to be re-evacuated to Wales:*

Evacuated to Wales.
Local Children In Large Exodus West.
A Warm Welcome.

Schoolchildren from the Medway Towns who had been evacuated to other parts of Kent at the outbreak of the war were among the several thousand scholars who on Sunday made the journey to find new homes in Wales.

Twelve special through trains took the children, who had enjoyed the kindness and hospitality of foster parents in Kent, Essex and Suffolk, to the West Country, which received them with no less warmth of welcome and affection.

And they left behind them with those who had been their foster parents for less than a year cherished memories and a feeling of real loss. It was a rousing send-off that was given them, but handkerchiefs were used for more things than merely waving goodbye.

'We couldn't feel worse about it if we were parting from our own kiddies,' said one Canterbury foster mother, and she was expressing the innermost thoughts of many.

Local children went mainly from the quiet coastal and country places pivoting about Canterbury, the Rochester ones from Whitstable, Elham, Chislet, Sandling Park and Saltwood, all of which areas were visited by the Rochester Education Secretary (Mr E. H. Webb) on Friday at the earliest moment after he received notification of the new exodus. With the exception of only two of them, the whole of the Rochester teachers who have been with the children in the reception areas have gone with them to their new billets.

The scenes at the departure railway stations were as quaint a mixture of pathos and fun as those other scenes at our own local railway stations nine months ago, when the children first started on their strange journey – but this time there were new and novel differences.

The kiddies brought with them gas masks, bags containing a change of clothing and other necessities, and a day's rations. Each had an identity card fastened to its clothing. And with them as far as the trains themselves came dozens of other kiddies, kiddies native to the reception areas who have found new companions during the first long winter of war, and were loath to see them go. . .

Ten thousand children in all have been expected to travel, but over two thousand of these had been taken home by their parents. Wales, they thought, was a little too far away; and who, after all, will blame them for that?

From all reports, it seems that the spirits of the youthful travellers rose steadily as they sped across the English countryside to the West. Later, when the relays of trains reached their destination junctions and distributing centres, there were scenes strikingly reminiscent of seaside resorts on bank holidays.

Chatham and Gillingham children had the honour of being the first to arrive; the train that pulled in at Cardiff punctually at 1.30pm contained thirty girls from the Chatham Technical School and ninety-two boys from the Rochester Technical School. They had been evacuated to the Sittingbourne area; their new homes will be in the Cardiff rural area. The children continued to arrive at regular intervals up to eight o'clock. By supper-time they were all in their new billets. Wales gave them a warm welcome and all arrangements worked as smoothly as in the first evacuation scheme.

At Pontypridd, for example, several thousand people were at the station to form a 'committee of reception', and the Salvation Army played the Canterbury and Faversham re-evacuees into the town. Most of them passed through Cardiff on their way, and on reception they were given hot meals and medically examined before passing on to their billets. Many will live in miners' homes in the almost derelict Rhondda Valley.

Some, seeing for the first time the queer aspect of colliery country, stared in amazed silence before starting to talk about it 'nineteen to the dozen'. Will they have something to write home about . . . ?

A special and unexpected thrill was reserved for a number of Kentish kiddies; their assembly station was nothing less than the banqueting room at St Fagan's Castle, Lord Plymouth's home. Will they have something to write home about . . . ?

And so another evacuation scheme has been planned, suddenly decided upon, and swiftly carried out. Unfortunate as it is in many ways, there can be little doubt that it is in the best interests of the children themselves that they have been thus separated from those near and dear to them. There will be many and blissful reunions when peace visits these isles again.

* * *

The bulk of the evacuees seemed to have had good billets with loving foster parents but, for some, the billets were less than satisfactory. The following personal accounts give some insight into how these children's lives were changed and how they all had to cope with the different culture.

Mr E. Towlson, Chatham Grammar School, remembers his evacuation to South Wales:

In mid-1940 we were shipped off to South Wales where I was lodged with a mining family called Thomas in Pontypridd. All the family are now dead and I regret that events never gave me the opportunity to return and thank them. I now realise that our schooling was a marvel of organisation, split as it was between Treforest Mining Tech, Harthonn Tech (near Taffs Wells), the Unitarian Chapel at Pontypridd, and any other secondary school that had spare facilities.

Attending all three schools in a day was not uncommon and one can only look back with gratitude to the head and his masters for keeping up standards and good humour.

I can only remember causing trouble once for which I received six of the best! This involved, with others, the adventurous crossing of the river Taff by way of an unsafe, disused railway bridge. The crossing might well have gone unnoticed but for the cheers of the onlookers.

Other than this instance I was a model evacuee to outward appearances and caused no further anguish to the staff. No doubt they had many welfare problems which passed unnoticed by the majority. All in all the time in Pontypridd was a happy and occasionally, due to the enemy, an exciting one. Probably the greatest shock was one of culture. Being C. of E. I was dispatched to Communion at 7.30am every Sunday and, as it was a 'minor' religion, quite often formed the entire congregation. This was followed by Baptist indoctrinations 10am to 12.30pm, Sunday School 3pm to 4.15pm and Evensong 6pm to 7pm with the rest of the day my own. I did enjoy the marvellous hymn singing and still have a great love of Welsh massed choirs.

Another plus from those days has been a continuing interest in mining and minerology. Due to this influence I still, whenever I can, venture into the hill and old mining districts of Britain.

About the summer of 1941 the senior class was moved to Caerphilly to attend the local grammar school. I remember I and another lad, whose surname I think was Richards, were boarded with the Griffiths family. This family also is dead. In fact all those we lodged with were past middle age and we must have been a handful for them.

At this period I remember being constantly short of money due to our developing tastes for the wild life. To overcome the problem 'Rich' Richards and I 'liberated' the Congregational Chapel window cleaning gear, went into business and became instantly rich, charging 2s 6d a front plus 3d a fan light. Such was the nature of the times we were welcomed with open arms and gained more female 'dates' than we could cope with. It was some time before we realised that our earnings were being spent on our customers.

In 1942 I gained a good position in the then Civil Service Commission examination and, determined not to be the only male in the family not in the services, I joined the Fleet Air Arm as an aircraft armaments apprentice. This was done in the face of the good advice offered and, despite all, it was a reasonable choice, as it has kept myself and family fed and clothed ever since.

*After **Derek Utteridge's** relatively short stay in Sittingbourne and then his return home to Chatham, he was off once again, this time with the Gillingham County School to Rhymney in the South Wales valleys:*

This time I took my younger brother, Roy, with me. We stayed with a couple in their late 50s, named Benjamin. They had four children. Mary, a 14 year old schoolgirl, Jackie, a railwayman of about 22, and two in their late 20s, Richie, a miner, and Annie, a nurse. We used the local grammar school's buildings, but kept our own identity, in entirely separate classes. We also used the local miners' club for lessons – and for leisure! We were expected to attend school on Saturday mornings, as well as the normal Monday to Friday routine, but I think this was mainly to keep us well occupied. My brother attended the local junior school.

Although the immediate area around the Medway Towns in the late 1930s and early 1940s was more rural than it is today, in Rhymney the countryside was on our doorstep. The hills were like mountains to us, and sheep wandering in the roads where we lived were a common sight. There were ponds close by where we sailed our model boats. The streams which fed the ponds were crystal clear, tumbling down the hillside.

Calvary Chapel, Rhymney
(The Tin Chapel)
(Photo taken in 1991)

We went to Sunday School at the English Wesleyan Methodist Chapel, known locally as the 'tin chapel', not far from where we were billeted. It never struck me as particularly evangelistic, for we had attended Sunday School in the Union Street Methodist Chapel at home, despite having attended a Church of England junior school, and the fact that our father was a Catholic. Our foster family were Catholic (except the father), but it was never suggested that we go to the Catholic church, or the local Methodist Chapel, but we went to this 'tin chapel'. I mention this because I know this chapel survives to this day.

Rhymney village was in Monmouthshire, on the eastern side of the valley of the River Rhymney. Below the village, the river formed the boundary with Glamorgan. On the far side of the river the land rose steeply again. Although there was a road crossing, it was much more fun to cross the river using the stepping stones. On the western side of the river there were derelict drift mine workings which were fascinating places for us kids to investigate. There were also very deep ponds, probably old mine shafts, which we were frequently warned against.

On one occasion half a dozen of us, all from our school, were wandering on the hills when we came upon a very distraught lady, who was threatening to commit suicide by jumping into one of these ponds. The older boys managed to restrain her and tried to calm her down, sending the two youngest, myself and one other, back to the village to get help from the local police. We arrived at the police station breathless from our exertions and reported the incident. 'Ah,' said the officer, 'that's in Glamorgan. We can do nothing from here, that's a job for the Pontlottyn Station!' However, he did agree to report to them and, as far as we know, the lady was saved. We were all sworn to secrecy at the time, which was very frustrating. Here was a great adventure which we were unable to talk about – and a secret I have kept for nearly 60 years.

During our stay, tragedy struck the family next door. The husband, Les, was killed in a mining accident, leaving his wife with a babe-in-arms. I saw then, at first hand, the community spirit of a mining village, typical, I suppose, of an area where almost the entire community was employed in the mines.

We remained in Rhymney until June 1941. My mother and elder sister visited us in Wales and we returned home with them. There was never any suggestion before she arrived that she intended taking us home. I will never know the reason; both my mother and elder sister have now passed away, but I've always assumed that once she had seen us she couldn't bear to go home and leave us behind. We may even have expressed a desire to go back with her – I don't remember. Anyway home we came.

In recent years I have read somewhere that prior to mid-1941, evacuees could return home free of charge. After that date any travel would have to be paid for. My mother would have found that expensive – probably impossible – and may have decided at the time that it was 'now or never'!

Looking back at that time, the local Welsh people must have suffered much disruption to accommodate us evacuees; a sacrifice I'm sure we didn't appreciate at the time. I have no doubt that we were homesick from time to time, but I can't be more specific. It was a great adventure.

Contrary to what I have heard about the mistreatment of evacuees by their host families, we were treated well, in fact we could not have been better treated. The Benjamins were a very caring family. I wonder what my reaction would be today if I were forced to take in two unknown 12 and 8 year olds from the inner cities? Hypothetically, I like to think that I would welcome them with open arms – but in reality?

My mother and Mrs Benjamin exchanged Christmas correspondence until 1945 when the latter died and the family lost contact. In 1965 I called briefly at the old house while on my way to west Wales, and found that the 14 year old girl I had known when I was an evacuee was still living there, but now she was a mother of three children. Her father had died and so had her younger brother Jackie.

Regrettably, I waited until 1990 before visiting again. Regrettably because I learned that the two older children, Richie and Annie, and a cousin, Annie Knox, who used to join us in walks on the mountains, had died during the previous couple of years. The old house had been demolished, and the daughter, now a widowed grandmother, was living in a council house with her unmarried son.

We have had her stay with us at our home for a couple of weeks holiday; a totally inadequate repayment for the kindness shown by her family all those years ago. We were able to show her Chatham Dockyard, the prime reason for us meeting in the first place, my old school buildings in Gillingham – and made a surprise visit to my brother who was unaware that I had found her.

One final point to my story is that one of my foster sister's daughters now owns a house in Rhymney near the river and hospital; probably the same house in which my fellow evacuee and best friend, Bernard Snow, was billeted.

*The following thoughts were expressed to Derek by his foster sister, **Mary**, which shows a Welsh perspective to the reception of English evacuees:*

During the depression in the 1920s and 1930s the children of Rhymney had received food parcels and clothes from the children of Kent, so she and her friends assumed that

An example of the postcards issued to most evacuees for informing their parents of their safe arrival and new address in the reception area

all Kent children were rich. It came as quite a shock to find that they weren't! Mary herself never received any of the parcels because her father was never out of work. She learned of them from her friends. In fact, she tells with some amusement that she had a 'deprived' childhood. During the hard times there was a soup kitchen in a local hall where all her classmates went for their soup and roll every lunchtime – and had a fine old time! Mary meanwhile had to go home to her meat and two veg! And for two weeks in the summer all her friends went off to a charity camp while she had to stay in the village alone! She even remembers complaining to her father that he ought to be out of work to enable her to join the fun!

Children of St Michael's School, Chatham, rallying round the school banner before departing to an unknown destination in 1940
(Photo by courtesy of the Kent Messenger Group)

When the evacuees came to the valleys, some families had been expecting to welcome dear little children parted from their mums and were taken aback to find that some of the evacuees were 17 and 18 year old sixth formers, at a time when most of the population was at work at the age of 14.

I reminded her once, safe in the knowledge that we were talking of events of 50 years previously, that she had been (to put it politely) the least welcoming of her family. She confessed to being aware of this and concluded that that was probably because she had been the baby of the family until the arrival of those two 'cuckoos in the nest', who because they were refugees were probably given more attention than she had ever been given. We agreed to let bygones be bygones.

Roy Utteridge, *younger brother of Derek, now puts his thoughts down on his evacuation to Wales:*

I was almost seven years old when war was declared in 1939, and was attending St Paul's School in Chatham. We were evacuated to South Wales the following year, 1940. I remember having a brown luggage label attached to my coat, with my name on it, and leaving Chatham by train, but of the journey I can remember nothing.

Our final destination turned out to be the village of Rhymney, and my brother and I ended up in our new foster home with Mr and Mrs Benjamin. They were very kind to me and I have only fond memories of my stay with them.

Derek and Roy Utteridge reunited with their Welsh foster sister, Mary, in 1991

As I recall I attended school just mornings one week and afternoons the next. We were taught Welsh and in time I could speak Welsh fluently. All my foster family were Welsh-speaking so I suppose it was inevitable that I would start to speak Welsh.

My strongest memories of Wales includes going up to a mountain lake with Richie, the son of Mr and Mrs Benjamin, and playing with a boat he had made. And of watching the pit ponies coming down the lane from the pit – and one of them pushing its way into the front passage of the house!

My mother brought us both back from Wales in 1941, and although we hadn't been in Wales for very long, it seemed to me that we had been there for ages. When I returned to Chatham I then attended Luton Road Boys' School. I stayed in Chatham until the doodlebugs began in 1944, when I was evacuated again, this time to Yorkshire, but that's another story!

Gladys Austin (now Mrs Gladys Hamer) from Gillingham recalls her second evacuation, this time to a village in South Wales:

In May 1940, we were on the move again, this time to South Wales. We went on a train which took us straight through to Pontyclun. When we arrived we were all taken to a school hall where lots of local children and their parents were waiting to meet us. There were long tables set out with all sorts of food to welcome us, then after we had eaten we were sent out into the playground until billeting arrangements had been made. Eventually, my brother and I and just a few other children were picked out and were sent to Penygawsi Llantrisant.

I and another girl named Vera were fostered by a Mr and Mrs Robbins, while my brother and Vera's brother Reginald were fostered by a Mr and Mrs Owen, just four doors away from our billet. Mr and Mrs Robbins whom I called Auntie and Uncle, were the most wonderful and kind people you could ever meet. They had no children of their own so they really spoilt us.

Our first day at school was an experience. All the local children came to look at us, as though we came from another planet. We attended Llantrisant School which was situated on top of a mountain and it was quite a climb every day.

I really enjoyed my life in Wales. In the spring time we used to go fishing for minnows in the river, and picked primroses and bluebells. In the summer we played in the tall ferns on the mountainside, and in the autumn I was always out picking blackberries so that Auntie could make jam and pies.

When I was fourteen I was sent home, much to my Auntie's regret because she wanted me to attend the Commercial College, but my mother couldn't afford it. I returned to Gillingham and went to work in Curry's radio and cycle shop. Meanwhile my brother, who was still in Wales, was extremely unhappy, so my mother went down and brought him back home as well. My sister was by now living with my Auntie and Uncle in Wales, where she stayed until my father returned home at the end of the war. My father went away when I was ten years old, and I didn't see him again until I was sixteen!

When the Germans started sending over the doodlebugs, the raids started to get very bad, so children were again being evacuated from the Medway Towns. My brother was off again, this time to a billet in Bolton in Lancashire. He lived with business people who had no children of their own, just a nephew. When brother Norman was 14 years old his foster parents wanted him to serve an apprenticeship in their business. So that Norman could do this, his foster parents built a house for our family, and we all moved, lock, stock and barrel, up to Bolton. My parents have since died, but my brother, my sister and I are all married and settled there.

Having been evacuated to the village of Shepherdwell in East Kent, **John Clark** *returned to his home in Gillingham and was later evacuated to South Wales:*

Having spent a delightful six months (although it seemed much longer) in Shepherdswell, I returned to Gillingham and later, I have no idea how long, I was sent to South Wales, to a village called Onllwyn, near Seven Sisters. I was billeted with a Welsh family with another evacuee called Julian Hunt, who was also from Gillingham. My foster parents considered me spoilt, and they were probably right! They lived in this tiny single street village overlooking the pit. Their house was quite modern, with a bathroom, but the bath was never used. 'Father', a miner, and the rest of the family bathed in a tin tub in the kitchen in front of the kitchen range.

Moira, the daughter, was in her early teens and when she and the others bathed, whatever the weather, Julian and I were required to take what shelter we could in the porch of the front door, also seldom used.

The food was disgusting being mainly stews made from swede and other root vegetables and lumps of fatty meat. Once a month we had fish and chips, a real treat! There was one tiny corrugated-iron shop, painted green, which as far as I can remember, sold only packets of 'Nipits', which weren't on ration. On Sundays we would go for a walk in the morning, attend Sunday School in the afternoon and go to Chapel in the evening – that was until we were unfortunate enough to meet a fellow evacuee from Gillingham on one of our walks who managed to 'con' us into going to church in Banwen, a mile or two up the road. So we were pretty well tied up on Sundays. Needless to say, in later years when I was old enough to object, I stopped attending organised religious services, and I have never looked back since, as I consider I put in enough church time during the war. Likewise, I seldom if ever eat root vegetables, especially in stews, not to mention beef fat!

The one good thing about Sunday was that the front room was opened and high tea was put on in this room with jellies and sandwiches, which was quite a treat. The only other time this room was used was when my parents came to take me home, nine months after my arrival in Wales.

For breakfast on the morning we left we had tinned tomatoes on toast, which my mother found very strange, but it was quite a treat for us. The last thing my foster parents said to me as we left in a tiny car en route for Neath and London was, 'Don't forget, you send us Christmas presents, and we'll send presents to you.'

Other memories I have of my time in Wales include going to a 'bug-hutch' cinema near Seven Sisters to see *George Formby at the TT Races,* being 'shopped' by my fellow evacuee for transporting a large lump of fat in my mouth from lunch back to school to spit into the raging stream outside, writing home pleading for a postal order and later pleading to be brought home, and seeing London burning from the train on our way back.

I had a nice collection of toys in Wales, which might have provided a potential source of income for my dotage, but these were confiscated by my foster parents for their young son, so I don't feel I exactly found a welcome in the valleys. It would certainly intrigue me to pass through Onllwyn again, but definitely without stopping and no tears!

Don Phillips *and his brother* **Jack,** *from Luton Council School, Chatham, had already been evacuated to Sittingbourne, now Don was leaving the Medway area for the second time:*

We stayed at home until late May 1940, when we were evacuated to Abercarn in South Wales. As we were saying our goodbyes to friends, relatives and neighbours on the day

Don Phillips' class, taken in Abercarn in 1940. The group includes Peter Robb, Peter Bernthall, Jimmy Phillips, Ronnie Sharp, Albert Terry and Don Phillips (back row, extreme right). The class teacher on the left is Mr Lowden

of departure, Mrs Scott who ran a little grocery shop from her front room at 23 Connaught Road, Luton, gave us a big bar of Cadbury's chocolate each. My brother ate his on the journey and I, after a little nibble and a lot of persuasion, sold mine for sixpence.

We walked to Chatham Railway Station and when we got on to the platform Jack spotted Mum in the crowd. He tried to point Mum out to me, but all I could see was a mass of faces. I was quite disappointed as well as being a little sad. My memory of the journey to Wales is a bit hazy, but I do remember that there were several stops on the way, all of them I suspect due to pressure of traffic on the railways at that time. The Dunkirk evacuation was in progress and we were held up several times to let the troop trains through. I can remember one stop where a kindly porter came along handing out cups of water in thick white china cups that were the style of the day. When the train started to pull out of the station I have a lasting memory of the porter haring down the platform trying to recover the cups. It was hilarious to watch; some of the cups smashed as he was trying to catch them and missed!

We arrived at Abercarn sometime in the late afternoon. We alighted from the train and were taken to a school hall at the bottom of Gwyddon Road. We were given milk and biscuits. Jack and I stood at the back of the hall while we watched as people came in, choose a child or two, and leave. It was reminiscent of an Arabian slave market! I think Jack and I were almost the last to be chosen. The lady who chose us was Mrs Davage, and we were taken by car to her house, which was not far away at 39 Gwyddon Road. Mr and Mrs Davage were a kindly couple. Mr Davage was, to me, a great big man who worked in the local tin works. He was in fact a gentle giant.

Jack and Donald Phillips with their foster father, Mr Davage, taken outside their billet in Abercarn in 1940

By and large I enjoyed my time in Abercarn. I made lots of friends with local children and also the adults. All of the local people seemed to be very friendly. I remember one in particular, Mrs Knight, who was a friend of Mrs Davage. She had two grown up sons who were both in the Royal Air Force. She also had a lovely black labrador whose name was Mick. Mick would often come round to the Davages during the spring and summer, to go for a walk with Mr Davage up into the mountains. I also used to tag along from time to time.

I cannot remember much about my schooling in Wales. The school was situated in a part of Abercarn known as the West End, about one and a half miles from where we were staying. As there were no school meals in those days it meant that I had to walk that distance four times a day. Very occasionally, and only if it was raining hard, I was allowed to catch a bus.

The house at 39 Gwyddon Road was to me a very large one. It had a front garden and the front door was about 20 feet from the road. There were three downstairs rooms

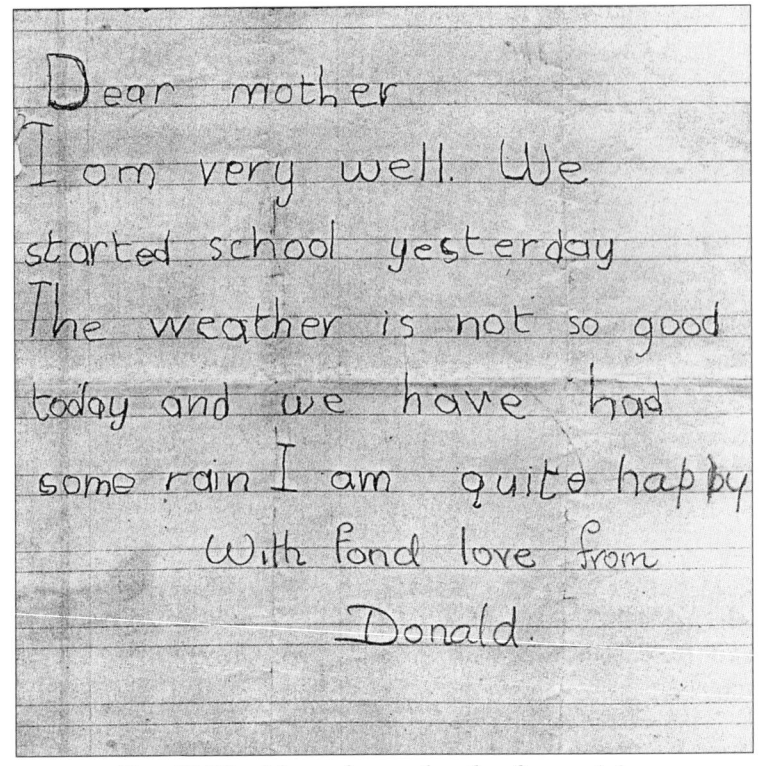

> Dear mother
> I am very well. We started school yesterday The weather is not so good today and we have had some rain I am quite happy
> With fond love from
> Donald.

Don Phillips' letter home shortly after arriving in Abercarn in 1940

plus a scullery. Upstairs there were three bedrooms plus a bathroom – unheard of in our terraced house in Connaught Road, with two up and three down with no bathroom. Our bathroom back home was a galvanised bath in the kitchen where the copper was.

Mr and Mrs Davage let some rooms to a young married couple named Selwyn and Olive Hyde. They did not stay long after an incident when Olive burnt my hand. Olive who smoked asked me if I would like to see the smoke coming out of her eyes. Of course I said, 'Yes, I would,' so she told me to place my hand on her stomach and watch her eyes while she drew on her cigarette. She then took the cigarette from her mouth and while I was concentrating my attention on her eyes she jabbed the cigarette on the back of my hand, which left a nasty burn mark. When Mrs Davage found out she was very angry, and needless to say they were not around for much longer.

My teacher for the first few months was Mr Lowden, who was billeted opposite me. His bedroom backed on to the recreation area where most of us played. He took it upon himself to be involved in our welfare. One of his ways to make sure we did not stay out too late playing in the evening was to hang two Union Jacks out of his window. The first one meant we had fifteen minutes left to play, the second meant that our time was up and we had to go in straight away or risk punishment. Mr Lowden eventually went into the army, although he still sent me a Christmas card. When we started school, we were doing half days – mornings one week, afternoons the next. Jack was on opposite half days to me. As my Dad said we were not to be separated, to my mind these arrangements were separating us and were wrong, so I stayed with my brother in the afternoons, but I was soon found out and punished.

In the midst of trundling all over the South of England and South Wales, Jack passed for the Math School. How he managed it in the middle of all that upheaval I will never know. At the end of the summer holidays in 1940 he had to move on to Porthcawl – so we were separated anyway!

Abercarn is set in a sort of a 'T' shaped valley surrounded by mountains; Mt Rhyswg to the east, Mt Mynydd Islwyn to the south and Llanfach to the west. In the valley running north to south was a mountain stream known locally as the Brook; when in spate it was wild indeed, but in summer was a nice gentle stream about twelve to eighteen inches deep carrying tiddlers, sticklebacks and some large trout. Once I saw a local man catch a large trout by tickling it. The Brook was dammed off causing quite a large deep lake which we called the 'Distillery'. I don't know why it was called that because I cannot recall any breweries nearby. What I can recall is that a local lad went swimming in the 'Distillery' which, even in the heat of the summer, was very cold. The locals thought that he got cramp and sadly drowned.

At the base of Mt Rhyswg and towards the village was an old quarry with several mounds of spoil known as the 'tumps'. The main one was about 25 feet high with several smaller ones around it. They were overgrown with scrub, small trees and bushes – ideal for playing war games, cops and robbers, Robin Hood and also my favourite, Cowboys and Indians!

I have one abiding memory of a walk on Mt Rhyswg on my own which was forbidden because I was only eight years old. I was about three quarters of the way up the side of the mountain, which was about a thousand feet, when I saw an aircraft

Don Phillips (with a sore head) and brother Jack, standing with their mother, Ethel, and Mrs Pat Davage. Abercarn, August 1940

which looked like a Gloster Gladiator flying down the valley below me. I was able to see into the cockpit and could clearly see the pilot with his helmet on.

During the summer holidays of 1940 our parents came to stay with us. Just before they arrived I was involved in a stone fight with the 'Gwyddonites' versus the 'Llanfachites'. We were always at a disadvantage because we had to throw our stones up a steep wooded slope. I think the point of the fight was to gain control of the high ground held by the Llanfachites. I was leading our gang up the slope when I decided to take cover behind a tree. After a while I poked my head out and wallop! I was hit on the head with a rather large stone. The Llanfachites immediately vacated the high

POST OFFICE GREETINGS TELEGRAM

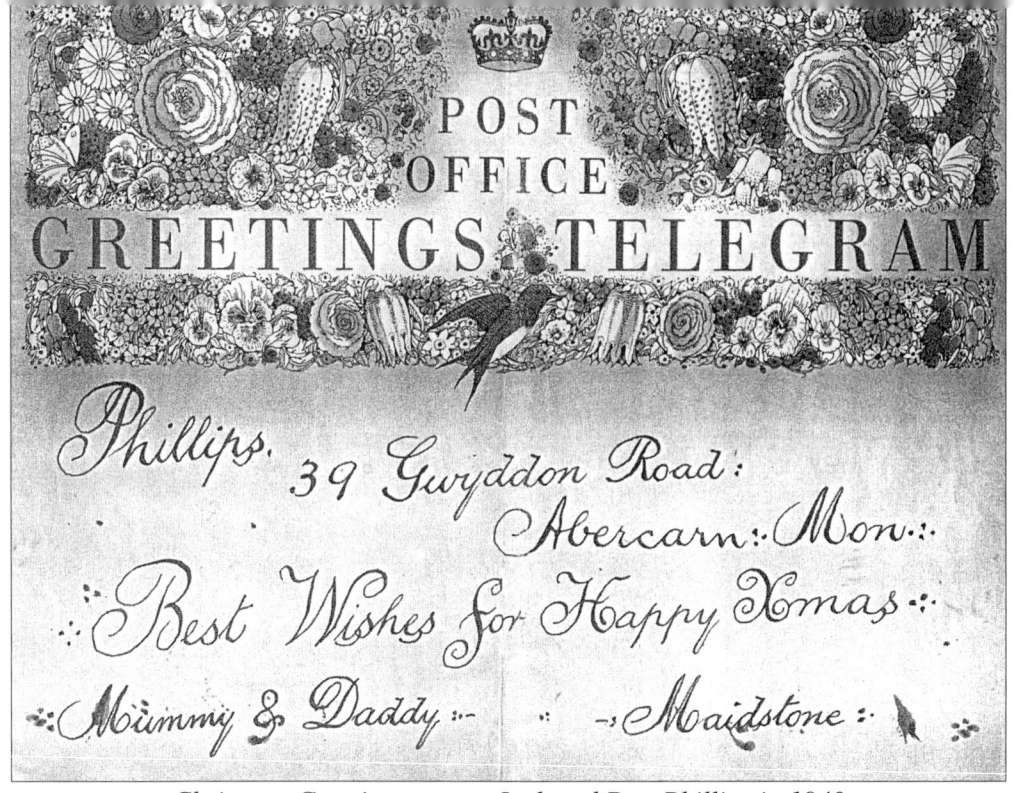

Phillips, 39 Gwyddon Road, Abercarn, Mon.

Best Wishes for Happy Xmas

Mummy & Daddy — Maidstone

Christmas Greetings sent to Jack and Don Phillips in 1940

ground, but unfortunately I was not in the slightest bit interested as I was a little concussed. Mrs Davage took me to the doctor and he stitched up my wound. A few days later we met our parents at Newport Station. Mum said the first thing she saw was someone with a large elastoplast cross on his head. That someone was me and I got precious little sympathy for it.

While our parents were with us we went picking whinberries on Mt Rhyswg. Whinberry pies, as made by Mrs Davage, were one of life's culinary delights. I used to love them.

Mum and Dad went home, Jack went to Porthcawl – and I was on my own! As I have already mentioned, our father had said before we went to Wales that we were not to be separated. My parents must have thought long and hard before they agreed to let Jack go to Porthcawl. Although his billet was not very nice and his foster parents were about the same, the decision was obviously right.

By this time I had made friends with a lot of the local children and there were still large areas of Abercarn to explore, so I had plenty to do. Abercarn was called a village, but it was more like a small town with a population probably between five and ten thousand people. It is situated on the main road from Newport that headed through Newbridge and Crumlin up into the valleys. It also had a river, the Ebbw, which was as black as the ace of spades. Abercarn also had a canal, all of which is now a dual carriageway. There were several ways to cross the canal. One was the main road bridge, the second was any of the lock gates and the third was by way of a very flimsy foot bridge. Both the last two were forbidden on threat of punishment, usually the cane if caught! This only added to the thrill and of course we could not resist the temptation occasionally, until one day when one of our lads fell off the foot bridge and was drowned. I think his surname was Fields and he came from Coronation Road in Luton.

Abercarn once had a coalmine called the 'Prince of Wales', and was situated in the village itself. It had been closed down earlier this century after a nasty accident when somewhere in the region of seventy miners were entombed and their bodies left underground. There was also a ramshackle cinema in the village. Films were changed two or three times a week, so in the long winter evenings a lot of my time was spent in the cinema. One evening on the way home from the cinema with the blackout in force and an air raid in progress, a bomb was dropped on the mountainside near Pentewaun about two miles down the valley. As the noise reverberated around the mountains and valleys, I think I was the first person to do the sub four minute mile. Roger Bannister would not have been in the frame! I got to know the cashier at the cinema and she used to let me in for nothing until one evening when the manager stood in the ticket office with her and I had no money on me. As the couple in front of me went to get their ticket, I panicked a little and dashed into the cinema and tried to make myself as inconspicuous as possible, expecting to feel a hand on my shoulder prior to being thrown out on my ear. But he must have been an old softy because he let me stay. After that experience I though it was best to stay away for a while.

When Jack came to stay with us at Christmas, 1940, I am sure Mrs Davage took particular notice of his condition and wrote to our Mum and Dad. Later, when Jack had threatened to run away, Mum came down on her own to pacify him and to see what his billet was like.

The generosity of the general public knew no bounds. This postcard acknowledgement was sent to Don Phillips' parents

Don Phillips in 1998, with his original evacuation haversack, standing outside the gates of Luton School, Chatham, where he stood in 1940.

> **WAR ORGANISATION**
> **OF THE**
> **BRITISH RED CROSS SOCIETY and ORDER OF ST. JOHN OF JERUSALEM**
>
> President: HER MAJESTY THE QUEEN.   Grand Prior: H.R.H. THE DUKE OF GLOUCESTER, K.G.
>
> **WOUNDED, MISSING AND RELATIVES DEPARTMENT**
> Chairman: THE DOWAGER LADY AMPTHILL, C.I., G.B.E.
>
> R.L.3a.
>
> TELEPHONE NO.: SLOANE 9696
> TELEGRAPHIC ADDRESS: "WOMIREL, KNIGHTS, LONDON"
>
> 7 BELGRAVE SQUARE
> LONDON, S.W.1
>
> Re. Sigmn. A. A. Phillips - 2346253 - R. Sigs.
>
> Dear Mr. Phillips,   5-9-42.
>
> We are pleased to hear that you have had definite news that your brother is a prisoner of war.
>
> As he is now known to be a prisoner, all correspondence concerning him will henceforth be dealt with by the Prisoners of War Department, St. James's Palace, London, S.W.1.
>
> If you will write to that address, you will be given whatever information is available and you will be told how you can communicate with him and how parcels should be sent.
>
> The Red Cross despatches food, clothing and tobacco to all Prisoner of War Camps, which are distributed to all prisoners.
>
> Yours sincerely,
>
> Margaret Ampthill
> Chairman.

Official notification that Jack and Don Phillips' uncle had become a prisoner of war

1941 was much the same as the previous year, except for the following incident. Jack had come to stay for the Yuletide period. One evening after Christmas we were playing marbles on the table (no such thing as television in those days and precious little radio either), when one of them fell on to the floor. On the hob in front of the open fire was a saucepan with some broth or stew in it warming for our supper. As I bent down to retrieve the marble, my trouser leg (short trousers) caught the handle of the saucepan, which was nearly boiling by this time, and pulled it over my right leg. I leapt across the room in two bounds. Unfortunately before anyone could stop me, I rubbed my leg which removed several layers of skin. Flour and butter were applied to the scalded area in an attempt to cool it, all of no avail. I went to bed to spend a very disturbed night. The doctor was called the following day, the same doctor who repaired my head. He was quite used to me by now. He dressed and bandaged the affected leg and he gave me some money, two or three pennies I think. He called regularly to see me until nearly Easter. While I was off sick I was able to go for short walks, and I would wave to an elderly man who would be looking out of his window. Sometimes on fine days when his window was open I would stop and talk to him, and in this way we became very friendly. After some weeks he died and I went to his funeral. I was still only eight. A Welsh funeral in those days was rather strange as only men attended. We all walked behind the hearse to the cemetery. It was rather a solemn and sombre experience for one so young.

Also in 1941 evacuees from Birmingham came to our school. This led to several fights between the 'Brummies', 'Taffies' and 'Chathamites'. The children from Birmingham seemed to me at the time to be very rough, and they also had something of a chip on their shoulder.

Another incident I remember happened in 1942 when I was walking home from school at lunch time. There were a lot of soldiers wearing some form of camouflage gear, marching down Gwyddon Road and through the village. The soldiers were marching down wearing slouch hats and with their rifles at the trail. in single file columns of about ten or twelve at a time, alternating on either side of the road. When I arrived home I asked Mrs Davage what was happening. She of course did not know but she did say that they had been going past all morning. When I went back to school after lunch, they were still marching down the road. There must have been hundreds if not thousands of them.

I can also remember the LDV (Local Defence Volunteers) drilling on the recreation area with their broomsticks, wearing civilian clothes with khaki armbands. During one exercise they set up an ambush in a derelict building in the west end of Abercarn, known to us as the Chapel of Ease. This ambush was supposed to be a secret, but a group of us kids got to hear about it and sat on the wall opposite, laughing, joking and generally taking the mickey out of them. They in turn, and in no uncertain manner, told us what we should be doing with ourselves. Although something of a joke at the time, each of these men was prepared to lay down his life for his country.

When I used to say my prayers at night, either kneeling beside the bed or in it, I used to ask God that should Hitler drop a bomb on my Mum and Dad, would he please make sure that one dropped on me as well.

Mum and Dad had decided by now that it was safe enough for me to return home to Luton. Mum came and collected me and took me home in July 1942. I can remember there was an air raid in progress as we approached Swanley. There was some machine gun or cannon fire, and I wanted to open the window to have a look, but Mum wouldn't let me.

In August, Jack and I went to stay with our aunt, uncle and cousin at Bexley. While I was there I was lacklustre, listless and very much under the weather, so much so that my Aunt Florrie took me to see their doctor, who, after being put in the picture, diagnosed that I was pining for Abercarn. I can't remember what the treatment was, if any, but I obviously recovered.

I did see Mr and Mr Davage two or three times after the war. It must have been very hard for them to take on two boys, not having a family of their own. They chose us on our arrival in Wales, and I think my brother and I will be eternally grateful for that. During the school holidays Mrs Davage would take me to places such as Newport, Cardiff, Barry, Blackwood and Crumlin, but a lot of the school holidays were spent playing by the brook and up in the mountains. All in all I had a pretty good time.

Pamela Costen *(now Mrs Pamela Chew) having been evacuated with her school, Fort Pitt Grammar School, to Sittingbourne in 1939, now departed again with her school to South Wales:*

I have a vivid memory of my mother standing alone on the platform as our train left Sittingbourne in May 1940. She looked so lost and upset. My mother had stayed the previous night with us so that she could be there to wave goodbye.

Arriving at Cardiff was so different from my first evacuation because this time there had been time to arrange things properly. We were taken to a school where food had been prepared for us, and cars were then laid on to deliver us to our new billets. Our new home was in Rhwibina, about seven miles from Cardiff. It was a lovely village and our road was built on a picturesque hill, perhaps one could even call it a small mountain. Bracken and Rowan trees predominated; it was altogether a beautiful area.

We shared a school with the Welsh children. At first it was with another grammar school, but only for the first few weeks. Then at another school we were one of three – the original Welsh school, a school from Tottenham and Fort Pitt Grammar School. The Tottenham school was, shall we say, different! And we were subjected to taunts of 'snobs', and 'who do you think you are!' Eventually, we all settled down together. Naturally, there was an acute lack of space. At one time I remember having a maths lesson in a dressing room while on the adjoining stage was a school singing in Welsh!

The first Christmas we were there a landmine was dropped on the school. It didn't explode at first, but the roof was damaged. The Royal Navy dismantled it, but I believe part of it did explode eventually. We had to have our Christmas party in a church hall and thereafter lessons as well, but when repairs to the school were complete we moved back. I sat my exams there and never returned to Fort Pitt School in Chatham, which I always felt sad about.

My sister sat the scholarship exams in Wales and returned home to attend Chatham Grammar School. I had started work in an insurance company in Cardiff, so I stayed on for another year or so.

Chatham school children, including those from Fort Pitt Grammar School. The photograph was taken on their arrival at Cardiff railway station in May 1940. Pamela Costen is fourth from the right in the back row

I made many friends in Wales and I still keep in contact with some of them. On my wedding day as I came out of the vestry, I was overwhelmed to be greeted by 'Auntie Win and Uncle Jack'. My parents were for ever grateful for their wonderful kindness to me and I still exchange cards and letters with their son.

My admiration goes out to the teachers who not only taught, but were mediators and social workers. I was doing my weekly stint in the office with the Deputy Head one day when an irate woman charged in. Apparently, her evacuee was being awkward, or so she said in no uncertain terms. Afterwards, my teacher sighed, 'You see Pamela, our life is very complicated now, we are even expected to take on the role of parents!'

The bombing of Cardiff was pretty intense at times and I remember Cardiff Docks being just a mass of flames. I also remember the poor people walking up our road on to the mountain every evening with their sleeping bags, just to be safe. We shed many a tear for them.

Once my sister returned home, I too felt the need to be with my family, and so I returned – just in time to witness the German V1s and the V2s. To sum up, I know the years I spent as an evacuee helped to make me the person I am. I certainly appreciated my family more and I realised how kind we were to each other as a nation. The fact that people were prepared to take complete strangers into their homes never ceases to amaze me.

John (Jack) Phillips recalls, with extraordinary detail, the events leading up to and including his second experience of evacuation, this time to South Wales:

After the BEF were plucked, *sans* weapons, *sans* dignity, *sans* just about everything, from the beaches of Dunkirk in 1940, and a major onslaught seemed only a matter of time, evacuation once again seemed a reasonable proposition, only this time there would be no messing about. This time the powers that be would make sure that I was far enough away so as to make it impossible to walk home!

Young Elizabeth Taylor and young Roddy McDowell went to the USA; we went to Abercarn in South Wales, which was quite far enough. I was still at Luton Junior Boys School, now ten and a half and recently having sat the scholarship entrance exam for Rochester Mathematical School. The exam seemed extraordinarily easy, and I finished the papers with lots of time to spare. I then simply forgot about it and concentrated my attention on the much more exciting war that was getting rather interesting for a change. At ten years of age I knew the ultimate outcome was never in doubt. Good invariably trounced evil: the Saturday morning cinema at the Palace on Rainham Road showed us that. But it was exciting, and although

Jack Phillips with his father (left) and foster father, Mr Davage, on Mount Rhyswg after picking whinberries in 1940

I wanted to see what Wales was like, I also wanted to see and be a part of the main contest. Wales seemed such a backwater with no action. But my parents knew best and again we donned our grey suits – perhaps a size larger now, shouldered the same gas masks and haversacks and were ferried once more to Chatham station in what were probably the same buses.

This time, although we had a special through train which took us all the way to Newport, the journey took most of the day. The train stopped and started dozens of times for no apparent reason and we spent ages in sidings while trains loaded with tired, filthy soldiers crept past at little more than walking speed, bound for special rehabilitation camps. These were the men from France, the British Expeditionary Force who, some eight months before, had blithely set out for France intending to be home by Christmas.

Our sandwiches had vanished long before we reached Reading. Eventually we went through the Severn Tunnel at a slow rumble, arriving at Newport late in the evening. At Newport we transferred to a local train which crawled slowly up the Western Valley via Tredegar Park, Risca and Crosskeys to Cwmcarn where we lost some of our party. Abercarn was the next station and we alighted in darkness. The dim gaslamps of the station were shrouded for the blackout and we were so tired that many of the younger children were sleeping and had to be carried. We were taken to a local church hall to be assigned to our foster parents. Ours were Mr and Mrs Davage, and I fear I could scarcely understand a word they said! My brother Donald was out on his feet and we were taken to the Davages' house at 39 Gwyddon Road, given a hot drink and put straight to bed.

Waking early, as one does in a strange bed, I peered out of the window the next morning and looked straight across a narrow valley at a dark, wooded mountainside which disappeared upward into the clouds. I wakened Donald and we got dressed and went downstairs while the rest of the household was still fast asleep.

The mountains ranged from about 1300 to 1600 feet in height, and they gave me my strongest first impressions. They weren't craggy, with cliffs and pinnacles. Rather, they were round-topped and cultivated or fenced with dry-stone walling for sheep pasture. The steeper sides of the mountains were generally unsuitable for arable farming and where they were too steep for pasture, were thickly wooded with birch, oak and mountain ash.

I was enchanted with the mountains and spent long hours in the following weeks wandering in these strange hills, often on my own, but sometimes with my foster father, Bill Davage, a large, softly-spoken, gentle giant of a man whom we both quickly came to love and admire. He worked in the tin works, processing rolled steel sheets. It was hot, tiring and dirty work, and he was exhausted when he came home in the evenings. But after a meal and a rest he always responded to our clamours to be taken for a walk. There was a large black dog called Mick, which belonged to a neighbour, and Mick would come around daily to escort us on our perambulations.

I cannot recall going to school in Abercarn. It was soon high summer, the school holiday period, and all the long days we played in the meadow, a large flat area on the valley floor beside the stream. It had slides, swings and seesaws, low and high for assorted sizes of children. It had a carousel and a rocking contrivance like a suspended battering ram, with a series of handles across the top and spaces for half a dozen kids.

It also had running boards like pre-war motor cars. We had nothing quite so sophisticated in Luton Recreation Ground.

When we tired of these ready-made amusements, we fished for sticklebacks and bullheads in the stream, skimmed flat stones on the Distillery Pond and gathered whinberries and blackberries on the high hills, or fresh watercress in the headwaters of the stream several miles up the valley. It was an idyllic time, so soon to end for me – but not quite yet!

Mrs Pat Davage, our foster mother, was the total antithesis of her husband. She was thin and angular where Bill was plump and rounded. She was hyperactive, whizzing about the house and garden, while her husband was slow and deliberate in all he did. There was not an ounce of spite in either of them and we counted ourselves the most fortunate of kids.

The house, typical of the area, was stone-built in the grey local basaltic stone with red-brick quoins. It was semi-detached and perched some fifteen feet up from the road. A short lawn sloped steeply down from the front of the house to a high, buttress stone wall encasing steps leading down to the pavement. We used to catch grasshoppers on the lawn and holding them captive in a jam-jar, we would run down the road to the letter-box set in the wall, and put the grasshoppers through the slot to frighten the postman when he came to empty the box. One day I ran down with my jam-jar hoping to beat the afternoon collection, but I tripped and fell headlong. The jar flew from my hands and smashed; I landed heavily, grazing knees and hands and gashing my forehead. Bleeding profusely in numerous places I might have expected some solicitude from brother Donald, but no, he was cross because I'd let the grasshoppers escape! Mrs Davage bandaged my wounds, then sent me back down the road with a brush and pan to collect the broken glass before 'some other English idiot injures himself'!

Abercarn also had a canal, which was still in occasional use in 1940. It was fed from the Ebbw River meandering along beside it. The Ebbw itself had already travelled some 30 miles from its source before it reached Abercarn, through some of the most heavily-worked coal-mining areas in the country. Its flow was augmented along its length by water leaching coal dust from the many spoil tips higher up the valley, and was the colour of Indian ink by the time we saw it. The canal, of course, was a similar colour. Our stream was different. Its waters were crystal clear and drinkable. It was shallow, except in spate, and there were no habitations of any kind above the meadow.

One of our fellow exiles called Meredith – Merry for short – was crossing the stream by the stepping stones, a little above the foot bridge, when a stone rocked as he trod on it and tipped him into the water. His first reaction had been to cry, but when we all laughed and clapped, he smiled to find himself the centre of attention and promptly fell over again on purpose! He was a simple soul. If he had a proper Christian name, no-one knew it. His trick with the water became his party piece and he would do it to order, always with a big grin on his little face, and always provoking much hilarity. He introduced variations into his act, balancing on one leg and toppling sideways, or falling backwards, straight as a tree, making a colossal splash. I daresay his foster mother wondered at the state of his clothes, but as it was generally a hot summer in 1940, doubtless the clothes dried out on his skinny frame most of the time.

If you have never tasted whinberry jam you have missed an experience! My mother

What you should know about
INVASION DANGER

YOU will shortly receive a leaflet "Beating the Invader," issued to all householders in the country, telling you what to do should invasion come. If invasion finds you in this town, and you are not ordered to leave, you must act on the instructions to stand firm. But you can help to defeat the invader by leaving now if you can be spared and have somewhere to go.

THIS APPLIES PARTICULARLY TO—

SCHOOL CHILDREN
MOTHERS WITH YOUNG CHILDREN
AGED AND INFIRM PERSONS
PERSONS LIVING ON PENSIONS
PERSONS WITHOUT OCCUPATION OR
LIVING IN RETIREMENT

If you are one of these, you should arrange to go to some other part of the country. You should not go to the coastal area of East Anglia (including Essex), Kent or Sussex.

School children can be registered to join school parties in the reception areas, and billets will be found for them.

If you are in need of help you can have your railway fare paid and a billeting allowance paid to any relative or friend with whom you stay. If you are going, go quickly.

TAKE YOUR—

National Registration Identity Card.

Ration Book.

Gas Mask.

Also any bank book, pensions payment order book, insurance cards, unemployment book, military registration documents, passport, insurance policies, securities, and any ready money.

[CONTINUED OVERLEAF]

If your house will be left unoccupied, turn off gas, electricity and water supplies and make provision for animals and birds. Lock your house securely. Blinds should be left up, and if there is a telephone line, ask the telephone exchange to disconnect it. Go to the Post Office and fill up a Redirection Notice so that they can forward your letters.

If you go and your house is unoccupied, your liability to pay rent, rates, mortgage charges, or charges under hire purchase agreements will be postponed.

It makes no difference if you leave your furniture in the house.

Private car and motor cycle owners who have not licensed their vehicles and have no petrol coupons may be allowed to use their cars or motor cycles unlicensed for one journey only and may apply to the Police for petrol coupons to enable them to secure sufficient petrol to journey to their destination.

If any of these matters are not clear, you will get further information at the local Council Offices.

ESSENTIAL WORKERS MUST STAY, particularly the following classes

THE HOME GUARD. OBSERVER CORPS.
COASTGUARDS, COAST WATCHERS AND LIFEBOAT CREWS.
POLICE AND SPECIAL CONSTABULARY.
FIRE BRIGADE AND AUXILIARY FIRE SERVICE.
A.R.P. AND CASUALTY SERVICES.
MEMBERS OF LOCAL AUTHORITIES AND THEIR OFFICIALS AND EMPLOYEES.
WORKERS ON THE LAND.
PERSONS ENGAGED ON WAR WORK, AND OTHER ESSENTIAL SERVICES.
PERSONS EMPLOYED BY CONTRACTORS ON DEFENCE WORK.
EMPLOYEES OF WATER, SEWERAGE, GAS AND ELECTRICITY UNDERTAKINGS.
PERSONS ENGAGED IN THE SUPPLY AND DISTRIBUTION OF FOOD.
WORKERS ON EXPORT TRADES.
DOCTORS, NURSES AND CHEMISTS.
MINISTERS OF RELIGION.
GOVERNMENT EMPLOYEES.
EMPLOYEES OF BANKS.
EMPLOYEES OF TRANSPORT UNDERTAKINGS, NAMELY
RAILWAYS, DOCKS, CANALS, FERRIES, AND ROAD TRANSPORT
(BOTH PASSENGER AND GOODS).

When invasion is upon us it may be necessary to evacuate the remaining population of this and certain other towns. Evacuation would then be compulsory at short notice, in crowded trains, with scanty luggage, to destinations chosen by the Government. If you are not among the essential workers mentioned above it is better to go now while the going is good.

A. C. GEDDES,
REGIONAL COMMISSIONER.
No. 12 (South-Eastern) Region.

March, 1941.

(10924) Wt. 47988/P1046 250,400. 3/41 K.H.K. Gp. 8

and father came down to Abercarn a number of times while Donald and I were there, but occasionally only one would come – possibly for economic reasons, I suppose. My father was working long hours on defence telephone works and could not readily take time off. But they too were very taken with our foster parents and Abercarn in general. I could not wait to show my parents where the best whinberries were to be found, high up on the Rhyswyg mountain across our little valley, and we picked bushels of them it seemed. Mrs Davage made jars of whinberry jam and it was totally delicious. My father especially, could not get enough of it and brought back to Kent as much as he could.

Donald was still only eight in August 1940, and at the end of those marvellous summer holidays he went to a local school, with a mixture of local pupils and evacuees. He even had to learn Welsh! But when that episode in our young lives ended, I had to change schools. I had won an excellent scholarship and was due to join Rochester Mathematical School. The school at that time was divided into two locations, (three if you include the residue remaining at Rochester) located at Porthcawl and Pontypridd. It was to be my unhappy lot to go to Porthcawl!

Porthcawl, of loathsome memory, is some twenty or so miles west of Cardiff. It was and presumably still is a seaside resort. Until I visited Atlantic City in New Jersey, I thought no place could come close in terms of sheer horror and, although Atlantic City on its worst day in the depths of winter runs it pretty close, I would say that Porthcawl still holds the record for terribleness! By this you will no doubt gather that I did not enjoy my seven months sojourn in Porthcawl.

Bill Davage took me there. By bus first to Newport, then by train to Cardiff and then by a local train to Pyle, some three miles away from Porthcawl. On Pyle station we were met by the acting headmaster, A. C. Cheeseman, known to all and sundry as 'Cheesy'. Headmaster Clarke seemed to divide his time between Rochester, Pontypridd and Porthcawl, spending most time at Pontypridd. It was several weeks before I met him. On the station platform I made a forlorn and I daresay tearful farewell to Mr Davage and left him to await a train back to Cardiff, while Cheesy in his little black Ford took me to my new foster home at Suffolk Place.

A greater contrast with the Davages' home could hardly be imagined. There were already eight people living in the small terrace house before I arrived; my new foster parents, their two daughters, Megan and Avril, their son John, and an ancient maiden lady called Miss Oram, who was originally from Maida Vale, privately evacuated to Porthcawl at her own expense and occupying a ground floor bed/sitting room, most comfortably furnished with her own bits and pieces carted down from London. The last two residents were two senior boys from Rochester Math School, John Hayward and Roy Baker.

I was horrified to learn that not only was I expected to share a room with those two older boys, but also a double bed! My foster father was a builder's labourer who regularly got drunk about twice a week. I had never seen anyone drunk before, and

Opposite – A leaflet issued in March 1941 by the Regional Commissioner, No. 12 South-Eastern Region, warning of the continuing dangers of invasion. The authorities were not to know that Hitler was about to turn his attention to Russia instead of invading Britain

when I whispered to John to ask him what was wrong with his dad, his mother said he was sick and I was to mind my own business. The two girls were both working. The elder, Megan, was a WAAF auxiliary at Stormy aerodrome where she stayed overnight when on duty, and otherwise shared a bedroom with her younger sister Avril who was a shop assistant as I remember. John was about my age and really quite affable. We got on quite well and he was about the only person in that wretched town whom I could call a friend. He slept in his parents' room. The house seemed to have a perpetual stink of cabbage being boiled to death, although I cannot recall eating anything in that house besides fish and chips. Another smell which persists in the memory is that of washing being boiled in an old gas copper. John's mother took in laundry! And when she wasn't washing and ironing, she cleaned twice a week in the local Baptist Chapel. She had no time to devote to her evacuated charges or matters like shopping or cooking, so we ate fish and chips *ad nauseam*! Her brother had a lock-up one-roomed cobbler's shop just around the corner from where we lived – and right next door to the fried fish shop! I had to have my leather shoes mended there, but still had to pay the going rate. My foster father, too, ensured that still more of my pocket money went into the family coffers. He fancied himself as a barber and every second Saturday morning he would sit me on a box on a wooden chair in the small back yard, throw a stained and smelly sheet across my shoulders and give me a short-back-and-sides for which I had to pay him 4d. That memory has lurked in my sub-conscious for half a century.

There was nowhere in that house where I could be alone to read or study, and if anyone ever needed a place for private study, it was I. When I had taken the scholarship examination in the summer of 1939, before even the first evacuation, I was some ten months below the average age of the rest of the boys. I was placed very high among the successful candidates and my age and marks were quite misinterpreted by the examining board. They placed me straight into the second year – bypassing the upper third entirely. In the fourth form I found I was about 20 months below the average age of the class. This meant that I was tossed into the deep end with no waterwings and expected to swim. Most of the older boys in the class had already enjoyed at least four complete terms of Algebra, Euclid, French, Latin and German and the specialised sciences, Chemistry and Physics. There was no opportunity for individual tuition or private coaching. The foster home was like a zoo and I knew absolutely nobody. I was ten years old and had never been more miserable. I was so reluctant to go back to the house – I simply could not regard it as home – that I used to hang about the school after staff and pupils had left, trying to make sense of these arcane subjects. The cleaning staff got used to me and allowed me to stay in the classroom while they swept, polished and dusted around me. Once when the school caretaker found me and went to put me out, I said that my mother was one of the cleaners and I had to wait for her. One fat old Welsh lady (she must have been at least 40) was delighted to enter into the conspiracy, and so I managed to get an hour or so private study most days in the empty school.

During the Christmas 1940 holidays I returned to Abercarn to spend two weeks with the Davages and my brother Donald, and I remember taking a number of school text books with me to revise in my weakest subjects. While I was there, Donald had a bad accident, scalding his right leg with boiling broth. His injury was very bad and he was away from school for a long time. All too soon the holiday ended and I went back to

Porthcawl. I think that the school authorities had become aware that we were sleeping three to a bed, but instead of transplanting me to another set of foster parents, they took the two older boys away so that I should be on my own. But that misfired, because I then had to share the same bed with John so that his parents could have their room to themselves.

What of the town of Porthcawl? I remember it hardly at all. It is as if I deliberately chose to exclude it from my memory. The abiding impression which does persist is of universal greyness. The winter of 1940/41 was mild and wet. The streets were grey, the buildings were grey and the sky, mostly, was grey. Even the people were grey. There had been a funfair with mechanical rides before the war, but it seemed to have been abandoned at the outbreak. The beaches were inhospitable places with pointed steel girders driven haphazardly into the sand and festooned with seaweed-covered, rusting barbed wire. Germans and tourists, keep away! All the bright, coloured trappings of a popular pre-war seaside resort were faded and peeling away. No seafront shops were still doing business. Sweet rationing was by now in force and whatever benefits that brought to our young teeth were hardly appreciated. The funfair was called Coney Beach, but whether that was the inspiration for, or was inspired by New York's Coney Island, I have never discovered. The funfair was surrounded by a high, palisaded wooden fence bleached and weathered by sun, wind and salt spray, but there were places where the boards had been prised away so that with some determination and at risk from splinters, ten-year old children of standard proportions could squeeze through.

Inside, it was even more fascinatingly awful than it had seemed from a distance. It was evident that the place had been shut down in a hurry and highly probable that no-one had been near the place since. Playbills advertising coming attractions for the 1939 season of concert parties and other entertainments hung, torn and faded, on the side-show stalls. Here was a derelict fortune-teller's cave, here a deserted coconut shy, and there, in one of the pay booths, an enamel cup with a desiccated brown mess in the bottom. It was as depressing as it could be and when, suddenly, it began to rain with huge noisy drops, we hurried back to our hole in the fence and gladly left the Coney Beach funfair to its ghosts.

To the west of the town, along the edge of the sea, the beach gave place to rocks, with tide-filled pools containing sea anemones, limpets and other shellfish. But even here, providence had decreed that such attractions should not be allowed to soften the grey squalor that was Porthcawl. Some little while before, an oil tanker, bound for Bristol no doubt, had been torpedoed by a U-boat in the Bristol Channel and its cargo now reposed on the beaches and littoral rocks of the South Welsh coast. It formed thick, tarry patches mixed with shells, sand and flotsam and was all but impossible to remove from our clothes if we were careless enough to encounter it.

At school I could make little headway against the handicaps that beset me. English was my only good subject, and History and Geography the only other lessons I really enjoyed. The teachers were on the whole helpful. Mostly they were elderly, or just plain old – sometimes even retired, but brought back again to replace younger men called to the colours. My favourite teacher was Mr Jenkinson – 'Jenks' to the boys, and he endeared himself to me when he gave me a shilling to replace one I lost when my purse was stolen at school. Jenks taught Chemistry and Religious Instruction and I tried really hard in his classes. Pop Fearnley taught us Euclid and Music, but preferred talking about Percy Chapman and Frank Woolley. Our German teacher was a sarcastic, unsympathetic man. Because he was unpopular he had the nickname of 'Fritz', and because he was relatively young and had not been called up, we all insisted that he was really a German spy! Cheeseman was everywhere – taking more classes than any of the other masters. He taught French, English and Algebra. He insisted on calling me 'John Henry' whenever he spoke to me in class and, unreasonably, this annoyed me. But he was friendly and helpful and I quite got to like him. Cheesy had a brisk manner and a rounded, rather puffy face with broken and distorted front teeth, rather discoloured. The story behind the teeth was probably apocryphal, but it was said that he was on the golfcourse with a friend and had taken his partner's sliced drive full in the mouth. But whatever caused it, the result was a gap which somewhat impaired his speech. During his French classes, the front rows of desks were always the last to be filled, for when he tried to bring his best Gallic pronunciation to bear in the silly way the French have of rolling their 'R's, he sent a fine spray of saliva several feet in front of him.

One afternoon after school was finished for the day, I dawdled down the road near the school, reluctant to go back to the foster home, and began carving my initials on a small tree. I was just finishing off when Cheeseman came along and stopped behind me. I thought he would tell me off, but all he said was, 'You should come back here in twenty years and see how much it has grown with the tree.' But of course I never did.

The wet winter of 1941 gave way to spring and I began to see a little of the hinterland of Porthcawl. On fine days I would go exploring, often alone and occasionally with my friend John Cook. We would walk over the sandhills to the west of the town to Kenfig Pool, an ancient inlet of the sea closed off by large sand dunes and now a freshwater lake. One fine Saturday John and I found ourselves peering through a chain-link fence into what was clearly an aerodrome. This was Stormy, a small airfield some three miles from the town and I think it was a training field. It was also possibly a decoy airfield for the operational field of St Athan, near Swansea.

The purpose of these decoy aerodromes was to delude German bombers into dropping their bomb-loads relatively harmlessly, and to heighten the illusion, unserviceable aircraft were dispersed about the perimeter of these fields. One such aircraft sat in front of us as we lay in the grass staring. It was an obsolete light bomber called the Fairey 'Battle'. It was a single-engined, low-wing monoplane, but too slow and underpowered to be very effective, and although this plane forty yards inside the wire seemed intact, a close look betrayed the fact that it had no propeller, and the engine bearers bore no engine.

As luck would have it there was a hole beneath the wire and this coincidence was too tempting to ignore. We wriggled under the fence, scurried under the fuselage, climbed through the hatch in the belly of the plane and sat in the pilots' seats. It was the first aeroplane I had ever been in and we had a fine time, pulling levers and switches, operating the working flight controls and imitating engine noises, machine-gun fire and exploding bombs. We were having so much fun that we neither saw nor heard the arrival of a big, uniformed RAF sergeant and his big Alsatian dog until he challenged us and called to us to come out – in the sternest of voices!

Quaking in our shoes, and scared half to death, we climbed down and stood in front of this burly airman. While his dog sat motionless, he walked right round us and although I can't recall the exact dialogue I remember that one of the first things he said to us was, 'Sprechen sie Deutsch?', and I answered him in German, falteringly, 'Ja, ein wenig, Sprechen sie Englisch?', and I said, 'I speak English better than German.' 'You had better come with me,' he said, and off we marched across the grass.

As we approached one of the airfield buildings an officer appeared and the sergeant saluted him and said, 'I've captured two enemy spies, sir.' They must have had a hard time trying to keep straight faces, but we were scared silly, and John was almost in tears. He hadn't said a word. But eventually it dawned on me that we weren't going to be shot or shut up in a cell, and eventually the double act they were performing broke down when I saw the officer winking at the sergeant. We got a lecture about trespassing on Air Ministry property, and lemonade and biscuits and a ride into town in an RAF staff car. We did not dare tell John's mother and father, but we did tell Megan on a vow of secrecy and she was not in the least sympathetic. 'I wouldn't have let you off so lightly,' was her response, 'I would have locked you up!'

After a big air raid on Cardiff and Barry Docks, my parents finally allowed me to come home. The Medway towns escaped relatively unscathed, compared with the raids on the larger industrial centres. There was never a concerted attack, although there were low-level sneak attacks in daylight, by aircraft flying up the Thames estuary and targeting the dockyard. Most of the bomb damage to Medway was caused by aircraft jettisoning bombs when under attack. Luton Senior Boys' School was actually damaged by a small bomb.

Once I had shaken the dust of Porthcawl from my heels, I never returned. Abercarn was different. Our family kept in regular contact with Mr and Mrs Davage long after the war was over. Donald of course stayed on for another fifteen months or so, only returning in the summer of 1942, and with an accent you could cut with a blunt knife, so much so that my father called him Taffy! During 1941 and 1942 while I stayed in Kent – enjoying the excitement of the war, my parents, usually singly, went periodically down to Monmouthshire to visit the exile. Once only did we all go down together and had a somewhat nerve-wracking experience of being in a darkened train confined in the Severn Tunnel for an hour while air raids raged simultaneously over Newport and Bristol. Total darkness and growing colder by the minute as the train's heating was shut down. The guard periodically walked the track carrying his oil lamp, checking to see that we were alright and, apart from the odd case of claustrophobia or nervous hysteria, we were mostly none the worse for the experience.

When the war ended, and before I began working, I spent a holiday in Abercarn with a cousin of mine – another John, John Sharpe this time. It was his first visit to Wales. He lived in Bexley and had himself been evacuated during the war, but privately, to our mutual Aunt Bessie, who lived in Suffolk. Then eight years later, my brother Donald, by now 22 years of age, took his bride-to-be to Wales to spend a holiday with the Davages in Abercarn.

I last saw Bill and Pat Davage in 1960. By then I was living in Belfast and doing a little private flying from time to time. With two friends we flew to Oakwood Common on the Gower, near Swansea for a three-day flying club rally. I left my colleagues to put the aircraft through its paces, and I hitch-hiked via Brecon, of all places, and Abertillery to Abercarn, to the surprise and delight of Mr and Mrs Davage.

I stayed two days. Pat put me in the tiny spare bedroom where Donald and I had been put exhausted to bed exactly twenty years before, and when I woke and looked out of that same little window on the Saturday morning, across the same valley, at the same dark hillside stretching up into the clouds, the feeling of *déjà-vu* was overwhelming.

Donald kept in correspondence with Bill and Pat Davage until their deaths. When I went back to Gwyddon Road in 1978, I called at the house, and explained to the young woman at the door who I was. She was local and as a child had known the Davages, but the lady next door, whose name, if I ever knew it, I had forgotten, had lived there since before the war and she was quickly summoned to meet me. Astonishingly, she recognised me, only erring in calling me Donald. I haven't been back to Wales since.

Nora Ticker-Fry, *having already experienced evacuation to Canterbury, now left with her school, Rochester Grammar School, for somewhere in South Wales:*

It was a long and tedious journey, with many halts along the route. This was because there were trains full of soldiers recently saved from the beaches of Dunkirk and they had priority. At last, in the evening, we arrived at Pontypridd – and what a welcome we received as we dragged our weary bodies from the train.

The mayor was there, the town band, crowds of people and a bag of food for everyone – corned beef, tinned milk and biscuits! We were quickly ushered into groups and marched off. The town had been expecting children of under ten, so they had arranged for us to be billeted all around the local primary schools. Our landlady was a widow, Mrs Davies. She gave us a warm welcome and soon my sister and I were in bed and asleep.

The school prefects from Rochester Grammar School pictured outside their new premises in Porthcawl

The next morning we were all assembled in the school yard where we were told that we would be sharing the local grammar school – which was several miles away. Sharing the school wasn't very easy. We used the school at different times to the local pupils and we also used several halls in Pontypridd. With part time schooling I was able to play a lot of tennis.

During those years I kept a diary and still have the ones for 1940 and 1941. We had quite a lot of air raid warnings during both day and night. We had to get up during the night and sit downstairs and if there was an air raid warning while we were at school, we all had to sit in the corridors.

I played tennis nearly every day. I also used the public library at Pontypridd which I thought was super. We walked a lot – over the common to school and for miles all around Pontypridd. Everyone was very kind to us and we were welcomed everywhere we went. I have very happy memories of my stay there. But I hardly ever mentioned in my diaries the reason why we were there!

We had left Canterbury on the 19th of May but some of the school that had been left in Rochester had now been evacuated to Porthcawl on the coast. Soon, we had the news that we were to leave Pontypridd and we were all heartbroken. We had made many friends there, we liked our billet and now we had to pack up and start all over again! We left Pontypridd on Sunday 14th July 1940.

The move was disastrous: we had all collected a good deal of gear, including bicycles, all our school books – even some trunks! The coaches arrived two hours late and we finally reached Porthcawl at 1.30pm. We hadn't had any lunch – and there wasn't any for us when we got there! My mother, my sister and I were billeted in a big house, about ten of us there altogether. It was very cramped and my mother felt we would be better off somewhere where she could look after us properly. So we moved to a Mrs Griffiths which was much better.

Porthcawl, being a seaside town, had lovely beaches and a fun fair. On the sea front was the Pavilion, used for dances, concerts and plays. A crowd of us would go most Saturday nights to the Pavilion, but only if my mother came with us! We couldn't go on to the dance floor, but we would sit upstairs on the balcony and watch the goings-on below! One of the Math School boys from Rochester, Ronnie Verral, got to play the drums in the band, and years later played with the Ted Heath band.

Sybil Thorndike and her husband Lewis Casson brought their touring company to the Pavilion, and we went to see them. Sybil Thorndike was an 'old girl' of Rochester Grammar School, and on one occasion she met us all back stage where we presented her with a bouquet of flowers in the red, white and orange of our school colours. She came several times to Porthcawl so we were lucky to see her in *Pygmalion*, *Macbeth* and *Major Barbara*.

Considering all the upheavals, moving and air raid warnings, and having different places for our lessons every day, we somehow managed to do quite well in our exams that year.

My father came down to see us several times. This was the summer of the Battle of Britain and nightly air raids over Kent and London. We worried a lot about him and all our family still in Rochester. Although we had constant sirens going in Porthcawl, there was very little bombing. Sometimes we heard explosions as bombs were jettisoned over the coast, and once we saw a German pilot being dragged from the sea after his aircraft had exploded over the Bristol Channel.

Somehow the war didn't seem to touch us 15 year olds very much. We were too wrapped up in our own lives. It seems to me now that what would these days be regarded as traumatic events, needing counselling and endless seminars on how it would affect us in later life, we just took in our stride. Perhaps children of that generation had the ability to cope better.

Most of us changed billets several times, sometimes disastrously and we all had to rally round and lug cases and sobbing friends from one place to another. This happened to everyone. My worst one was when, in August 1941, my mother decided she had spent enough time away and would take my young sister back home. I had just finished my exams and would stay there to go into the sixth form. My mother chose my billet, but it was a mistake. I was expected to do the cooking, look after a four year old and do quite a lot of cleaning. Well, I stuck it for six weeks and then I fainted at school because I wasn't being fed properly – no breakfast and not much of anything else! As soon as this was discovered I was moved. This time I was much luckier and went to a retired couple. They had been farmers and they had a nice house – and I was certainly well fed there! They had a car and a petrol ration, so sometimes I was taken out for a drive.

When I went home for Christmas 1941, my case was stuffed full with 'goodies' like dried fruit, glacé cherries, chocolate and things like rice which I hadn't seen for several years! While I was home, I decided I wanted to stay there. I had been away for two and a half years and I wasn't sure if staying in the Sixth Form was very helpful as by then, many of the girls had drifted back to Rochester – and the staff had to go where most of the pupils were.

So I went into the civil service, but I rushed back to say goodbye to Porthcawl. Goodbye to the Pavilion where we had so much fun and enjoyment, goodbye to the lovely beaches like Rest Bay and Coney Beach, goodbye to the fun fair and the cafe on the front where we could always get ice cream, and goodbye to all my friends there.

I don't think anyone had thought in September 1939, when keeping children safe was a priority, that we would all be away for so long, separated from our parents by so many miles. Was it worth it? I really don't know. When I came back to Rochester, there were many more air raids to come, and the very danger we were supposed to be shielded from was to be present for a very long time.

Did evacuation affect us in any way? I don't know the answer to that either. I understood quite clearly why we had been sent away and I was confident in my parents love and care for my sister and me. Many times I have talked it over with old school friends and all we could say was that it was an experience which perhaps made us more mature and independent. But we were young and it didn't stop us laughing and enjoying life, so perhaps it didn't do us any harm at all.

Joan Quarrington *(now Mrs Joan Poynter) had returned home to Chatham after being evacuated to Sittingbourne in Kent in 1939. Now her school, Chatham Grammar School, was on the move again:*

A hot day in early June, 1940, saw us boarding trains at Chatham station for unknown destinations. However, the journey was not to be just half an hour as in the first evacuation. Our new journey was to take most of the day. Our train spent a large part of the afternoon in sidings as troop trains took priority. On one occasion we happened to be alongside one such train filled to capacity with Dunkirk veterans, and for a few minutes both trains were at a standstill. We viewed each other with mutual compassion. The picture of old/young faces, weary, begrimed with mud and in some cases blood, stays with me still. The only way the soldiers could express sympathy was by throwing money through our open carriage windows. Thinking that the silver coins were sixpences, we scrambled for them, but on discovering that they were centimes, we pocketed a few as souvenirs and let the rest lie.

The day wore on and it was almost dark when the train finally pulled into a small country station. We piled out and gathered on either side of our headmistress, while the reception committee, which consisted of local dignitaries and a brass band, bade us welcome. After a speech, the members of the band raised their instruments to their lips. Alas, only a strangulated wail emerged, to die away immediately. It was too dark for the lads to read their music! An apologetic and embarrassed silence followed, before we walked to a hall where we were literally selected by prospective foster parents.

A group of girls from the Chatham County School at Porthcawl in 1940

A friend and I were fairly soon deemed suitable for a couple, who then walked us to their home. It was only then that we found that we were in the small Welsh town of Crumlin, whose only claim to fame was a magnificent viaduct straddling the valley, underneath which, our new home nestled. Only a few memories remain of the time spent there – the walk each morning over the mountainside to a pleasant new school with a lovely playing field; being woken one morning by shouts and oaths coming from our otherwise placid host – I was in time to see a red faced, angry Mr Dix pushing a reluctant sheep through the gate, before turning to contemplate a row of grey stalks, which until a few moments before, had been supporting splendid heads of carnations! These had been Mr Dix's pride and joy and were almost ready to be entered for the flower show!

The people of Crumlin were kindly folk and I could have happily settled there, but it was not to be. Less than a week later we were on the move again. This time we were deposited at Pontypridd. I remember being whisked away by car to an imposing Edwardian house, the home of a retired bank manager, and his wife and a middle aged schoolmaster son. It was an orderly, quiet, respectable household. The front room had permanently lowered blinds to prevent the sun fading the carpet and upholstery. To this room Mr Lewis retired to read the paper and to have a nap. I was summoned one day to this vanilla ice cream coloured room for a conversation. Sitting on the edge of an uncomfortable chair, I engaged in 'talk', escaping as soon as possible into the fresh air.

My host family were decent, nice people, who in their way really tried to make me welcome, but an incident within an hour of arriving prevented this!

After being shown my bedroom, I was taken into the back kitchen and with my head over a bowl of water my hair was thoroughly washed. I was surprised as there was a perfectly adequate bathroom upstairs, but it was only when I complained about the

Eugene Brooker's home was vulnerable near Short's aircraft factory. Pictured above are the Maia and the Mercury sitting on the River Medway just before the war. Rochester Bridge can be seen in the background

awful smell of the 'shampoo' did the truth dawn. It was presumed that I had head lice. Anger welled up within me on behalf of my most fastidious but absent mother. How dare anyone insult her like this!

In those days children didn't express their thoughts to adults and so, within me, resentment grew. I became sullen and unco-operative and it was with relief all round when I ran away! A group of friends were in the Treforest area of the town, and it was to there I made my way. One friend introduced me to a lady who was already housing an evacuee from another school, but was willing to have me as well. I stayed there for over a year. The other evacuee was replaced after a few weeks by my long standing friend, Winnie. On returning from the Easter holidays, it was discovered that Winnie and I were suffering from a mild case of scabies and we found ourselves incarcerated in the general hospital where our fellow patients displayed various forms of open sores. That wasn't the end of our troubles as I succumbed to diphtheria, caught from a nurse. I was speedily dispatched to the isolation hospital where I languished for a further three months – picking up hepatitis on the way. The only consolation was that the scabies disappeared within a few days of admission!

On release at the beginning of August, my mother, to my delight, came and took me home. If I was going to be ill in the future, she wanted to be the carer.

By September 1941, so many evacuees had returned home that most of the schools re-opened and so at last I received full time education in the right buildings, with our own teachers – just two years later than intended.

Eugene Brooker recalls his own evacuation with pupils of Troy Town School, Rochester to Twyn-y-Deryn, Nantyglo in South Wales:

At the outbreak of the war I was living between two very important military installations – the Royal Naval Dockyard at Chatham, and the Short's Aircraft Company at Rochester so I was a prime candidate for evacuation if the situation made it necessary.

In May 1940 the German Army had overrun Belgium and Holland and had reached the Channel ports. Britain was now well within easy reach of German aircraft. The decision was made to evacuate the school children from the Medway Towns, including my own school, Troy Town School, so I was now going to embark on a very traumatic experience that I would remember for the rest of my life.

Early one Sunday morning in late May 1940 we assembled in the school playground. We were only allowed to take what we could comfortably carry and, being only eight years old, that wasn't very much. I had a rucksack because my mother thought it would be easier to carry than a suitcase. We each had a buff coloured luggage label attached to us listing name, age and home address. After tearful farewells to our parents we marched to Rochester Railway Station. Each class was accompanied by a teacher. My class of 27 children was very fortunate. Mr Holliday, our teacher, was a very nice, kind man and he turned out to be a person to whom I would be grateful for the rest of my life.

As we stood in bright sunshine on the station platform, it was like going on a day to the seaside. A great cheer rang out as a train steamed in. Then class by class, we boarded the train. A whistle blew, a flag waved and off we went into the unknown.

At first there was a holiday atmosphere on the train. It was fun being on a train with school friends. We didn't know that we were going to Wales and that the journey would take more than seven hours. After a while, boredom began to set in and a slow realisation of what was actually happening to us. Children began to get tired and upset. Relieving the monotony were two stops en route. Kindly ladies boarded the train, handing out sandwiches, cake, chocolate and lemonade. Teachers tried to keep our spirits up by encouraging us to sing but an air of gloom and despondency spread throughout the train. After what seemed like an eternity, we arrived at our destination – Nantyglo, in South Wales.

I shall never forget my feelings of horror and disbelief when leaving the train at Nantyglo station. I saw the huge, ugly slag heaps dwarfing the rows of terraced houses. What a dreadful place it seemed after the greenery of Kent. My spirits were at a very low ebb. From the station we had a short walk to a school hall and were given more sandwiches, cake and tea. When we finished eating we were led outside by our teachers and boarded small buses and dispersed in various directions. Our bus trundled through rows of ugly terraced houses, dwarfed by more and more huge black slag heaps.

Eventually we arrived at a street called Twyn-y-Deryn and were met by a billeting officer. Women came out of the houses and surrounded our group of 27 bewildered, dishevelled boys and girls. Glancing at his clip board the billeting officer read out children's names and allocated them to the women standing nearby

When our group was down to about six, a lady asked the officer if she could have one! 'Yes,' said the officer, 'which one would you like?' 'Him,' she replied pointing to me. 'Go with the lady,' I was told, so off I went following her to number 24. Once inside, the door closed behind me and I really felt scared.

'Look what I've got,' said the lady to a man seated in a wooden armchair beside an unlit fire. These two people were to be my foster parents for the next two years and at that moment I didn't know how happy I would become, living with them in South Wales. Mr and Mrs Arnold, who became Uncle Arthur and Auntie Annie, were two of the kindest, nicest people one could ever wish to meet.

My first problem was trying to understand what they were saying to me. Their Welsh accent was very strong. As I was not hungry, still full from the meal at the school hall, the three of us went for a short walk to Mrs Arnold's mother's house. I was introduced to her and her family. I was very conscious of being looked at and shyly answered their questions. On the walk back I managed to get about twenty yards ahead of the Arnolds, as I wanted to be on my own and have a good cry. I felt very lonely and homesick, but they were very tactful, pretending not to notice my obvious tears.

Once back at the billet, I was taken upstairs and shown my bedroom. From the window I had a nice view of a green grass-covered mountain which I was to discover, divided Nantyglo from the steel making town of Ebbw Vale. Auntie Annie unpacked my rucksack and put my clothes into a wardrobe and chest of drawers. My belongings seemed very meagre. She told me later that apart from giving me a helping hand, she wanted to check what clothes I had, and more importantly, that they were clean. Word had spread that some children, mainly from London's East End, had arrived in Wales previously in a dirty state; some even had ringworm and head lice.

Downstairs again I was shown the toilet, which was of the non-flush type and situated at the bottom of the front garden. During my first week I got up in the middle of the night to use this toilet, and as I went out of the front door, it blew shut on me. I was too embarrassed to knock on the door for someone to let me in, so I spent the rest of the night sitting on the front door step!

The only tap in the house was in the scullery. There was no bathroom and once a week I had a bath using a wooden tub in the kitchen. The tub was filled with buckets of water heated on the coal-fired kitchen range. As there was no electricity or gas in the house, all cooking and water heating was done on this kitchen range. A large kettle was always simmering on top of this stove and I never knew this fire to go out, summer or winter, during my stay there.

On that first evening in Wales, after a cup of cocoa and a biscuit, I went to bed tired out after such an eventful day. I nestled down into a very large double bed and cried myself to sleep. My first day as an evacuee was over.

I woke the next morning to the sound of Mrs Arnold singing. She had a beautiful soprano voice and chose to sing mostly hymns and other religious songs. Sitting up in bed, I became aware that for the first time in my life, Mum was not there to tell me what to wear. Anyway, I dressed myself and sat on the edge of the bed, too scared to go downstairs.

Mrs Arnold must have heard me moving about because she called out that my breakfast was ready. It was a beautiful sunny warm summer's day. 'Isn't that pullover too warm to wear on a day like this,' she asked. 'No, I'm fine thank you,' I replied. I was uncomfortably hot for the rest of the day! She also asked me if I had washed before coming downstairs. Although there had been a jug of water, bowl, soap and towel in my bedroom, I had been reluctant to use them. Anyway, I told her I had washed, but realised too late that she would see that no soap or water had been used. She never mentioned it that day. The following morning she called to me to make sure I had a wash before coming downstairs.

The house was built of yellow stone blocks and had a black slate roof. The thickness of the walls kept the house snug and warm during the winter, and cool during the summer. The ground floor consisted of a scullery, a kitchen, a large pantry, a parlour and two front rooms. One of these front rooms was quite large, the other small and used as a reception room when visitors came. The larger room was used only on very special occasions such as Christmas. In fact, I did not go into that room more than six times in the two years I lived there.

The parlour was the hub of the house. Meals were taken there and we sat there in the evenings and at weekends. It was a nice cosy room in which I spent many happy hours. Mr Arnold used to tell me stories of a sporting past such as the time Wales beat the All Blacks at rugby, and the exploits of boxers such as Jimmy Wilde, Tommy Farr and Ronnie James. The whole house was kept spick and span.

Upstairs were three bedrooms, all nicely furnished, and the beds had deep feather filled mattresses and colourful eiderdowns. The toilet was near the front gate and there was no back garden because the house backed on to a hill. The house was quite high up and on a clear day one could see the Brecon Beacons.

We had a ton of coal delivered each month. The lorry would get as close as possible then dump the coal in a big pile about thirty yards from the coal house. Buckets were then used to carry the coal inside. I was expected to help with this task and I wasn't very happy on delivery days, especially if it was raining. The Arnolds keep about 100 free range chicken which were let out first thing in the morning and they would roam the neighbourhood until evening. Mrs Arnold would call to them and they would come running from all directions to the hen-house. With all these chickens we were never short of eggs. The chicken house became another task for me; it required cleaning out once a week.

There was no school for us on our first day, so I went out and met up with some of my classmates who lived nearby. We discussed the merits of the houses, laughed about the toilets and compared the people we were living with. The local children formed a group and stood some way off just looking and talking about us. We were unprepared for the hostility the Welsh children were to show to us in the next few weeks. We soon found out what it was like to be a member of a minority group.

One day I went to meet Mr Arnold from work and as I waited at the end of the road I took no notice of a group of men that passed by. A voice from the group said, 'Hello Snowball, aren't you going to talk to me?' It was Mr Arnold. I hadn't recognised him. I expected a coalminer to come home from work covered in coal dust and carrying a pick! I didn't know some pits such as Rose Colliery, Blaina, where he worked, had pit-head baths. I didn't expect to meet such a clean, well dressed coalminer coming home from work. Snowball or Snowy was to be my nickname for the whole of the time I was in Wales.

The Thomas family who lived nearby, had a father and three sons working in a mine with no washing facilities. The four of them would come home each day wearing dirty clothes and covered in coaldust. They had no bathroom and cleaned themselves in a tub in front of the kitchen fire.

'The Spirit of Britain'
An example of morale boosting postcards issued during the war

When we started school I met up with my teacher, Mr Holliday, and the rest of the class. To the rest of the school we were the centre of interest – 27 'Londoners' among some three hundred Welsh children. During our time in Wales we were always known as Londoners, although we came from Rochester in Kent. For the first few months we were not very well accepted by the rest of the school. Our greatest fear was being caught alone. I often arrived home with a back eye or split lip. As time went on things got better as the novelty wore off, but we never felt as though we belonged to the school.

Mr Holliday became a father figure to us all, always showing the utmost concern regarding our welfare. Every Friday afternoon we were made to write a letter home. Mr Holliday wrote a weekly column for the *Rochester & Chatham District News* under the heading 'News from Gwent', and as part of our English lessons we were encouraged to contribute to this column. A poem I wrote was published and my mother was very proud to read it. I gradually settled in on the home front, losing my shyness and homesickness, and life became quite pleasant.

I had my 9th birthday in July 1940 and my mother sent me two books, Ballantyne's *Coral Island* and Percy F. Westerman's *The Young Fur Traders*. I really enjoyed these books and I read them again and again.

Religion was very strong among the mining communities. I went to chapel three times every Sunday, and to Band of Hope meetings every Tuesday and Thursday evening. All chapel services were conducted by laymen. Some of these preachers were renowned for their sermons. The preacher who was of the 'fire and brimstone' and 'hell and damnation' type tended to frighten me. On the other hand, keeping awake during long boring sermons was always difficult!

The nearest town to Nantyglo was Brynmawr, a half hour walk away. Each Saturday, market day, I went with Mrs Arnold to help with the weekly shopping. Mr Arnold had made me a small cart consisting of a wooden box mounted on a set of cast iron wheels which I pulled along with a rope handle. I used this cart to take eggs to the grocers and to bring home the vegetables, with the corn and meal for the chickens.

Some months after my arrival in Wales, the Arnolds took in another evacuee, Keith White from Frinsbury, a small village near Rochester. Keith was a year older than me, and although we got on quite well, I wasn't too pleased at sharing the bedroom and what had been the personal attentions of Mr and Mrs Arnold. However, he was good company and in the summer holidays we went fishing, built camps, played cops and robbers, cowboys and indians or what ever took our fancy. In the autumn we picked whinberries which grew in abundance on the hills. Keith passed for the local grammar school and completed his education in Wales, taking up a career in mining engineering. He eventually married a local girl and continued to live in Nantyglo.

We were never physically punished at home. For misdemeanours we were not spoken to for a set number of days. A card listing the number of punishment days was placed on the kitchen mantelpiece. The months passed very quickly and I settled down to my life in Wales. Even the local children became less hostile. In fact I became friends with some of them and joined in their games.

As for the war, it seemed very remote to us. In her letters my mother told me how bad the air raids were. An Indian Army regiment was garrisoned near Brynmawr and they were certainly looked upon with curiosity. Then one day they were gone!

AUTUMN 1940   Uncle Bill.

Dear Aunty Bassett & Uncle.
                    Please excuse note
but as mam is writting I must put my
bit in as I must say if it had been
under more pleasant curcumstances it was
very pleasant happy moments we all spent
together when you were here with us
and I must say we are all looking forward
to the time when we shall have the pleasure
of meeting Mr Bassett. and for goodness
sake if it gets too bad for you, you know
there is always an open door at 132 Wood Rd
and bit of bread and cheese and Welcome.
I dont think I can say anything about Win
other than she seems happy and is eating
well I should like for you to be able to see
them both here some nights they make our
sides ache with laughter, Will mam has
stopped so I must for a cup of tea good night
and God Bless you all,
                            yours sincerely
                              Uncle Bill.

A letter from Winnie Bassett's foster father to her parents shortly after her arrival in Treforest, South Wales

In May 1942 I passed my eleven-plus. My parents had the choice of me attending the local Welsh grammar school or returning home to Rochester. They chose the latter so in August I returned home – much against my wishes. After two happy years in Wales I didn't want to return to Kent. My father came to fetch me and I was devastated to be leaving Nantyglo. My parents and brothers seemed as strangers to me and once again I felt homesick, this time for Wales!

Having acquired a Welsh accent I soon found out that the local children were reluctant to accept me. I was called 'Welsh Boy' now and there was more teasing, black eyes and split lips. I felt quite alone and I never again felt as though I belonged anywhere. Although I was only eleven I had already been through traumatic experiences which I have never forgotten. It is impossible, without living through it, to make anybody fully understand what evacuation was actually like.

Winnie Bassett *(now Mrs Winnie Rolfe), first evacuated to Sittingbourne in 1939, was unaware that she was to be evacuated yet again:*

Things began to alter in 1940 after the fall of France and Dunkirk. There were more air raids. My uncles joined the Local Defence Volunteers, later called the Home Guard, and we had rifles in the hallway. I wasn't too keen on the sight of guns, or the khaki

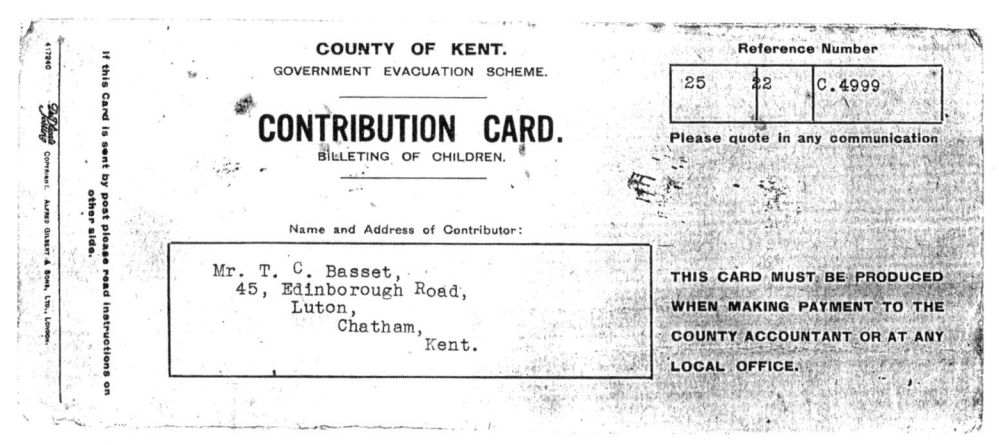

Contribution card issued to parents of evacuated children so that payment could be made towards the upkeep of the children in their new surroundings

uniforms that went with them. We watched troop trains going by with soldiers, rescued from Dunkirk, hanging out of the windows. Most of my friends had returned home and I knew that some of them had already been evacuated again, this time to Wales. I stayed in Sittingbourne until the end of the summer term and then returned to Chatham. The Battle of Britain had already started.

After weeks of indecision about my being in the Medway Towns during the air raids, my parents made up their minds to send me to Wales. Arrangements were made by Chatham County School for my mother to accompany several of us to Pontypridd on Friday, 13th September 1940. After a sleepless night because of the air raids we were away from the Medway Towns by the early coach to London. It was useless to consider the train as quite possibly the railway lines had been bombed during the night. We arrived at Victoria Coach Station at breakfast time – in an air raid! A policeman pushed us into a taxi and off we went to Paddington Station. There we were hurried out of the taxi and taken down to the connecting passages under the platforms where it was safer. The station had a domed glass roof and shrapnel and glass was showering down everywhere. Once the train pulled into the station we were hurried aboard it and away we went.

We left Paddington Station at about 15 miles an hour with the carriage blinds down and a man in a corner seat giving us a running commentary on the dogfight going on overhead. It wasn't until we reached Reading that the train picked up a bit of speed. Just before we arrived at Newport we stopped again. We had been travelling for hours. This time a barrage balloon had come down and wrapped itself round our engine. We eventually arrived in Cardiff, changed trains for the Rhondda Valley and arrived at Treforest just as the School Billeting Officer, Mrs Peters, had more or less given us up for lost. It was nearly 5pm and we had had nothing to eat or drink since our dawn breakfast.

When we arrived at Wood Street it was tea time. On the table there was a dish with a large bunch of bananas in it – we hadn't seen bananas for months! I was billeted with Joan Quarrington, and my mother was invited to stay as well. She had expected to try and find herself a room at a hotel and return home the next day. She was invited to stay for a while to give her a rest from the air raids. We never expected to find such kindness. It was a good start to my new life in Wales. The relief of being in an area free from raids was indescribable. Apart from November 1940 when the German bombers flying over the Valleys to bomb Coventry kept us awake for hours, we heard very little of the war. Cardiff, Newport and Swansea were just far enough away not to disturb our sleep.

I soon realised what it was like to live near the coal mines; the afternoon I arrived home from school to see a huge pile of coal in the road. I was told to get changed and hurry up – the coal had to be off the road before dark! I had never seen such large lumps of coal before, and they had to be split into smaller lumps before we could carry them. A ton of coal took some clearing and it was such a dirty job.

I stayed with 'Auntie' and 'Uncle' Field and their adult daughter Betty until I returned home in 1942. They were marvellous and they always included us in their family life. In 1942 I was Betty's only bridesmaid. She had a real wartime wedding complete with chocolate iced cake.

We went to school in a chapel in the town in the mornings and to Treforest County School for Girls in the afternoons. At school I shared the desk of a girl called Buddug Jones. I never met her because of the difference in our hours of attendance, and it took me ages to learn how to pronounce her name correctly – 'Bithig'! We also went to school on Saturday mornings, partly to keep us busy I suppose. We also attended during the holidays and played table tennis, held beetle drives, played tennis and rounders and a couple of times I joined a group ramble over the mountains. That was really doing something different, the mountains were wooded on their lower slopes and then grass to the summits. The wild flowers were beautiful and there were streams of clear water everywhere. It was much softer scenery than around the Medway Towns.

The only thing that went wrong was when Joan and I caught scabies. There was an epidemic of it after the London evacuees arrived. It was no one's fault, they had lived in the shelters and slept on Underground Stations for such a long time. Joan and I were sent to the local hospital, the infirmary, because the isolation hospital was full. My infection kept me away from school for most of that summer term! There was an outbreak of diphtheria in the hospital and poor Joan caught the disease. She spent a long time in the isolation hospital and when she finally recovered her mother took her home, so I was on my own. No other evacuee came to take her place, but my Mum and Dad came to see me regularly so I was very lucky.

Uncle Will was a baker by trade so food and cooking was a speciality in that house. Every Sunday for tea we had a large plate apple pie and cream. Welsh cakes were another favourite. My mum always wanted to eat them straight from the bakestone. At times meat was very short. The first Christmas I was there we had a huge Christmas tree from a firm in Cardiff where Auntie's father worked. It was free to us so long as we paid the cost of delivery on the railway. We went to Treforest Station with an old barrow to collect it. It must have been at least seven feet high – and cost 1/6d! My mum arrived to spend Christmas with us and the best thing of all was that dad managed to get some time off and joined us for the new year. I remember we all went to a pantomime in Cardiff and had a box adjacent to the stage. The rear door of the box opened suddenly during one scene and the pantomime dame rushed in, took a couple of our chocolates and climbed up on to the stage. Looking back on it all, the war barely touched my life.

After the majority of the girls from my school returned home, some of us who stayed behind were enrolled into the Treforest School and I stayed for nearly a year. It was an experience I would not have missed. We learnt to take part in the morning assembly every other week in Welsh, although I was not among girls having Welsh lessons.

The results of my nomadic existence only really surfaced after returning home to school in Chatham. I felt so lost and unsettled. The class was divided into those who were evacuated and those who stayed behind, and I felt like an interloper, far worse than I ever did in the Treforest School. Half the mistresses were complete strangers and they were intent on ensuring we fitted into the mould that Miss Mitchell the headmistress required for her girls. She was a stern, forbidding figure, and I had always heaved a sigh of relief when her periodic visits to Treforest were over. She would conduct an icy interview with each of us and I can never remember her asking me if I was happy or had any problems – only how many baths I had a week, and how many clean blouses. The gaps in my education were many. To this day I cannot do maths properly and decimals are an unknown language to be avoided at all costs.

Recently I discovered my old school reports and, before I hid them again, I read them through. I realised that apart from a note on one that the next term would begin on such a date in Chatham and a different date in Treforest, no one reading them would ever know that I had been at any school other than at Chatham. The whole episode of being evacuated was ignored as if it had never happened.

I have never forgotten my time in Pontypridd, and have valued the friendship of my foster family over the years, as have many others who found themselves in similar situations. On the rare occasions when I have seen Tom Jones on the television, I reflect on the fact that he was born in the road behind where I lived, at the time I was there. Uncle Will's niece, Jenny James, lived next door to us in Wales and in 1951 she swam the Channel; we all went to Dover to see her.

I have some fond memories of Wales and they will stay with me for ever.

Emily Bubb *has many happy memories of her stay in South Wales:*

When evacuation came I was living in Gillingham. I had five cousins living in Rochester and they all attended Troy Town School, so arrangements were made for me to be evacuated with them to Nantyglo in South Wales. I can't remember much of the journey except that the train was very crowded, and I remember the long tunnel as the train went under the River Severn.

When we finally arrived in Nantyglo, my cousin Nen was billeted with me at 15 Gwent Terrace, two cousins lived next door and the other two lived a little further along the road, so we were all living quite close to each other. My foster parents were Elsie and Bert John, and they had a daughter, Ceinwen.

Our teacher was Mr Holliday, who was a well known figure in Rochester. He was a keen botanist and also very interested in Charles Dickens. I still have a book of *David Copperfield* in which he wrote a poem about me and my cousin. In the summer we used to play a lot on the mountain and, when they were in season, we would pick whinberries which our 'Mam' would make into gorgeous tarts. All our food scraps would be saved and would be given to a woman who lived nearby and kept pigs.

At Christmas 'Mam' used to pluck the chicken herself and everyone would take their Christmas cakes to the local baker for him to bake them. Coal was delivered by the ton and tipped outside the gate on the pavement. We then had to carry it into the house in buckets. The milk was delivered from a milk churn with a special ladle, and we had to have a jug ready when he called.

We joined the Band of Hope and we would go every week to sing hymns from a large written sheet hanging over a blackboard. I also remember the schools' walk, which took place at Whitsun. Every Saturday night a dance was held at the local British Legion Hall, and we used to go and help in the cloakroom. If we wanted to dance we had to go to the centre of the dance floor so that we didn't get 'under the feet' of the adults.

'Dad' had been gassed during the First World War and as a consequence he had terrible trouble with his chest. When we came home after the dance, we both used to push him from behind to help him up the hill. He was a lovely man and he used to let us put ribbons in his hair. We were in Nantyglo for about three years and, although we were very well looked after, we were getting a little homesick. By this time most of my other cousins had returned home. When we did finally leave for home, I remember 'Mam' being very upset and she was crying when we left. I took my family down to visit in 1960 and they all made us very welcome.

Our foster parents are both gone now, but I am still in touch with their daughter Ceinwen.

Jean Jones *(now Mrs Jean Dyer) remembers when she, aged eleven, and her brother Colin, aged eight, were evacuated from Rochester in June 1940:*

I remember Rochester Railway Station being packed with children, with labels on our coats, gas masks and a case with a few clothes in, waiting for a train to goodness knows where! When we finally left, the train eventually took us to Cardiff. From there we were put on a coach to Cowbridge Town Hall. At the time we had no idea where we were!

I can remember very well sitting around a room and people coming to choose which child they wanted. A lady chose Colin and he left with her. Soon afterwards a man chose me; I was one of the last to leave that room and I felt no one wanted me. I went up the High Street with him to number 65 and found Colin crying outside the house next door. He just didn't want to go into the woman's house, so Mr Yorwerth let Colin stay with me.

There were gas cookers in the window of my billet. I suppose my foster parents were agents for the local gas company. Living with Mr amd Mrs Yorwerth was their daughter-in-law and grandson, Dean, who was 20 months old. Dean's father was away in the army. They also had a live-in maid named Annie.

Our school in the Broadway was quite a distance away. Colin had to go to school in the mornings and I had to attend in the afternoons. I spent the mornings meeting my class and teacher in a farmyard not far from the school, but when it was raining we met in a chapel.

On Saturday mornings I was given our ration books to get our rations from the small grocery shop a few yards up the road. If I needed to get milk I had to take a jug with

'Warship Week' at Pontypridd – one of many events to raise money for the war effort

me – there were no bottles in those days! I spent Sunday mornings taking Dean out in his pushchair to the local recreation ground to watch the Local Defence Volunteers marching. We also went to church in the morning and Sunday School in the afternoon.

My brother Colin wasn't very happy and was quite homesick so Mrs Yorwerth decided to find a friend for him to play with. Two boys, Melville and David, from the grocery shop came round to play, but I was to find out at the local recreation ground that Melville was more interested in me than in Colin. We were given permission to go to the cinema on Saturday afternoons with our two new friends, and were given sixpence each to go in and a penny each to buy chips on the way home!

I can remember Melville having a lot of different birds' eggs in a cardboard box. It is of course illegal nowadays to collect wild birds eggs. I also remember the air raids over the RAF Station at St Athan.

One Saturday afternoon we were playing with Dean in the hay field behind our billet, and my brother threw some hay at Dean and something went into his eye. That was enough for Mr and Mrs Yorwerth to get Colin moved to another billet. When I got back to the house my brother had gone and I didn't know where he was staying until I went to school the following Monday. I found Colin sitting on the pavement outside a house in The Broadway. Colin was one of four boys who had to sleep on the floor in a cupboard under the stairs! I felt unhappy at the way Colin had left so I complained to my teacher that I wanted to move as well.

I was soon moved to the headmaster's house next to the school. Mr and Mrs Roberts were very nice and I was lucky to have a double bed in a lovely bedroom – a bit different to Colin's circumstances!

My parents came to see us one weekend. Soon afterwards my father came back to take my brother and me back home. When my father arrived I was playing in the front garden, and he called out to me, 'Get your things, I am taking you home!' I had to leave in a bit of a hurry. I didn't want to go, because I was quite happy there. So, after just a few months we returned to Rochester.

I had a letter from Melville after I got home, but I never replied. My brother went back in the 1970s to the house in The Broadway, but they said they couldn't remember him. He also found Mr Roberts (his wife had died by then) and Colin was made very welcome. He went in search of Mr and Mrs Yorwerth but he could find no trace of them. I have been back to Cowbridge several times. The last time was in 1988 when my husband and I walked from the Town Hall to number 65 High Street. The gas cookers had gone and it was now an estate agent's showroom!

Karen Moller *(now Mrs Karen Lodge) was excluded from the first evacuation from the Medway Towns, but remembers well the time in 1940 when she and her two sisters left for South Wales:*

I was 13 years old when the war broke out on 3rd September 1939. We lived in Higham, a village two miles from Rochester, and since it was deemed to be outside the danger area, we were not allowed to be evacuated with the school on 1st September 1939.

On that day there was a mass evacuation of children from all the schools in the area, including the school my sisters and I went to, Rochester Grammar School. They were evacuated to Canterbury.

As far as I know, no educational provision was made for those who were not evacuated, so my father had us enrolled at the Rochester Art School for one day each week. Shortly afterwards, two teachers from a secondary school in Northfleet were billeted with us, and my parents arranged for them to teach us each evening for an hour or so, as part of their lodging payment. This worked very well and all the main school subjects were covered, with plenty of homework to be done during the day.

In January 1940 the Rochester Grammar School re-opened, as there was a number of children who were either returning from Canterbury, or who, like us, had not been evacuated. We attended just once or twice a week for half a day. However, with our tuition continuing in the evenings, and at the Art School, we felt we were well catered for.

By the end of February the whole school returned and we started regular lessons five mornings a week. The Rochester Mathematical School for Boys used our school in the afternoons and we shared their teachers. We never met the boys, but I remember my friends and I leaving them notes in our desks, and finding replies the following day. It was all quite innocent, but tremendously exciting!

By mid May the war situation was getting pretty tense. Denmark and Norway had been invaded, the King had broadcast to the country and we had been drilled in using gas masks, stirrup pumps to put out incendiary bomb fires and had had innumerable air raid practices.

Then on 20th May there was another mass evacuation of school children from Rochester Railway Station. This time Rochester Grammar School was sent to Pontypridd in South Wales; again we were supposed to be in a safe zone and were not allowed to go. We did start all day school though, but not for long.

On Sunday 2nd June 1940, the remaining girls were at last to be evacuated. My parents drove us to school where we were grouped in our classes and conducted in a long crocodile to Rochester station, carrying our gas masks and food for the journey. Our trunk was sent by luggage in advance and actually arrived thirteen days later!

I remember standing in line on the station forecourt, with hundreds of children from various schools, all rather apprehensive of their future, yet nevertheless excited at the adventure. Our train left at 11.35am and steamed into Porthcawl at 7.30pm, stopping four times at stations on the way where we were given cups of cold water to refresh us on the hot journey.

We needed a good wash too, because the steam train was none too clean and it was hard to resist opening the carriage windows now and again to watch the curve of the long train as it chuffed along the meandering countryside.

The rhythm of wheels on the railway lines stay with me still and remind me of endless journeys and clouds of acrid smoke that filled our nostrils – not to mention the sooty smuts that flew in through the open windows!

When we arrived at Porthcawl, we were thrilled to see a fairground next to the station, but thought it most unfair when later we were told that it was out of bounds. Supper was waiting for us in a large restaurant, after which we were introduced to our new foster parents. We three sisters were among the last to be billeted, because we wanted to stay together and few people had the room.

At last Mrs Blundell, who lived in the village of Nottage, a short distance away, agreed to take us. She lived in a large Tudor house, which had been given to Anne Boleyn by

King Henry VIII. The stately rooms were hung with tapestries and huge portraits, with priceless furniture and ornaments in every room. The building was set in magnificent grounds, with ponds, rolling lawns, rockeries and herbaceous borders. There were two tennis courts which we were allowed to use, and a walled kitchen garden.

We really were tremendously fortunate and Mrs Blundell was very kind and generous though quite strict, so I was a bit afraid of her. She was a land owner and Guide Commissioner, and frequently took us out to the woods or the coast for picnics at the weekends, where she taught us so much about the wild life, flora and fauna. We gathered edible fungi which would be cooked for our tea, and we learned to recognise various birdcalls. To round us up, Mrs Blundell would cup her hands and hoot like an owl. It took some practice to be able to reply, but master it we did, probably to the bewilderment of the resident birds.

The Pavilion, Porthcawl, in 1940

Our bedrooms were on the second floor where we also had a sitting room and bathroom, so the only time we went downstairs was for meals. The parlour maid rang a huge gong in the hall, and Mrs Blundell and her secretary joined us at the large polished table, set with a silver service. It was all very grand and, though the atmosphere was friendly, I never really relaxed and was quite shy.

We shared the Central School with the local children. In the mornings we used the various halls in the town for lessons, supervised homework or country dancing. Sometimes we would be taken for walks or sea bathing. The latter was always very popular and good fun, till an oil tanker was blown up, and the rocks and sand became covered in oil.

In the afternoons we used the school building. Holiday times were also organised with rambles, scavenger hunts, games, sand castle competitions, walks and swimming. The teachers worked really hard to make sure we enjoyed ourselves and, though we respected them, we never took advantage of their relaxed attitude. It was good to have fun with them and to know them as friends and confidantes when we were so far from home.

On 17th July 1940, six weeks after arriving at Porthcawl, the girls who had been evacuated to Pontypridd came to join us and so the school was complete once more. Later in the year we were all taken to the Pavilion to see Sybil Thorndike, Lewis Casson and their daughter Anne Casson, in *Macbeth*. Sybil had been a pupil at our school and, when she heard we were in the audience, she came out to meet us at the end of the performance.

She had us in fits of laughter as she shared her classroom memories and recalled the pranks she and her friends got up to. I have never forgotten the contrast she displayed between her serious character as Lady Macbeth and the warmth of her naturally bubbly nature when she spoke to us afterwards. It was an amazing experience.

Two years later, by the summer of 1942, most of the girls had returned to Rochester. The headmistress, Miss Butterfield, had re-opened the school and it was decided that it was no longer practicable to keep such a small group in Porthcawl. I was then in the 5th form, and there must have been fewer than fifty pupils left. It was a time of very mixed feelings. Wonderful to be going home again after what seemed almost a lifetime away, though we did go home each Christmas.

I was sixteen years old, and had done a lot of growing up in Porthcawl; I was to miss greatly the friendly atmosphere of the small school where we all knew each other so well. Back in Rochester, the classes were more than twice as large, and the routine much more rigid.

Mrs Blundell, our second Mum, continued to keep in touch with us all and it was a great privilege and joy to have her at my wedding. She was much loved and respected; later, when she came to live in a flat near her sister in Camberley, we could visit her more often to share our reminiscences.

I look back now on my two years as an evacuee as a time of colourful memories and experiences that shaped and matured me in many ways. It was often hard, but I accepted it and, because my sisters were with me, I wasn't homesick. But oh, what a joy it was when we at last got home – to stay!

Roy Godden *was approaching his seventh birthday when he was evacuated with his school, St Matthew's School, Borstal, to the village of Blaina in South Wales:*

We left Rochester Railway Station in May 1940, bound for South Wales. The journey was long and tiring and I remember the train stopping at Reading, Swindon and at Newport where we changed trains and puffed up the valleys to our destination, the village of Blaina, near Abertillery. George Ribbens and I were almost the last to be billeted as our mothers had instructed us to stay together. However, we were finally chosen by Mrs Wakely who really only wanted one evacuee, but she took us both.

Mr and Mrs Wakely owned a little general store, which was really the front room of the house, in Railway Terrace. We arrived at the house very tired and dishevelled. That first night I remember that we two evacuees and Mrs Wakely's son Bernard, all slept in the same bed. There were only two bedrooms in the house, and you had to go through one to reach the other. Eventually, both Bernard and his sister Mary had to sleep at their grandmother's house on East Side to make enough room for George and me.

Blaina was a typical mining village situated between two mountains. It had a main street, with mostly stone houses on either side of it spreading back to both mountains. The only cinema, situated on the High Street, was named the 'Gaiety', and I remember going there on five consecutive nights to see five different Deanna Durbin films. Mrs Wakely gave me the money for the cinema and also gave me bars of chocolate from the shop (no sweet coupons required!!). I also remember going with some older lads to a cinema in Abertillery to see the film *Dr Jekyll and Mr Hyde*. I spent most of the time under the seat, too frightened to watch! To add to my fright it was thundering and lightning when we came out of the cinema. I think I slept in Mrs Wakely's bed that night – as I invariably did when her husband, Bryn, was on night shift at the local Beynon Colliery.

Memories of school are a bit vague although I recall we only did part-time schooling while we were there, mostly in the British Legion Hall. The older evacuees mixed with the Welsh children at the Westside School.

I remember when a little girl evacuee from Essex arrived next door. She was about my age and her name was Doris and I grew very fond of her. Mrs Wakely used to pull my leg about something I was supposed to have said to Doris – that, 'When I grow up I'm going to be a cowboy and you can be my cow!'

I enjoyed climbing the mountains, playing hide and seek in the tall ferns, exploring the quarries, and walking over to the other side of the mountain to look down on the Ebbw Vale steel works. I also remember an eventful bank holiday when my foster parents took me to Barry Island. The train was so full of holiday makers on the return journey that we younger children had to sit on the luggage racks!

Roy Godden pictured left with his foster parents, Bryn and Helen Wakely. The other boy, George Ribbens, was also an evacuee. Photo taken in Blaina, Monmouthshire, in 1940

I stayed with the Wakelys until I returned home in February 1943. My time in Blaina, mixing with older children, climbing the mountains and exploring had made me a lot more confident. My foster parents were very kind to me and treated me as one of their own. Mrs Wakely used to call me her 'Chicken Little'.

My wife and I visited Blaina a few years ago and we managed to contact Mary Wakely, the daughter with whom we had had no contact for over 40 years. She lives only about a quarter of a mile from her mother's old house. From that visit we managed to contact Mary's brother Bernard who now lives in Mid-Wales. They both have children and grandchildren of their own. It was a tremendous thrill for me; the only sad thing was that their older brother Harry had died. I remember playing truant from school and going with Harry on his baker's round!

I was well looked after by my foster parents and I shall always remember them with affection.

Chapter Five

MORE MEMORIES OF WALES – THE GOOD AND THE BAD.

Having experienced a few months in Sittingbourne, **Joan Prosser** *was off again, this time with the Chatham County School for Girls:*

This was to be my second evacuation, but for me this was a much happier time. Our mothers were very brave about saying goodbye as we were bundled on to the trains, gas masks over our shoulders, cases, and name labels in case we got lost! No one knew where we were going although Wales seemed to be the most likely destination.

I finally ended up at a place near Newport in Monmouthshire, and I was pleased to find myself billeted with a friend, Joan Quarrington, and in the care of an amiable housewife. This lasted scarcely a few weeks and we were shepherded off again – this time for Treforest and Pontypridd. There I was really happy, mostly thanks to 'my family', the Robothams, who had a nice shoe shop. They also had a daughter Peggy of nineteen. Peggy was great fun and spent a lot of time with me. She bought a mongrel called Raffles whom I took for long walks up the mountains. Sheila Peters and her mother lived close by and Mrs Peters encouraged my friendship with Sheila. We spent many hours happily trying to dam mountain streams and make waterfalls.

Another close friend was Joyce Geldhart. She was not as adventurous as I was and I clearly remember taking her to some lock gates on a canal and firmly saying she could walk across provided she did not look down – 'just follow me!'

School seemed quite a happy place. We were all aware of Miss Mitchell's strict presence but in a curious way it gave us security with very definite boundaries of behaviour.

Apart from my time in Sittingbourne I adapted quite well to being evacuated. This was mainly due to the caring people I had in Wales – my teachers and foster parents! After I returned home, Peggy and I wrote to each other for many years. I cannot remember how it all ended but I will always think of them with gratitude for the way they looked after me during those dark days.

Patricia Hughes (*now Mrs Patricia Kay*) *now recalls her second evacuation when she went to South Wales in 1940:*

My first billet was at a tiny house half way up a steep hill in a village called Crumlin. I can remember that the front doors in all the houses were left wide open all day! After about a week we went to Treforest near Pontypridd. My sister was, by this time, separated from me because she went to a different school. My foster parents at my new billet were Mr and Mrs John, and they had a grown up daughter named Marjorie. They were all very nice to me and I was very happy there. Mr John was an insurance man and had a small green car with the registration BNY7. It was most unusual for people to have cars in those days.

We were still going to school part time and I think the school we used was the Treforest Intermediate School. The local adults treated us very well, but the other children did not like us. The called us 'Silly Vacuees'. One of them said to me, 'I bet you keep your teeth in a glass of water,' but it did not worry me.

I think I was quite a naughty little girl and I used to talk to the boys. That was considered very forward when I was a child. I had a tall, dark, handsome boyfriend called Idris, but I don't think he considered he was my boyfriend. He preferred the company of his mates. My foster parents were not religious, but I had to go to chapel a great deal. I went to morning service, Sunday school and evening service every Sunday. I remember seeing people baptised. They were laid right down in the water from a standing position. Our minister was very holy and hated seeing people enjoying themselves. I remember we had a new year party and he walked across the hall with a large bible under his arm, looking very cross! I also remember having to sing a solo in chapel. I was very nervous. The tune was *Humoresque* by Dvorak.

I helped at a forces canteen one evening a week, I went to Speedwell on Tuesday, Band of Hope on Wednesday, Christian Endeavour on another evening. I can't remember much about these activities, except that at Band of Hope we had to swear never to drink alcohol! I was twelve years old.

After a while I had to move from Mr and Mrs John's because they had to move away. I was very sorry to move to another billet, which was with Mr and Mrs Culliford, who lived in the same road. They had two very good looking children, grown up to me, a boy named Gerald and a girl whose name I can't remember. They went out every evening and when they came home, there were always rows.

We seemed to have liver every day for dinner. It took me years to start eating liver again after the war! I was not with the Cullifords for very long when I was suddenly made aware that I was going home. Again, no reason was given, but I suspect that my foster parents could not cope with an extra child in the house.

I went back home in 1941 to air raids, doodlebugs and all the horrors of war. We hadn't an air raid shelter, so when the sirens sounded, we sat in the cellar, which my father had strengthened with large wooden joists. It was damp down there and dark. My eldest sister refused to join us in the cellar, and I can see her now, sitting at the top of the cellar stairs, on a little stool, knitting!

We still shared schools, firstly at the Technical School on the New Road (Fort Pitt), then finally at our own school, Chatham County School for Girls. This we shared with Gillingham County Boys, and lots of letters were passed between the boys and girls. Life at school was mostly normal, but evenings were still disrupted by air raids.

My sister stayed on in Wales for quite a long time after I came back. She was very happy there. Eventually the war ended and life returned to normal, whatever normal meant! But food was still rationed. I remember the excitement of VE Day and I vividly remember the street party. By this time I was sixteen and had left school and started work at the education office, feeling very grown up!

Freda Kingsnorth *(now Mrs Freda Oliver) was another Chatham County School pupil who was whisked off to South Wales:*

Towards the end of May 1940 it was obvious that France was about to fall and then England, particularly Kent, would be the new front line. So parents were given the opportunity to re-evacuate their children. We had to meet at Chatham Station at 3pm on Sunday 2nd June. We were told to bring sandwiches but nobody said anything about drinks. I don't think we were even told where we were going although I vaguely remember a teacher telling us where we were when we arrived at Crumlin station. It was a terrible journey across country, with stopping and starting all the way. We were held up for a long time at a place which somebody said was Salisbury Plain. We were all very thirsty by then. Local village children came along the tracks selling water for a penny a cup. I along with many others had not been given any money so we stayed thirsty.

We arrived very late at Crumlin which was a small mining village outside Newport. Doreen Crowther and I were billeted with a young couple with two young children. I do not remember much about the place except there was a viaduct nearby and lots of slag heaps – and the fact that we were sent out to play for most of the daylight hours! We stayed in Crumlin for six days and were then moved on to Pontypridd, at about the same time the Faversham evacuees arrived in Pontypridd.

Doreen and I were handed over to Mr and Mrs Webber and I stayed with them until I returned home. They were so kind to us, but we were not spoilt. There were rules which we were expected to observe but I do not remember ever receiving or being threatened with corporal punishment. There were two grown up children in the family. The boy was 19 and worked as a research chemist at the pit in Pontypridd. The daughter was 26 and was a nursing sister at a mining hospital in Bargoed.

I don't know how long Doreen stayed, perhaps about a year, then Rosina Wood came to stay. She was two years below me and was having trouble settling in, so it was my job to act as an older sister to her. The school was at Treforest and our foster home was at Rhydyfelin. Unless the weather was very bad I could walk to school, but some lessons were held in a church building in Pontypridd.

One of the girls, Daphne Bradley, broke her leg and was off school for a long time. She ran to get on a moving trolley bus and was dragged along for some yards. She became the subject of a long sermon to us at school!

From Pontypridd to Cardiff was 10 or 12 miles. I remember when Cardiff was bombed. We all stood in the backyard and heard the bombs falling and saw the fires. The sky was red and we were all in tears!

In December 1941 I returned home to Kent.

Daphne Bradley *(now Mrs Daphne Hawes) is the Daphne mentioned in the previous account, and now relives her memories of her time in Wales:*

We took the train to Pontypridd in either May or June 1940, and we were given fruit and drinks on the way to Wales. The boys' school was at the rear of the train and every time we went round a bend there was a lot of waving and shouting between the girls and the boys. I don't remember much of the journey except that it took a long time and

Evacuees leaving by train in June 1940

we arrived very tired. We went to a hall where we were allocated to various families. We went to an elderly couple, Mr and Mrs Green, who for some reason expected us to be ill-educated, scruffy and dirty! They had never had children and really had no idea how to treat us. I remember feeling envious of two of the County School girls, Joan Churchman and Daphne Gordon, who were billeted next door in a much happier household.

Six weeks later I fell off a trolley bus. I was on the step and just got thrown off. It was very frightening and I was terrified that I would be in trouble from Mrs Green, my foster mother. I spent nearly three months in Cardiff Infirmary. We had a lot of bombing raids there and lost the windows in our ward. Every morning we woke to new patients who had been caught up in the bombing and there were many horrendous sights. I think I must have been drugged every night as I always slept through and would wake in the morning to find my bed had been pulled down the ward and the nurses busily moving them all back again.

We were able to have our beds on the balcony on fine days and that was when I realised Welsh really was a different language. There was a men's ward opposite and they would call across to the women in our ward and I could hardly understand a word! Mind you it might have been just as well. I ended up speaking with a Welsh accent which horrified my teacher, but I was quite unconscious of the fact that I had developed one. I was very lucky with visitors and everyone there was so kind.

When I finally got back to Pontypridd, Mrs Green decided she did not want the responsibility of looking after an injured child – my leg would break open at the least activity. So I moved to another billet, this time to a Jones family. Mr Jones and his brother were miners and they came home every night absolutely black and would have a bath in front of the fire.

It was in Wales that we found out that teachers were human beings! They appeared to be different people and were so friendly and jolly. They would take us out and they really became pals. One of our outings was to the coal mine at Cwm, which was supposed to be the deepest pit in Wales. I hated it because I suffer from claustrophobia.

On Sundays we used to go to go to church in the morning, Sunday school in the afternoon and chapel in the evening. I liked chapel best – lots of singing and much less preaching! We never saw much of our parents who only came on very rare occasions, but I think by then we were used to our new way of life. I remember one time they came down and decided to come to the school to meet me; they were told to catch the Rhydyfelin bus. Well, they did not arrive and were still waiting at the bottom of the hill when I got there. 'There hasn't been a bus,' they said. When I pointed to one, Dad said, 'But that says Ride Feeling, not what you said!'

We would pick whinberries on the mountainsides and play on the Rocking Stone on the common. We frequently walked to school over deserted mountains and sometimes we had to pass a flock of geese who would attack our knees, but that was the only danger. We hardly knew there was a war on!

Ione Bates, *having spent the first part of the war in Faversham, Kent, now recalls the second evacuation of her school, Chatham County School for Girls, this time to South Wales:*

Because of the possibility of German invasion we were re-evacuated on 19th May 1940, and went to Pontypridd in South Wales. Our parents were asked not to come and see us off and so it happened that I did not see mine until a year later!

We boarded the train at Faversham and did not get off again until we arrived at night in Pontypridd. I believe the Boys' Technical School shared the train and they may have gone on to be evacuated to Caerphilly. Our own experience in this was just one small part of a huge project organised so skilfully by the government.

Being by now experienced evacuees, Daphne Hawkins and I asked that we might be billeted together. From an assembly hall we boarded a bus and we were taken with others to our various billets. The two of us alighted at the Pwllgwaun Vicarage, where the vicar, his elderly housekeeper and her husband, and Gladys the maid, greeted us. To our surprise we were to share a single bed alongside a wall with a very heavy immovable mattress sloping steeply to the outer edge. The promise of a bigger bed never materialised so we took it in turns to sleep on the wall side hoping we would not fall out on the alternate night from the outer edge! The vicar did fix us up with a pull cord so we could switch off the light from the bed, so at least we enjoyed one luxury! On our first morning there we awoke to see a varied scene with a railway line down in the valley, a nearby colliery and surrounding mountains. It was quite a surprise as we had arrived in the dark and had no idea of our surroundings.

Our schooling was at Treforest County School for Girls. At our first assembly there the headmistress of the school welcomed us and explained that when we went to our allotted form room, we were to open our desks to find a letter from the regular resident of that desk. The letter was a further welcome and suggested a place to meet in the grounds to get acquainted, and this we did. It was a kind and thoughtful gesture of friendship.

All our lessons were in this school and great flexibility was made for both schools to operate and dovetail their timetables as separate schools. Again we acknowledge the upheaval to the resident school in making it possible to continue with our education.

The school always had a flourishing Girl Guide company under Miss Moorcroft in Chatham. This was revived in Pontypridd under the guidance of Miss Best, the history mistress. We were proud to include in our camp fire songs the refrain:

> There's none so rare as can compare
> With the 7th Pontypridd Evacuees!

We obtained our Welsh badge by learning quite a bit of the language and to this day Daphne and I can still pronounce: Llanfairpwllgwyngyllgogerychwyrndrobwll-llantysiliogogogoch – even if it is difficult to spell!

So the war continued, we listened to the news and read the papers anxiously, we were concerned for our relatives in the services and we longed for the war to be over. In the meanwhile we tightened our belts literally with the rationing of so many foods. Very occasionally we would see a queue at a sweet shop. Word had spread that chocolate was in stock – a rare commodity with one small bar being a real treat shared among us!

We were lucky enough to see something of the countryside as the vicar kindly took us out in his car a few times. By now, after three months the vicar's elderly housekeeper was finding it difficult to cope so we moved to Maesycoed, part of Pontypridd, joining two of our school friends already established in an averaged sized terrace house. The householders generously gave up a room to us both by taking their two small sons to sleep with them. They also gave the four of us complete use of the front parlour – such a kindness!

Bath night on Fridays was quite a performance. It was in a tin bath in front of the kitchen range. We had to heat the water in a huge heavy enamelled pan over the fire, and being small of stature, I always struggled to lift the pan off the range. One night disaster struck as I slopped a lot of water over the fire which promptly produced a mass of hissing steam and ash all over the place. The kitchen got a good clean with my flannel that night – but I didn't! How I worried about that incident and hoped that no one would notice!

By July 1941 most of the school had returned to Chatham. The Blitz was over and, although the Medway Towns were classed as a danger zone, I suppose there were good reasons to bring the school back. Daphne and I returned later on 19th December 1941 and it was wonderful to be home again. We often look back on that time we shared. It made us friends for life.

We owe an enormous debt to the school staff who did such a marvellous job looking after us and giving us a great education. They were unsung heroines. We also owed much to all the people in Faversham and Pontypridd who opened their homes to us and cared for us for two and a quarter years – more unsung heroes and heroines.

We grew up fast in that time! We had to take on responsibilities and decisions at an earlier age than usual. We must give credit to our parents for bringing us up to cope with this. While we did not want to be away from home we made the best of it, had a lot of laughs and learned to get on with people. We did everything with zest – even if we got none from oranges!

Edna Eacott (*now Mrs Edna Everitt*) *remembers with clarity her evacuation to South Wales:*

I was evacuated to Wales on Sunday, the 2nd June 1940. Our school was the Luton Infants' and Junior Girls' School. We all gathered at our school on the day at about

1.30pm, before marching down the slope to the buses, marked 'Private', waiting on the Luton Road. Our mothers met us at Chatham Railway Station; they had used the normal bus service after checking us in at our different schools. We said goodbye to Dad before he went to work at the dockyard that morning, so Mum had to see us off on her own.

Our train was in on the 'down' platform, normally used for the trains going to the coast. It was the longest train I had ever seen. Across the line standing at the 'up' platform to London stood another train. It was full of very tired and sad looking soldiers returning from the Dunkirk beaches. It was very frightening. We had been told all about Dunkirk a few days earlier.

Mum had been into town to buy two small cases because we were not allowed to carry anything very heavy. I was eight and a half years old and my sister was two years younger. Mum also had twin girls and a baby of nine months to look after. Mum cuddled us at the station and told me not to cry because that would start my younger sister and her crying as well. I tried to fight back the lump in my throat as I had to be the 'big sister'. Then we were told to get on the train, so we had a quick kiss from Mum, who stood there on the platform waving – and crying, pretending that she had something in her eye. They closed the doors and I said my prayers, 'Please God take care of my mum and dad and Jean and Joyce and Shirley.'

Mum had also bought us a haversack like the soldiers wore. I had it on my back with the sandwiches in it. The train journey was very long and tiring. At some time during the journey some boys had pulled the communication cord and had stopped the train. Everyone was in a panic in case a German aeroplane came over, and they had to check to make sure everyone was on the train before we could move off. This made us quite late in getting to our destination, but we finally arrived at Newport and went to a hall where we were given hot drinks and biscuits. After that it seemed that we were all sent to different places. I was upset because I was separated from my friend Doris who lived in our street back home.

Our bus took us to Pentwamaur, near Newbridge, and we assembled in another hall. The boys were running around and making a noise. My sister and I sat down, we were both very tired. The local people started choosing children and they were leaving in ones and twos. My sister fell asleep on my shoulder. I had my feet on my suitcase and dared not move as I did not want to wake her up. We were dressed the same, like twins, and I was saying to myself, 'Please God, let someone nice choose both of us.' I was sort of half asleep, when I looked across the hall to the door. This tall broad shouldered man came in, spoke to the lady in charge and she looked at her big book. She pointed to us and as he walked towards me our eyes met. I felt as if I had known him for years, although I was very nervous. I had had meningitis when I was three and it had left me with bad eyes and bad nerves. The man gave me a big beaming smile and asked my name, then asked me if I would like to live with him and his wife and little boy. I said, 'Yes please, sir.'

I saw that he was wearing a minister's collar and, as we were taught about God at home, I thought that God had really answered my prayers. His name was the Revd Leonard Rees. I told him that I must look after my little sister, and she had to stay with me. He said that he would never think of splitting us up. A big lad from the Scouts took the two small cases and someone from the St John Ambulance carried my sister on his back, still fast asleep. I held the minister's hand as he told me not to be afraid. We walked down a dark lane and then an alleyway; I was afraid of the dark. We arrived at a lovely house, nicer than ours at home, and bigger. This lovely lady with hair all curly and fair bent down and gave us a cuddle and said, 'Oh, you poor little babies!'- then I really did cry.

They took us to a lovely bedroom and we fell asleep as soon as our heads touched the pillows. It must have been about one o'clock in the morning by this time. When I woke up I looked out of the window. I heard a cockerel and chickens, then saw a big field at the end of the garden. We were behind a small farm with pigs and chickens. A little way along the road were a few terraced houses and shops. Our school was about ten minutes away.

We used to go shopping once a week in Blackwood and the bus stop was just to the left of our billet. To the right of the house was the bus stop for Newbridge, which took longer to reach. While I was in Wales I learned to speak the language and I could sing in Welsh. I always told everyone that my auntie was pretty and my uncle was handsome. They chose us – we were not forced upon them. I miss them both so much, our friendship lasted until their deaths some years ago. I have wonderful memories of them and of my time in Wales. People were brave taking in evacuees and giving them homes. It must have been a struggle and I shall always be grateful for the way we were looked after.

Pat Mortley *(now Mrs Pat Blackie), having survived her school's first evacuation to Canterbury in 1939, now faced her second evacuation:*

In the second evacuation in June 1940, our school, Rochester Grammar School for Girls, travelled by train to Porthcawl, a seaside resort between Cardiff and Swansea. Once again we endured the distasteful business of the 'picking and choosing'. I was very late in being chosen and was billeted on an elderly lady. Her idea of having an evacuee was someone to do her housework for her. Eventually I was moved to more suitable accommodation and went to live with a village blacksmith.

The family consisted of the blacksmith in his sixties, his son and his daughter who kept house for them all. It was a rather old fashioned household, 'very much chapel'. We were happy there and they loved having us. 'Pop', as we called him, and his son spent a great deal of their time playing the harmonium, mostly hymns as far as I can recall.

I had not been there very long before I produced a pack of playing cards – on a Sunday! I was gently reminded by Pop that one did not play cards on a Sunday. One would not even dream of hanging out so much as a tea towel to dry on a Sunday.

On Sundays I attended chapel in the morning, then church in the afternoon. After church I took tea with the local vicar. It was back to the chapel for the evening service. After chapel we would go to the Pavilion where there were classical types of concerts, which included male voice choirs and the like. We enjoyed going to the concerts, they were the highlights of the week. I remember that the Dutch soldiers rescued at Dunkirk were billeted in the vicinity. They also attended the Sunday concerts and we all sang the Welsh national anthem followed by the Dutch national anthem.

Part of the Math Boys' School from Rochester was also billeted at Porthcawl. We were friendly with them and all shared our troubles at being so far from home. I stayed at Porthcawl until March 1941 and then returned to Rochester.

Helen Cross, after not having a very nice experience in Sandwich during her first evacuation, was now on the move again with her school, Napier Road Girls' School, Gillingham:

The journey to South Wales was long and tiring and when we finally got to our destination I can vividly recall all of us children standing in a large playground, and being moved around by adults, among them the dreaded 'Nit Nurse'!

Because of the problem we had in Sandwich on our first evacuation, my sister and I were hurriedly segregated. I didn't know what had happened to my brother at the time and no one saw fit to tell me. This small group of girls we were in were moved very quickly to what can only be described as a Dickensian orphanage. The only good thing about it was that my little sister was still with me. We had obviously brought head lice with us from Sandwich. The humiliation I had felt in Sandwich was nothing to what we were subjected to in this cold grey concrete building.

We were kept isolated in one room most of the time. Although I was of an age where privacy should have been considered, we were all bathed and had our hair scrubbed with some lotion that burned our skin, and then put into calico-type dresses and mop hats. This treatment was carried out every day and the mop hats kept on, even at night. During the very miserable time we spent there, it would not have been surprising to see Oliver Twist walk by!

Finally came the great day and we saw the sun as we were led to some waiting vehicles. We didn't know where we were, but that didn't matter. My sister and I arrived at a very nice clean house, which had a lovely homely feeling about it. It turned out to be the home of the local officer in charge of evacuees. Shortly after our arrival the officer's wife came in with their young daughter. As we sat not knowing what to say, the little girl came up to me and asked if I would take her bonnet and shoes off. I received a lovely smile and a thank you from her.

Then the evacuation officer asked me if I would like to stay there, and stated that my sister would be just two houses away. Knowing my little sister would be nearby, I was very happy to agree. It didn't take me long to find that kindness, love and care was in abundance. I felt very much at home and was treated like one of the family in every way. Their names were Mr and Mrs Mansfield and their little girl was Cynthia – and the place was Whitchurch.

When I became 14 years old I left school and despite these wonderful people wanting me to stay with them, my mother made sure I returned home.

*Having spent some months in Canterbury, **Frank Turner** and his school, Sir Joseph Williamson Mathematical School, from Rochester, left the city in May 1940 for Wales:*

Of the railway journey to Wales I have only a hazy recollection, other than it was long and tedious. My first real memory is of the train finally stopping at a station where the name boards had not yet been removed. I was convinced that I had arrived in a foreign country, the name of the small town was YNYSYBWL. We set off again and soon arrived at Pontypridd, a larger town at the beginning of the Rhondda Valley. This time our billets had already been allocated to us. I went to Mrs Morgan at 81 Middle Street together with Harry Harnet. David Wallis was billeted next door to us. Mrs Morgan was a widow with two sons. She was not well off financially but made us very welcome. It could not have been easy having us living there as well as her own two sons.

We were very lucky as we lived very close to Ynysangharad Park in the centre of the town. The townspeople were fortunate as they had a large park which included many different sports facilities. All evacuees were allowed free use of the swimming pool, so I was able to spend a great deal of my spare time swimming. While I was at Pontypridd I entered for a sports day in the park. Quite how I became involved I cannot remember, but I entered for the javelin throwing and did well at it. I was asked where I learnt to throw the javelin as well as I did. I explained about the Math School and the schoolboy championships. I spent the rest of the day instructing anyone who was interested in the art of javelin throwing.

At the time of our evacuation to South Wales the Math School was divided between Pontypridd and Porthcawl on the Welsh Coast. At a later date the boys in the Porthcawl group joined us at Pontypridd. After the passing of so many years it is difficult to remember the finer details of our stay in Wales. For our schooling, we shared the facilities of the Pontypridd County School for Boys in the centre of town. I sat and passed the School Certificate in the summer term of 1941. I was sixteen years old by this time, so I left school and returned home to Chatham. I was successful in obtaining an apprenticeship at the Short Brothers Seaplane Works at Rochester.

I have never forgotten the time spent with Mrs Morgan and her family, and her efforts to make us feel welcome in their home. Unfortunately, by the time I visited Pontypridd in later years, Mrs Morgan had died, as had her eldest son. He was about my age, so it was a shock to hear that he died as a result of an accident while playing rugby.

After a period in Canterbury with his eventual return to Rochester, **Peter Hoad's** *school, Sir Joseph Williamson Mathematical School was leaving the Medway towns once more, this time for Porthcawl in South Wales:*

On arrival in Porthcawl four of us from the same form were placed in one household in the care of Mrs H., a middle-aged widow. Conditions there were not as comfortable as my Canterbury billet, in fact they were quite spartan, but more importantly our guardian was a kindly person who worked hard on our behalf.

Porthcawl would normally have been thronging with holidaymakers at this time of the year (June), but now it was overflowing with our own troops and Dutch troops evacuated from Dunkirk. The incident I recall most vividly from that time is of the four of us walking along the seafront on a warm summer evening and being joined by Mr Stone, a popular teacher whose views we would respect. Britain was then more vulnerable than at any other time of the war, but we could not bring ourselves to admit the possibility of defeat. Mr Stone with more experience may not have been as confident, but he was careful to leave us on an optimistic note as we concluded that the Royal Navy would pull us through. In fact the Royal Air Force was about to play its part in the Battle of Britain.

Schooling on a half day basis got under way very quickly due to the generosity of the local grammar school in allowing us to share their premises, and the efforts of our own school staff. I am sure I never gave it a thought at the time, but our teachers, like ourselves, had already had to uproot themselves twice in the last year; additionally they had their own families to worry about and had to organise our schooling under difficult circumstances. We were able to take the London University General Certificate examination without any delay using our host's school and an old church hall. I was probably least confident in the French oral test, but I need not have worried. On the day of the test the elderly Frenchman examining me seemed pre-occupied with other matters; I am sure that he was more concerned about what the German army was doing to his country than the damage an English boy was inflicting on his native tongue!

Being at the seaside meant that we had no problems in occupying our time during the summer holidays. The funfair with its roller coaster had closed just after our arrival due to the critical war situation, but we could use the beach and swim in the Bristol Channel. Without our cycles we still managed to see much of the surrounding area on foot, and on one occasion got as far as Bridgend. There were at least two local cinemas and a concert hall to visit should we so wish, although as I recall we were much more occupied with outdoor activities. Porthcawl then had no public library but there was a small private library run from a terrace house on the road to Newton from which you could borrow books for a penny.

Mrs H. took her responsibilities as our guardian very seriously and encouraged church attendance on Sunday mornings. The walk to Newton Church on Sunday became a regular feature of our stay in Porthcawl; after the service we could look forward to our Sunday dinner which was by far the best meal of the week, an important consideration then, what with food rationing and our healthy appetites. The four of us must have been a bit of a handful for Mrs H. but for all her hard work in looking after us she received just fifty shillings a week. I was surprised when she told us that out of this meagre sum she was able to save ten shillings which was just enough to pay for her favourite Woodbine cigarettes. I marvel now that so many were prepared to look after us for so little in return.

I heard that I had obtained the School Certificate but had just failed to get sufficient subjects at the right level to be awarded matriculation exemption. As this had been my aim it was suggested I should retake it in the autumn term. Such was the shortage of senior pupils that those who stayed on were immediately made prefects. Our first task was to call on local householders warning them to expect another batch of evacuees. A decision had been made to move the Rochester Girls' Grammar School from Pontypridd. In retrospect it would appear that the opportunity was lost of uniting the Math at this time and we were to continue to have two Welsh homes for another year.

Mr Clark, our headmaster, was with us in Porthcawl and so a deputy must have been in charge in Pontypridd. There were just 17 pupils in the Upper 5th and Mr Jenkinson, our form master, in addition to chemistry, also taught physics and RE. Our other teachers at the time included Mr Stone (History), Mr Hadlow (English and Geography), Mr Cheeseman (Mathematics), Mr Pearce (French) and Mr Fearnley (Art). Of these, Mr Hadlow had joined the school about the beginning of the war, but the remainder had been with the school ever since I started in 1936. Anyone who was with the school at this time in Porthcawl will recall that we were taught PE by an attractive young member of staff from Rochester Girls' Grammar. She did her best to pass on some of the enthusiasm she had for her subject and certainly succeeded in making our school day more interesting, but unfortunately for us she soon left to marry. During the autumn term a touring repertory company led by Sybil Thorndike and Lewis Casson visited Porthcawl. They put on a special performance of *Macbeth* to a combined audience from the Math and Rochester Girls' Grammar. During the interval Sybil Thorndike reminisced about her time as a pupil at the latter, and it was probably in an effort to include us that she recalled how it was our predecessors who delighted in pulling the girls' pigtails as they walked to school. It might have been this visit which inspired the Girls' Grammar to put on their own performance of Oscar Wilde's *The Importance of Being Earnest*.

While we were in Porthcawl our families back in Rochester had experienced at close quarters the Battle of Britain and, following this, nearby London was still being blitzed nightly by the Luftwaffe. In contrast to this, Porthcawl was something of a backwater as far as the war was concerned and was certainly not bombed while I was there, but we still had to put up with spending many hours in the claustrophobic atmosphere of the school shelters whenever an air raid warning went.

Porthcawl didn't entirely escape the Germans, as an oil slick covered the beach and the rocks by the shore. Prior to this we had seen a low flying German plane over the Bristol Channel and, rightly or wrongly, we assumed the oil slick was caused by the sinking of a tanker by this plane. Apart from this there were just the RAF air sea rescue launch moored in the harbour and army units stationed nearby to remind us of the war. It was this difference between the life we led and that of our families back in Rochester that made me decide that whatever the result of my examination I would not be staying on beyond the end of term.

I travelled back home just before Christmas and, crossing London between Paddington and Victoria, I saw for the first time the damage caused by the Blitz. Strangely enough I heard that I had obtained my Matriculation exemption from a local firm of accountants rather than from school, when they wrote to my father offering to train me in accountancy. Unfortunately I was unable to accept the offer because a high premium was required. I soon found an alternative position with the City of Rochester Surveyor's Department. Ironically our offices were on the first floor of the Rochester Girls' Grammar School whose pupils I had left back in Porthcawl.

As a postscript to my time as an evacuee, I returned to visit my Canterbury hosts immediately after the end of the war. Many years later I went back to Porthcawl but by that time my wartime guardian there had moved away. I have mixed memories of my evacuation, but the fact that I still retain an affection for both Canterbury and Porthcawl is perhaps a true measure of my experiences.

Mrs E. Whale's first experience of evacuation was not a happy one and now she was off for a second time:

I think we were only home from Herne Bay a matter of months when it was decided we should be evacuated again, this time to South Wales. I remember going to my school, Holy Trinity School in Brompton, and then to the railway station in Gillingham before being herded on to a train. We had our gas masks hanging from our shoulders, and a bag containing a few belongings and sweets and sandwiches. We had eaten all the food within an hour of being on the train! After the initial excitement of the day had passed, it began to sink in that we were on our own again.

Coming from a big family, ten in all, we tried to keep together. Going to Wales were my three brothers, two sisters and myself. The others were too young to go. The journey was long and I remember eventually arriving at Llanharan Station rather late in the afternoon. By this time we were all very tired and dirty.

I clearly remember the hall we were taken to. There were lots of Welsh ladies there, taking their choice of the children, and how many each one could take. My brothers went to a farm in the village, but there was no way my two sisters and I were going to be separated! Eventually a Mrs Evans, who later became known to us as Auntie Vi, took us to live with her. She and her husband, Uncle John, were very kind to us and we stayed with them for four very happy years. While we were there we attended the local Dolliur Mixed School.

I kept in touch with Auntie Vi and Uncle John after we returned home to Gillingham. In fact I kept in contact with them until they both died within months of each other.

Colin Manley *was another evacuee who was sent to the village of Llanharan in South Wales:*

In 1941, my brothers, Alan and Ivor, and I were evacuated to Wales, to a small mining village named Llanharan. Alan was taken just up the road from us and Ivor and I were taken in by Mrs Reid.

Mr Reid was a miner and they had two children, Alan, the son who was about a year older than me, and a daughter Betty, who had just got married to Hector, another miner. We went to school in the village, but I am told by my elder brothers that nobody seemed concerned if we went or not! I can only say I have almost no memories of the school.

We spent a lot of time helping a farmer with his livestock or in the fields haymaking and generally enjoying ourselves. We were in Wales approximately nine months. My mother became so depressed at not having her children with her that Dad decided that we were to return home.

I visited Llanharan a few years ago and met Betty the daughter, who had married again. Her first husband Hector had died. Betty is now in her late seventies with a poor heart, but still gets around; they took me back to Llanharan and I was able to take some photographs of the place. I saw the school, so very small, and the cinema, now a baker's shop! There were no coal mines. The three that were there have all gone along with the slag heaps.

Freddie Rickard *recalls his evacuation with his school, Glencoe Road School, Chatham, to Pontardawe, South Wales:*

I was at the tender age of eight and three quarters when, in the company of many children from my school, Glencoe Road, Chatham, the government of the day decided that we would be safer from German bombing if we were sent to Wales. Even looking at the school atlas we could not imagine how far away Wales was let alone know that this country existed. So with my name tag on my jacket, my gas mask and sandwiches, not forgetting my suitcase, we boarded the train at Chatham Station for the journey to Neath, South Wales. Apart from going hop-picking with my family every September I had never left the Medway Towns before!

I honestly do not remember much of the journey except that we were to go through a long tunnel under water (River Severn Rail Tunnel). It was dark when we arrived at Neath and from there we were taken by bus to Pontardawe, a very small town about five miles away. After I arrived in Pontardawe it was discovered that I had left my suitcase on one of the buses, so all the clothes I had with me were those I stood in! It took my teacher, Mr Semple, a week to track down my suitcase of clothes.

I was taken to stay with a Mr and Mrs Hamer who had a son Dennis, who was six years old and even though they wanted a boy his age, they took me in and did their best to look after me. My first Welsh cup of tea had cream floating on the top of it, and since that day I have always made sure that the milk is shaken up before putting it in my tea! In the kitchen of my billet, hanging from the ceiling were huge gammons of bacon. Being a townie boy I had only seen bacon in the local Co-op shop. Later I found out that Mr Hamer's brother had a farm, hence the bacon. Extra rows of potatoes and vegetables were also grown for the family.

Going to Pontardawe Junior School was no ordeal as quite a few of my classmates from Glencoe Road School were also there. One lesson I remember was the weekly letter we all wrote home. On the blackboard was a 'dictated' letter which we had to copy and it was then sent to our parents. The journey to school each day took me alongside a wide river – or so I thought! On revisiting Pontardawe in 1997 I discovered that the wide river was in fact a narrow canal. Such was the imagination of an eight year old boy.

On reflection it seems ironic that I was sent away from the dockyard town of Chatham to live at 16 Ynisderw Road, Pontardawe, a road several hundred yards long with a huge steel works at one end, and at the other a huge tin plate works – prime targets for the German bombers, and the port of Swansea about eight miles away.

My evacuation to South Wales was cut short when my mother died quite suddenly. My father came to Pontardawe to take me back to Chatham to be reunited with my younger and older brothers. I think a lot of evacuees from all over the country returned to their home towns early, not realising that the worst of the war was yet to come. Before returning to Chatham, my father offered to take Mr Hamer to the local pub for a drink and was horrified to find out that the pubs did not open on a Sunday in Wales. All was not lost though, because Mr Hamer knew the publican and was able to give the 'secret' knock at the back door!

The thing I didn't miss when I got back to Chatham was having to go to church twice and occasionally three times on a Sunday.

My story turned full circle one day in August 1997 while on holiday in Neath. I had the opportunity to visit Pontardawe to show my wife where I had been evacuated to all those years ago. On visiting the Pontardawe Library a very kind lady librarian made a telephone call and, to my surprise, she told me that the lady I had stayed with as an evacuee was still living in Pontardawe, in warden controlled accommodation at the end of the road where she had lived for over 50 years.

In September 1997 I finally met Mrs Hamer again. We spent a lovely day chatting about the time she gave a home to her little evacuee, way back in 1940.

Fred Silver *had first been evacuated to Sittingbourne with his brother and two sisters, and now in May 1940 he was on his way to Wales with Rochester Technical School:*

We duly arrived at a place called Rhiwbina, near Whitchurch, Cardiff. Once we were taken to our individual lodgings. My sisters were again kept together, as were my brother and myself. My sisters were on one side of Rubbella Road and we were on the other. What a difference it was for us all. This was a high class area. We had really good accommodation and the families were so friendly. David and I were taken out most days in one of the family cars and given treats. Again no school could be found in this area and our happiness was to be dashed after only one week with these lovely people.

*Rochester Technical School
taken outside the main entrance of the Grammar School in St Martin's Road,
Caerphilly, 8th April 1942*

We were on the move again, this time to Caerphilly. We were taken to the grammar school in St Martin's Road and from here we were taken to our respective billets. My sisters Olive and Peggy went to live with a young couple in St Martin's Road, and David and I went to an elderly couple in Bryn Gwyn Road. I think we both had a cry; this was so different from Rhiwbina.

My sisters had a nice home and were really spoilt. My older sister Olive was very happy there and even learnt a bit of Welsh. My other sister Peggy was not quite so happy and could not accept being away from home.

As for my young brother and myself, we were not so lucky. The people we were

A group of pupils from 'Holcombe' (now Chatham Grammar School for Boys) at the top of Pen-y-Fan in the Brecon Beacons in the glorious summer of 1940, including, (rear): Len Griffiths, 'Dickie' Bird, Bill Churchman, Denis Gady, Alan Pearson, 'Podgy' Rogers, Ron Noot, Bob Chambers, Gus Gardiner, Fillingham, (unknown), Ken Kidney, Ginger Lawson; (front): Jamie James (chemistry) and 'Happy Harry' Thurston (woodwork) – both teachers from Holcombe, Mrs Thurston and another unknown

A reunion of Chatham Grammar School for Boys on 20th March 1998 to celebrate the 90th birthday of Bill Killen, for many years a teacher at the school. In the picture are some 1940 evacuees: Bill Churchman, Denis Cady, 'Dickie' Bird and Alf Lawson

with had a poor life, living in a small terraced house. The gentleman was a caretaker of the local grammar school and the elderly lady was his housekeeper. She also had her grandson, 19 years of age, living with them. The man used to come home much the worse for drink every Saturday night, so David and I had to be in bed before he came home. Apart from this they were never unkind to us in any way, but life was certainly different from what we were used to.

My sisters and brother were found places in three different schools in Caerphilly. I cannot remember why they went to different schools; it was probably due to the difference in their ages. My younger sister Peggy went to Twyn Junior Mixed School and my elder sister Olive attended Pontygwindy Girls' Secondary School.

Rochester Technical School boys were at last able to have full use of a technical school which consisted of annexe buildings to the main grammar school in St Martin's Road. We also used some of the classrooms and the gymnasium in the main building. On occasions we had the use of the local swimming pool and the playing fields.

Everywhere we went we were under strict orders to wear our school uniform and to carry our gas masks and identity cards. We did make friends with some of the local lads, but mainly we kept with our own mates from our own technical school.

In October 1941 my sister Olive was called home to assist my mother who was expecting an addition to the family. Olive was not very happy about this, as she had settled in and was content with her new life in Wales. However, Olive continued to keep in touch with her foster parents over the following years and, when she got married, she and her husband spent several holidays with them in Caerphilly.

In July 1942, having sat and passed the Civil Service examination for entry as an apprentice in Chatham dockyard, my technical education was now complete. So I came home ready to start work in August of that year. My other sister Peggy and brother David also returned with me.

After his stay in Faversham, **Bill Churchman** *now relates the arrival of his school, Holcombe (Chatham County School for Boys), in Pontypridd, South Wales, in May 1940:*

We arrived by train at Pontypridd and the process of billeting began again. A coach took a group of us Holcombeians to the mining community of Cilfynydd, close to Pontypridd where two of us were welcomed by Mr and Mrs Seymour and their daughter Brenda, who was about our age. The Seymours had been expecting small children and could have been forgiven if they were surprised by two large teenagers, and privately wondering how to feed them on reducing rations. However, I do not recall being hungry at any time throughout the war.

Wales was a new experience to us, with its hills, its mining, its language – its music! Mr Seymour was a lay reader. Both he and Mrs Seymour were Welsh speakers, but it was not the language of the house. However, in the same street lived a diminutive old lady whose only language was Welsh.

As at Faversham, schooling under our own teachers was carried out wherever a suitably equipped room could be found. This was sometimes at Porth, a town in the Rhondda Valley. Mr James, our energetic chemistry teacher, lead us on some quite strenuous rambles on nearby hills, presumably when classroom accommodation was not available. On one memorable occasion we were taken by coach to the Brecon Beacons – what magnificent scenery! – returning to Pontypridd via the length of the Rhondda Valley.

The Seymours operated a small shop, but food supplies were becoming tight and I believe this affected their business. I became friendly with the Carini family who ran a confectionery business and a small cafe a couple of doors away. They were of Italian origin, indeed the senior members of the family still had Italian nationality which made them enemy aliens when Italy entered the war. Frank Carini, who had served in the Italian army and had been wounded in World War I, was taken into custody. His wife and daughter were made to move to a less sensitive area. Frank Carini perished when the SS *Andorra Star*, on which he was being transported to Canada for internment, was torpedoed and sunk in the Atlantic.

The large local workmen's hall was the venue for prayer meetings on Sunday evenings. Servicemen on home leave were made welcome and, in particular, Dunkirk survivors were honoured, but the lovely singing made those Sunday evenings for me.

A practice which I have not seen elsewhere was the baking of home prepared bread at the local bakery. The charge was a half-penny per loaf. The open-air swimming pool in Pontypridd was well used in temperatures which makes me shudder to recall!

At the time of evacuation, my age group, 13-14 years old, puberty probably welcomed comparative freedom from parental control, in fact it was all rather an adventure. I do not recall that we gave our teachers too much anxiety, but perhaps their recollections were different. And what of the feelings of parents? I am ashamed to admit I gave little thought to the feelings of my parents.

My sister missed home more than I, especially when we were in Wales and quite cut off. My sister was so miserable in Pontypridd, especially after my departure to take up an apprenticeship, that our father decided that, war or no war, she was to return home.

I returned to Chatham to take up apprenticeship in the naval dockyard, from which dangerous vicinity we were initially sent away!

David Murray *writes from Australia about the time he and his brother were evacuated to Wales in 1940:*

First I should explain something about my own upbringing prior to evacuation. My father had died of tuberculosis in 1935, when I was eight years old. My mother was profoundly deaf, and we, the children, conversed with her by sign and lip reading. There was little love and caring in our family, especially during the war when food was scarce and necessities like boots and shoes and clothing were not only too expensive for us, but which also had to be bought with special clothing coupons which Mum had had to sell in order to survive.

I had two brothers, Lionel, four years my senior, who was called up in 1939 and served in both the Army and the Royal Air Force. He came home after the war unscathed. Then there was Leslie. He is two years younger than I, and he was evacuated to South Wales with me.

Having given some background information about myself, it is not surprising when I say that I had a very hard time relating to grown ups as a child. I was therefore very apprehensive about going to live with a strange family in a strange place. And, because

I had been ordered to go, like it or not, I already had my 'shackles' up! Anyway, off we went in 1940 to some unknown destination. There were about twenty children in our bunch, both boys and girls. We were taken by train, and then by bus to the small village of Ynysmeardy in mid-Glamorganshire, in the Rhondda Valley. It was late afternoon when we arrived.

A recent photo of the village school in Ynysmeardy which David Murray attended in 1940

We were then lined up in a single file in the main village street. Residents of the village, mostly miners and their families, lined the footpath. They were asked by the person in charge of us to please select a child and take the child home for now, and then next day report with the child to the postmaster.

Many of the miners' wives walked up and took a female child by the hand and went off home. Twenty minutes or so later there were only two children left, both boys – Leslie and I! The local residents looked on, but no one came to offer us a home because we did not want to be parted. Eventually, Mrs Newton arrived. She walked up and put her arms around Leslie's and my shoulders and said, 'Come on boys, let's go home.'

Home was Mr and Mrs Newton's small house which they shared with Raymond, their eldest son, Mealgwyn their second son, and there was also a very young baby daughter. There were only two bedrooms in the house; Mr and Mrs Newton and the baby used one, and we four boys all slept in the other.

For the first few days I hardly spoke a word to anyone. I ate very little, the chip on my shoulder getting larger by the day, then Mrs Newton took charge of me and showed me a love I had never known before. She showed me that she truly cared about me, showed me understanding, and almost immediately had me in the palm of her hand. By the end of the first week I was calling her Mum, just like Raymond and Mealgwyn were. Mr Newton, a tall and very muscular miner, turned out to be the kind of man I wished that I could have had for my Dad. He was so understanding, so easy to talk to, so warm and welcoming. We were treated no differently than their own children.

Soon Mrs Newton took Leslie and me to the little school and introduced us as her 'visitors from England', and we were accepted both by the teachers and the children as though we were just other village kids. Even the teachers made allowances for the obvious trauma each of us was suffering and unsuccessfully hiding.

It may seem strange to some that I did not know what love and caring for others really meant until I met the Newton family, but they brought it into my life, to keep for myself for ever, and it has been with me ever since. In the eight or nine months that we were with the Newton family, Les and I became equal family members. Yes, we were chastised when we did wrong, but that was very well and evenly balanced with plenty of praise when we did the right thing.

Our real Mum came one day to take us back home to Kent. She had been living alone and, on the meagre rations that one person was entitled to at that time, it showed markedly in her face; she looked quite ill! Mother had pawned something or other to pay for the train journey, so it was obvious that she was not about to go home without us. She explained to Mr and Mrs Newton that the main danger at home had passed, and that she needed me especially, because I was old enough to find a job and bring in a little money. Reluctantly and tearfully we returned to England and our home.

I have never forgotten the Newtons. On my 21st birthday I drove from Hempstead where we lived, to South Wales, and found Ynysmeardy again. I also found the house and knocked on the door. A beautiful young lady answered the door (she had been the baby of the family during our evacuation). I told her who I was and what I wanted and she gave me the address of the house where 'Mum and Dad' were now living in retirement.

I drove to that address some twenty miles away and tapped on the door. Mrs Newton answered the door and I told her who I was and that I had come to say hello again. I put my arms around her and thanked her for all she had done for me and Leslie all those years ago. Mr Newton was there too, and I shook his hand warmly and thanked him for the untold attributes I had learned from him over that all too short a time.

They have both passed away now, but today I have the friendship of their youngest son, Mealgwyn Newton. I can only say that the terrible start that I had in my life was somehow short-circuited and changed for ever by the experience of meeting and living with my Welsh Mum and Dad, their family, and the Welsh people as a whole.

*Ironically, **Sheila Rusted** was another young evacuee who had lost her father at such a tender age. Sheila was evacuated with her school, the National C of E School from Sheerness, on the Isle of Sheppey:*

In late May 1940, at the time of Dunkirk, my friends and I were told that we were being sent to a safer place. The Isle of Sheppey had then, as it still has today, only one bridge with road and rail access to the mainland. It was also a military area with an aerodrome at Eastchurch, various army camps, and naval units in the dockyard. We knew nothing of the letters and meetings which led up to the arrangements made by our parents and school until the very last evening.

My mother had thought deeply about what she should do. I was her only child and she had been widowed since just before my second birthday. In the end her fears for my safety outnumbered her wishes to have me with her, so with much reluctance she signed the necessary forms for my evacuation.

At first she, like many other parents, was expected to pay a small sum for my upkeep. This was soon rescinded when her circumstances were known. I was still only eight years old. It was explained to me that I was being sent away for safety reasons, and I don't recall at that stage being particularly nervous at the idea. As all the other children seemed to be going, it was like some great big adventure.

The following morning, with a bag which I carried over my shoulder holding only the bare necessities, we set off for school. I wore my best red blazer, and I had a luggage label attached to it with my name and school written on it. It was at school that we said our goodbyes, so that the parting would not be too protracted. Then it was off to the railway station.

We waited in the station yard for ages while soldiers rescued from Dunkirk were dealt with. We eventually boarded a train and set off on our journey. It was exciting, and we chatted as we ate our sandwiches. Our teachers came along and checked up on us from time to time. Every so often the train would halt and we would see troop trains passing by.

At last, late in the afternoon, we arrived at Mountain Ash in South Wales. Here in a large hall we were fed and medically examined before being sent on to Abercynon, our final destination. By this time we were exhausted. We were assembled in a large school and Welsh officials came and took us to our billets. Their voices were strange, but they tried their best to cheer us up. Hilary and I were delivered to a temporary overnight billet on the other side of the River Taff.

I don't recall getting any supper. There was no bathroom and the toilet was outside. This was strange to both of us. We didn't really have much of a conversation with the people of the house and, because we were so tired, we were put to bed. We shared a double bed and chatted between ourselves for some time before crying ourselves to sleep in

'The gardener's pride and joy.'
Sheila Rusted with her foster father at Abercynon, 1941

the early hours. The next morning, to our horror, we were sent to wash under a cold tap in the yard! We weren't offered breakfast, but Hilary had some stale lemon marmalade sandwiches left from the day before. Later we were escorted by someone back to the school where we were to be reallocated.

Gradually as time went on, all the other children left until only Hilary and I remained. We were becoming more and more anxious as time went by. Several adults, including our teachers, were standing in the doorway talking, and we felt they were discussing us. Finally, we were told we were being parted, but would be living near to each other. Hilary was taken away by a lady to a house in Woodlands Crescent where a number of prominent town's people lived. Her foster parents, the Gabriels, owned the seed merchants on the same side of town as the colliery, railway station and the senior school.

At the same time, I was taken by another lady to the same area as Hilary, just round the corner from her to another large house. It was quite a long walk and the lady tried to put me at my ease. On arrival I was taken into a large sitting room and introduced to

Mrs Smith. She was a small thin lady about 60 years of age. She had quite bad eyesight and wore strong glasses.

She had not been on the original list of foster parents because of her health reasons – and probably because of her age as well. Her husband, I was told much later, felt sorry for the little girl in the red blazer and decided that I should be sent to his home anyway. While we waited for Mr Smith to arrive home, I was shown my bedroom and the layout of the house. Then when Mr Smith arrived we had lunch.

Mr and Mrs Smith soon became Aunty and Uncle and I was encouraged to write home to say where and how I was. Over the next few months more of my belongings arrived from Sheerness. I also accumulated presents from birthdays and Christmas as friends and relatives of Aunty and Uncle got to know me.

I sent and received weekly letters from home, and as time went on, I got to know the local children – and the special group of children who lived in the area. We attended the same school and played together in each other's gardens or spent time exploring the locality and wandering over the mountainside. We knew little of the war.

The Smiths had a dog called Mij, of whom I was very fond. I'd always had a dog, so that too made me feel more at home. Uncle had built the garden himself out of the mountainside, and he grew his own fruit and vegetables. I spent many hours with him in the garden and I have enjoyed gardening ever since.

Sheila Rusted, aged nine, in her siren suit at Abercynon

Almost immediately we were settled in our billets, we were sent to school, to Abertaff, Uncle's own school. I had to call him 'Sir' when we were in school. At last the English children were in one room, also used as Uncle's office. Occasionally he would watch us over the top of his glasses, but as soon as he was able he gave us our own classroom.

I was always very nervous of one of our teachers, Miss Lawrence, but as soon as she had left (Christmas 1940) I was happier and thrived no doubt in the most part due to the environment in which I lived.

In school we had most lessons from Miss Perkins and Miss Skinner, but for special occasions like St David's Day, we mixed in with the Welsh children. I knew the Welsh National Anthem long before I knew our own!

I soon became used to my surroundings. Life went on much as it had back in Sheerness, but I had the advantage of a father figure to look up to and admire. Aunty hadn't been able to have children so she and her husband had adopted their nephew Mervyn when, at the age of twelve, his parents had been killed in an accident. I too was accepted as a member of the family, although I was frequently introduced as their 'little evacuee', a practice common even when I grew up. My mother also agreed that if

Local residents and evacuees at Abercynon, summer 1940

anything were to happen to her, they would accept guardianship of me. At the time I was unaware of this.

The highlight of the week was Friday evening when I was taken to the cinema on the far side of town. Uncle would collect tobacco for his pipe and get our sweet ration, some of which I was allowed to eat during the picture.

On Sundays, we children attended the local Church of England Sunday School. In the evening Aunty and I attended the same church while Uncle went to his chapel on the other side of the river. Life in these first few months seemed quite peaceful. Each Saturday we went off to Cardiff. Aunty had appointments for her eyes. While she was busy, Uncle and I frequently visited the museums, especially the Welsh Folk Museum. If the air-raid siren sounded we would shelter at the castle. After meeting up with Aunty, we would all have a meal before returning by train to Abercynon.

Sometimes we visited relations in Ynysybwl. There were also visits to the seaside at Barry and Porthcawl, and shopping trips to Pontypridd.

Aunty was a local councillor and was also a governor at Mountain Ash Girls' Grammar School and the Boys' Reform School at Quaker's Yard. When she attended meetings at the latter, Uncle and I would explore the district around the school. It was also explained to me that many of the boys, some not much older than myself, were there because of their family backgrounds rather than that they were criminals. I always enjoyed those visits especially when we had tea afterwards – where I was always fussed over!

As time went on, my life in Wales became my whole world and I thought little of life back in Sheerness. Once my Uncle Jim and Aunty Edie came to Llandaff to see his sister and brother-in-law who worked for the Admiralty. I was taken to see them and spent the weekend there. In the summer of 1941 Mother came to Abercynon. She stayed in lodgings, but had some of her meals with us. I enjoyed her visit but she seemed almost a stranger.

We did not have any enemy raids on Abercynon itself, but we were not many miles from Cardiff or Bridgend where the munitions factories were. When the night raids first started, we walked down to the communal shelter built into the mountainside. We children slept in bunks, but most of the adults chatted, smoked or drank tea at the other end of the shelter. When morning came we went about our normal affairs and no-one stayed at home because they had had a disturbed night.

If the sirens went while we were at school, we were initially sent home. There were no shelters at the school itself, nor had many of the private houses. Soon the teachers realised that although the children hurried home when the siren sounded, it was not the same story with the 'all clear', for then we dawdled back to school. Another problem was that many of the children lived too far from the school if there was more than one warning during the day. It was soon decided to send us to houses near school so that less time was wasted during air-raid alerts.

At the end of 1941 the children in my age group sat their preliminary examination for the grammar school. If we did well enough, we sat another examination in the spring – on St David's Day, which was also my mother's birthday. Hilary, Pauline and I were considered suitable for grammar education and were visited by Miss Capone from the Sittingbourne Grammar School. Because of my results, I received a scholarship which meant my mother would have no fees to pay for meals or travelling expenses. That year Uncle's school had the highest number of boys and girls going on to grammar school education. I now had a choice; I could continue my education in Wales and attend the school at Mountain Ash or, as there seemed less danger at home, I could return to live at Sheerness.

Sheila Rusted with her foster father, Mr Smith, summer 1941

There was much correspondence between Uncle and my mother as to what was best for me. Uncle felt that it was not a good idea to start at one school and then return to another, so he suggested that I stay with him and Aunty for the seven years of secondary education. Mother decided she would have me back, because she felt she was already losing me. I returned to Sheerness! I did not want to return and for the first year I found it very difficult to settle, both at home and at school.

I kept in contact with Aunty and Uncle, and they came to visit us in Sheermess. I also spent time with them in the summer holidays. In 1949, the year I started teacher training college, Aunty and Uncle retired to Caswell Bay, on the Gower Peninsula near Swansea. My visits to them continued. Aunty was in her eighties when she died, but Uncle lived on alone for a number of years. After my own mother died in 1977 my visits to Uncle became even more regular. We would work together on his garden and make visits to Abercynon and other old haunts. At the age of 92, he paid his last visit to Kent, and I took him to London, Canterbury, Sheerness and Tunbridge Wells, all in the space of one week.

Just after his 98th birthday on 19th October, 1986, Uncle planned a big family party for relatives and close friends. We had a wonderful time! Did he have a premonition that this was to be the last gathering? I don't know, but when I telephoned him on 1st January, 1987, he was starting a heart attack. He died the same day. I attended Uncle's funeral and stayed with friends for a few days.

I miss Wales and still think of it as my home. I find it difficult to think of myself as entirely English, regarding myself as Welsh by adoption. My time in Wales has had a great effect on my life. My time spent there is more important than the rest of my childhood. It moulded my character. I was so lucky that I had such wonderful foster parents.

After spending her first evacuation experience in Canterbury, **Dorothy Shilling** *(now Mrs Dorothy Lower) and her sister Beryl were now on the move again:*

I was about to embark on my second evacuation in less than a year. This time my younger sister Beryl came too. On a sunny Sunday in May 1940 we departed from Rochester by train and eventually arrived in Pontypridd, Glamorgan, in South Wales. Shortly after our arrival we found ourselves billeted in the vicarage of St Catherine's Church. Again we were very fortunate and had a wonderful time there. However, there was a further evacuation from Medway, this time to Porthcawl on the coast. That meant there were girls from Rochester Grammar School in two places and also boys from the Sir Joseph Williamson's Mathematical School in both places. Ultimately there was an exchange and on a Sunday in July, very sadly, we were taken by coach to the seaside and the boys were moved to Pontypridd.

My sister and I were again very well looked after. 'Uncle' was a master painter and decorator, 'Auntie' was a real mother figure and a great housekeeper. Maurice, their son, worked with his father, and Mary, their daughter, who was about two years my senior, worked in a nursery and was a good pianist.

My sister Beryl went to the local school (and even did well at learning Welsh!). I continued to be taught by my regular teachers in a variety of places, but eventually moved into the local school buildings at rather unusual times on a shared basis. We had a school Guide company run by a local Guider. We met on Saturdays and did all the usual things, including joining the Red Cross depot to roll up bandages.

Sybil Thorndike was an old girl of our school so we were very excited when she came with a theatre company and performed *Candida* at the Pavilion. I also attended my first symphony concert in Wales. The BBC Symphony Orchestra gave a performance at the Brangwyn Hall, Swansea, and Mary, the daughter of my hosts, took me along. This was just after Swansea had been bombed so I got my first sight of that sort of devastation. We had seen the glow of the fires across the bay, as we had also

COUNTY OF KENT.

GOVERNMENT EVACUATION SCHEME.

Please Quote Reference No.

2A/I 11026

347/33

Room 311,
County Hall,
Maidstone.

6.7.40.

Dear Sir or Madam,

    I have to acknowledge with thanks the receipt of the form forwarded by you, stating that you are prepared to pay at the rate of ....12/-........ a week in respect of the maintenance of your child(ren) billeted under the Government Scheme. (The total amount due from you up to the ....5.7.40........ is therefore ....£2-8-0........).

    An envelope, a remittance slip and a contribution card are enclosed. The remittance slip and contribution card should accompany any payment you make. If a cheque is sent it should be made payable to the Kent County Council and crossed.

    The card will be returned to you after your payment has been recorded and will act as a record of your payments.

    If you prefer to pay in cash, payment may be made at ....The City Treasurer, 40, St. Margaret's St, Rochester,........ ~~between the hours of~~ ....and......... at the usual office hours.

    I have to remind you that you should inform me immediately of any change of address.

Yours faithfully,

John Lord

Assessment Officer.

Mr. T. W. Shilling.

Initially parents had to pay something towards the maintenance of their evacuated children. This letter is an example of how Kent County Council assessed and collected contributions seen the glow when Cardiff was burning – yet we always felt safe in Porthcawl.

Our foster family, apart from Uncle, attended the local Gospel Hall. We went along to the Sunday School there, and I still have the book presented to me 'for regular attendance'.

We only saw our parents twice in two years, but our pocket money and letters came regularly. My postal order was for 2/6d, but I had to pay for my piano lesson out of that; my sister had 1/6d. Our relations kept us in stamps to write home.

We came back home in July 1942 when the numbers had reduced greatly and we were going to be grouped with other dwindling groups at Merthyr Tydfil. Our parents felt it was just not on for us to be re-located at that stage.

We were very well cared for and treated as part of the family by our foster parents. After the war I went back regularly on visits for quite a few years, but unfortunately they are all gone now. I know we were some of the lucky ones, but I also pay tribute to the school staff who accompanied us. They not only provided our education, but looked to our welfare very thoroughly and kindly. Our headteacher, Miss Butterfield, commuted regularly between Rochester and Porthcawl – no mean feat in wartime conditions, maintaining the school in both places.

Rosemary Macey *(now Mrs Rosemary Hill) relates her memories of the time she and her brother were evacuated – a time when her family had already experienced a great tragedy:*

My brother Brian aged 11 years and myself aged 9 years were living with our grandparents in Strood as our mother had just passed away. She was only 36 years old. It was a very tragic time for us. Dad was on war work, so I guess he didn't really know what to do with us at the time. It was November 1940, and we were experiencing very heavy raids every night.

Our first experience of evacuation was to a camp school in the East Grinstead / Forest Row area, but unfortunately my brother was found to have a chest complaint, so after three weeks we returned to our grandparents. The next thing we knew was that we were told we were going to Wales; so in January 1941 we found ourselves in a hostel just outside Newport in Monmouthshire. I think we were there for about a

Rosemary Macey, bottom left, and her brother, Brian, centre top, with a group of their evacuee friends, taken at the school in Wattsville in 1943

147

month because nobody wanted a boy and a girl – everyone wanted two of the same sex (so we were told!).

Eventually, they found a couple in Wattsville, a small mining village, who were willing to take us both. Mr and Mrs Hoskins, whom we called Auntie Rhoda and Uncle Ray, were a middle aged, kindly couple, and we stayed with them for three and a half years. Unfortunately, brother Brian was so unhappy, probably due to the death of our mother, that he ran away several times, but Auntie and Uncle always took him back, and slowly he did settle down. He even went on to pass his eleven-plus examination.

We lived a very care-free life in Wales. No-one seemed to worry if we went to school or not, and I must admit I often played truant and went up the mountains picking whinberries instead! Sundays however, were very strict indeed. In the mornings it was Sunday School followed by a service in the Baptist Chapel; in the afternoon it was Sunday School again in the Methodist Chapel – with a service in the evening! Going to two churches meant we always went to two parties and two outings, which was great.

Brian and Rosemary Macey with foster parents, Rhoda and Ray Hoskins, outside their billet in 1944

I remember my dad coming to visit us about once a year, but I don't remember ever being upset when he left, so I guess I must have been very happy. In fact, when it was time for us to return home, I didn't want to go, as by then Dad had remarried, and we were coming home to a different house as well.

On our return my brother had to go to Welwyn Garden City, where his school was at that time. He was now 15 years old and I was 13. It was the first time ever that we had been separated and I was very unhappy about it, so when the doodlebugs started coming over I put my name down at school to return to Wales, hoping it would be to the same place. But this time I went to a place just outside Merthyr Tydfil. I was only there for six months but, once again, I had a very nice billet with Mr and Mrs Appleby in the village of Pennidarren.

Years later I took my daughter on a trip down memory lane to Wattsville. I found my foster mother, Mrs Hoskins, by writing to the local paper. By then she was well into her nineties and living in a warden assisted flat, but she remembered us so well. Sadly she died just three months after our visit. My brother has also gone, having died at the age of 59. My father lived with Mum No.2 for 51 years and finally passed on at the age of 91. I shall always look back on my time in Wales with affection.

Jean Lyons *(now Mrs Jean Spashett), having experienced evacuation to the Canterbury area with her mother, was now to experience evacuation for a second time – this time without her mother:*

On 2nd June 1940 all the girls met at Napier Road School, Gillingham, and were shepherded on to the roof, a hitherto forbidden area. There we awaited the signal to start out for Gillingham railway station. It was a very hot day and the route of the train was planned to avoid any changes, so we travelled directly to Wales. One girl was taken ill with a mastoid infection and was taken off the train en route. The rest of us grew hourly more desperate for water, but it appeared that there was none on board. By the time we drew into Bristol Station we were hanging out of the windows crying out for water! Fortunately they were prepared for us and I shall always recall the trolleys coming towards us with water and cups at the ready.

By the time we had pulled out of Bristol, we had already been told of the village in Wales that was to be our home. It was the village of Resolven in Glamorganshire, and when we arrived, we were very tired and ready for something to eat and drink. We were taken to the local village school where we were given refreshments, then we awaited the people who were to foster us. People came and went, but it seemed that my cousin and I were the last to leave. I was by then a gawky 13-year old, and my cousin Barbara was just seven.

In the end we were taken to the home of an elderly couple, who had not long married. Resolven was a mining village and most of the billets were in miners' cottages. The elderly couple Barbara and I were billeted with were quite unused to children and I asked to be given a change of billet. The result was the elderly couple accused me of ill-treating my cousin! Sadly, my teacher appeared to believe this because Barbara and I were separated and we were moved to miners' cottages a few doors from each other.

I had gone from the 'frying pan into the fire', as my new foster mother was epileptic and had frequent attacks. She had quarrelled with Barbara's foster parent and was furious that I'd asked for help when one of her attacks had caused her to fall and cut her head badly. I became more and more unhappy, being used to an entirely different background with a more relaxed and happy atmosphere.

However, the mountains were a delight and I would go with friends as often as possible for walks, and we would dabble our feet in the freezing mountain streams. Sadly, this was soon forbidden as someone claimed that a 'nasty man' had followed them during one of these outings!

Not long after arriving, the school nurse visited to examine our hair and shortly afterwards we were summoned into the classroom for a telling-off by our teachers. Only one girl had clean hair among us – we were a disgrace to the old school! The one girl who had clean hair was the one who had been taken into the home of the Welsh headmistress! The rest of us were surrounded by coal dust which seemed to get in everywhere. No wonder we had nits!

The miners would arrive home black with coal dust, and a small bath would be placed in front of the fire and filled with hot water from buckets heated on the stove. We would have to go outside or upstairs while the master of the house cleaned up. Later we would sit round the table for tea. The men of the house were given the choice of everything on the table. I was limited to just a few items. For dinner mid-day, I was given a penny to buy a penn'orth of chips. I had a cooked dinner once a week.

I went home for Christmas, a blessed release from what I had come to hate – life among the Welsh! I returned, crying, but at least a chance of a permanent release was given to me. I had not been allowed to enter the exams earlier at home for the grammar school as my maths were not up to standard. Now there was to be a new exam for entrance to Fort Pitt School, a technical school in Chatham. I was determined to escape a life I hated. We were given three courses to choose – Domestic Science, Business Studies and Art-Needlework. Upon asking what the last consisted of I was told it probably meant making embroidered cushion cases. That sounded alright to me so that's the course I chose.

I worked hard during that winter. The snow looked so beautiful up on the mountains, but I still hoped it would be my last winter in Resolven. Meanwhile, Sybil Thorndike and her husband Russell had arrived in Resolven and were to give a performance of *Macbeth* in the Welfare Hall. We were all given a chance of getting autographs from Sybil and Russell. Everyone at the play that night could hardly fail to be enthralled at the performance we were treated to – an unforgettable night. I believe the company must have traversed the whole country during the war, giving so much pleasure at a time when so many people needed something to take their minds off the war.

Having taken my exam, I waited impatiently for the results to come through. Eventually they did and there, on the blackboard, was my name, I had passed! The Art-Needlework course was a very different thing from my teacher's description of making cushion covers. I spent half my week at Fort Pitt Technical School and the other half at the Art School in Rochester – I could hardly have been happier.

It was a long time before I was able to admit that not all Welsh people were narrow minded and unkind, but it did take time! In actual fact, it was what is nowadays called 'a learning experience'! I wouldn't have missed being evacuated for anything, but it was tough at times!

Audrey Jean Brown (now Mrs Audrey Markwell) was one of twelve children, and before the war she lived in Westcourt Street, Old Brompton, Chatham, and attended Holy Trinity School. Her first evacuation in September 1939 to Herne Bay was not a success and she returned home after only a month. Later that year five children from her family, including herself, were evacuated to South Wales:

I was billeted in Llanharan and my brother ended up on a farm where he was treated badly. We didn't see him for the whole of the time we were in Wales. One of our sisters lived just down the road from us and was treated like a lady. My other two sisters and I lived together in the same billet. We didn't have a very nice time. Our foster parent used to sell everything. When our mother used to send us parcels, we never got to know what was in them because they were sold.

I remember one Christmas the parcel post came with three large parcels wrapped in brown paper and our foster mother put them upstairs behind the wardrobe, and every night when we went to bed we would tear a piece of the paper until a face appeared. They were three big Sally Ann dolls for us for Christmas – but we never got them!

Our older sisters back home knitted us some little suits and we only wore them once

– we didn't see them again! We never had any decent shoes or socks, everything was sold, but for all that we were happy; she was not a cruel lady.

School was a traumatic experience. They didn't like us evacuees and they used to call us 'bloody London kids'! One teacher was really nasty to me. I am naturally left-handed and she used to push my arm behind me and kept hitting me in the back, telling me to use my right hand. One of my older sisters came down for a holiday and saw the bruises on my back and demanded that the teacher stop hitting me. The beatings continued so my sister hit the teacher – I didn't get hit in the back again! – and I'm still left-handed.

My poor brother who was billeted on a farm was treated so badly that he ran away several times. In the end our mum came to Wales and took him back home. He didn't have any boys' clothes to travel in. Mum had to take him home in a pair of baggy trousers that were miles too big for him, and a pair of women's high heel shoes. He also had hair down to his shoulders and it broke Mum's heart to see him like that.

My sister who lived close by was always beautifully dressed and didn't want to know us little scruffs, so we really didn't have a lot to do with her. She stayed in Wales after the war and married a Welshman.

They were poor times in South Wales and when I returned home in 1945, I was so glad to get back to Mum and Dad, my sisters and brothers and to be a family again. I have never been back to Wales!

George Prager, *having experienced life in Sandwich with his school, Gillingham County School for Boys, was now off to Wales:*

In May 1940, during the Dunkirk evacuation, about 40 boys including myself, with four masters left Sandwich en route to Cardiff in South Wales. This journey, which took the best part of the day, was by train again and we were routed along the south coast. We finally arrived at Cardiff, but our stay there was to be brief. Our main school at Gillingham was despatched to Rhymney in Monmouthshire on 2nd June and on the 8th June we forty-odd were uprooted and journeyed once again to join them. The only clear memory I have of our stay at Cardiff is a visit to Llandaff Cathedral and that we attended the Whitchurch School.

My new billet was at the extreme end of the town with the school being located almost at the other end. Again accommodation for two schools on the same premises was impossible so at first each school worked a half day shift in the Lawn School until extra premises were found. The Workmen's Institute, the Masonic Hall and the Social Centre were pressed into service. Until then we took part in games, mountain walks, table tennis, cricket, rugby (what else in Wales?) and trips to the next valley for swimming at Tredegar. We also found that the Workmen's Institute billiard hall was available to us at certain times. Here, soft drinks were a bonus if you had the necessary cash and most of the Gillingham boys learned to play both billiards and snooker.

In our early days in Rhymney, whenever we ventured to the Pontlottyn end of the town we had to run the gauntlet of the local boys throwing stones and or lumps of coal. It was resolved by the evacuees deciding to fight back with similar missiles. Since a few of us were reasonably good at cricket, our returns were quite accurate. The battles finally ended with both sides becoming reasonable friends. It was remarkable that none of us was permanently damaged.

I remember joining the Army Cadets and 'enjoying' a route march over the mountain into Tredegar and being bussed back. Once I became a messenger at the nearby ARP control centre, being allowed to do a full night duty – and afterwards falling asleep in the high backed Windsor armchair for about fourteen hours!

After the Battle of Britain, about the end of October 1940, there was a gradual drift back to Gillingham and since there appeared to be few serious bombing attacks on the Medway Towns, most of the evacuees returned to Gillingham at the end of the summer term of 1941. Farewell concerts were arranged and there were many tearful partings as many friendships had been forged that were to be long lasting.

However, about thirty boys, of which I was one, stayed on with one member of staff. Our expected stay was to be for one more year. We were absorbed into the Lawn School and joined in all the school's activities so completely that at least three Gillingham boys won first prize for singing in Welsh at the School Eistedfodd.

In September 1941 the County School for Boys reopened in its own premises in Gillingham and by the end of the summer term of 1942, all the remaining boys – except myself and two others in another form – returned to Gillingham. I stayed on in Wales and was integrated with the Welsh pupils of the fifth form which numbered just eleven and, during the summer term of 1943, I sat the exam for the Central Welsh Board Certificate of Education and the Civil Service Commissioners' Dockyard Apprentices Entrance Examination.

The school staff were convinced that I had no hope of passing the latter examination since the subjects I had been studying were biased towards art. However, since by this time my grandfather had reached normal retirement age it was foreseen that I would have to become the breadwinner. The end result was that I passed both exams well and after journeying to Newport for a medical at the direction of the Civil Service Commissioners, I returned to Gillingham at the end of the summer term of 1943. It was a sad occasion when I finally left Wales for home. The lady of the house, Jennie, had become a surrogate mother to me since from the day I entered her home I was treated as a son. Indeed her own son, a few years my junior received no treatment preferential to mine and we became firm friends. Contact was maintained over the years with visits to Rhymney on several occasions, one with my wife very soon after our marriage. Jennie also visited us in Gillingham and when sadly she died, some years ago now, we both had to say our farewell in Rhymney. Contact with Douglas, her son, continues to this day.

Albert John Smoker now recalls his second evacuation with Rochester Technical School in 1940:

We had a very long journey before ending up at Cardiff. We were again billeted out with local people and I went to stay with a very dear oldish lady in a very big house where she and her spaniel dog lived on their own. I liked it there very much, mainly I suppose because the lady of the house spoiled me. Unfortunately, after about six weeks, we were on the move again, this time to Caerphilly, some 12 miles away.

My first stay here was with a family of three, the Gays, who had one daughter who was away most of the time at boarding school in Pontypool. I stayed at this billet for well over a year and was very happy. The house was situated at the top of the town and

I was very fortunate that Mr Gay was the local water engineer with a car for his work.

We evacuees shared premises with the local technical and secondary schools but, because of numbers and lack of teachers, we alternated with the local school children. One week we would work mornings only and the following week, afternoons. I found this arrangement ideal because when not at school Mr Gay would take me out with him on his daily visits to pumping stations and reservoirs. In this way I was able to see much more of the area than many of my classmates.

We had some of our own teachers with us – those who had not been called up for military service and we struggled through the set curriculum, taking our exams each term. I don't think our education suffered unduly despite our overriding interest in being at war with Germany.

I well remember one Saturday when a few of us went by train to Cardiff for the day. We had a hectic time wandering all round the town but unfortunately we missed the last train back to Caerphilly. We started to walk the 12 miles back, hoping to hitch a lift, which didn't materialise! By the time we reached Caerphilly Mountain, just above the town, it was getting quite late. This was the night that the Germans chose to bomb Cardiff Docks, so we sat on top of the mountain watching the bombs exploding in the distance. We eventually arrived back in the early hours of the morning – to a good telling off by our foster parents!

Eventually, Mrs Gay, my foster mother, became ill and I was moved to another family at the other end of town. This time it was a Mr and Mrs Hughes and their son David. David was about two years older than me – and a right bully! Unfortunately, I had to share a room with him, but I steered clear of him as much as possible. That apart, I was reasonably happy there, but I missed my daily trips with Mr Gay, although I kept in touch.

The Hughes were Welsh Baptists and I was made to attend chapel on Sunday mornings, afternoons and evenings. I did not like this at first because most of the services were in Welsh but everybody was very kind and encouraged my participation in the services. In the end I enjoyed going to Chapel where I made quite a few friends, particularly among the girls.

The Hughes took a holiday to Llandudno one summer. David was not able to go with them but they kindly took me and I had a wonderful time during that week.

During all this time my brother had been evacuated to Pontypridd and I was able to visit him a couple of times. However, he was not as fortunate as me and he returned home early to our parents. My sister was also evacuated, and she went to a little Welsh village in the mountains of Monmouthshire called Blaina. I was only able to visit her once. It was an all-day trip with three changes of buses, so I was only able to stay a couple of hours – and I was expected to pay for my lunch! I later found out that she and her friend were treated like skivvies and were abused. My sister also returned home early.

My mother was able to visit me only once during the time I was away from home. It was not easy for her as she had had my baby sister just after the war had started. My father worked on the railways in a reserved occupation and was not able to get away at all.

In July 1942, I finished my time at school and was very pleased to return home. My stay in South Wales had, on the whole, been a pleasant one and I know I was more fortunate than many of the evacuees because I had caring families looking after me.

Within eighteen months of returning home I joined the army and spent the next few years abroad. I unfortunately lost touch with the good people I stayed with, but I have never forgotten the kindness shown to me during that very traumatic period of my life.

Margaret Ostler (*now Mrs Margaret Williams*) *recalls her evacuation in June 1940, with Fort Pitt School, Chatham:*

At the outbreak of World War II my father was farming on the Hoo peninsula, some 15 miles from the Medway Towns, and it was very difficult to get to and from school. When Fort Pitt School was preparing to be evacuated, my parents decided that I was likely to get a better education by going with the school. How wrong they were! Anyway, my second sister, who went to a school in Gravesend, was evacuated to Suffolk and then to Plymouth. My younger sister and brother stayed at home; I went in June 1940, to South Wales.

We arrived hot and tired in Porthcawl in the early evening. The place seemed crowded with troops rescued from Dunkirk. We only stayed in Porthcawl for about a fortnight and then moved to the Whitchurch/Rhiwbina area, within the confines of Cardiff, where we stayed for the next couple of years, sharing a school with the local children. My first billet in Whitchurch didn't last long because I did not get on with the son of the house, so I moved to Rhiwbina, to a retired Welsh-speaking couple where I was very happy. We seemed to have spent a lot of the time rushing home during alerts and suffered quite a lot from night bombings.

By September 1941 so many pupils had returned home to Kent that those of us who were left were amalgamated with another school in Treharris, which meant another change of billet – and where I met my future husband! My stay at this billet lasted two months when I went back to Kent to train as a children's nurse. However, I failed the medical and in fact I had to take things easy for the next couple of years. After this long convalescence I started working in a nursery in Tunbridge Wells. Little did I know that when the doodlebugs started, I was to be evacuated again. The nursery (and staff) were evacuated by coach to Kenfig Hill in South Wales. The children were housed in a 'prefab', and we were billeted around the village. Looking back, we worked hard, no dances or late nights, but we enjoyed ourselves.

I never went back to the Medway area to live. I married my Welsh boy in 1951, and we finally moved back to Wales in 1954 where we have raised four children and have had a happy life.

Maurice Coultrup *and his brother were evacuated in June 1940 with the Council School from Gillingham, to the village of Resolven in Glamorgan, South Wales:*

Our parents took us down to Gillingham railway station on the day we left for Wales and that is where we said our goodbyes. The train journey was long and tiring, but we finally arrived at our destination of Resolven. I can't remember much about our arrival, but I remember we were soon taken to our billets. My brother and I ended up at Noddfa House in Coronation Road.

Our foster parents were Mr and Mrs White; also living in the house was their daughter Nancy and her husband and they had a little daughter named Ann. Our foster parents were very good to us, looking after us very well and, once we had settled down, we enjoyed every minute we were there. We did eventually settle into school and we got on very well with the local children.

Our parents came down to Wales several times to see us and they were always made welcome by our foster parents. We always enjoyed their visits – it meant more time off from school!

One of our favourite pastimes when they were in season, was to go up the mountains and pick whinberries, which we used to sell for 4d a pound! Another memory is of the fish and chip van that used to come up our road, driven by a man called Ned. Sometimes the van used to catch on fire, much to the delight of all the kids.

Although my brother and I took a while to settle down when we first arrived in Wales, we really enjoyed our time there and we didn't return home to Gillingham until 1945.

My brother and I returned on a nostalgic journey to Resolven a few years ago, and called on the off chance at our old wartime billet. When the door opened it was Ann, the grandaughter of our old foster parents. She was very surprised to see us and she made us very welcome, insisting that we had dinner and tea before we left. The village itself has not changed a great deal over the years, and it certainly brought back many old memories.

(Although Maurice casually mentions that it took him and his brother a while to settle down in Wales, the following letter, sent to their father by the headmaster of the Council School in Resolven highlights that particular problem):

Council School,
Resolven, Glamorgan
2nd July 1940

Dear Mr Coultrup,

I am very sorry to have to let you know that your two sons have been the cause of a great deal of anxiety since they have been here.

They have the fixed idea of going back home. They are billeted with exceptionally kind people, and have no cause for complaint on that score.

Yesterday they were absent from school without permission, and I found from the police that they got as far as Cardiff by means of a platform ticket at Neath. The police were very kind to them and in the evening they were brought back to Resolven.

I want you to let me know if you want your children back, as the whole thing is very unsettling to the other children. If you want the boys back, then you must do one of two things:

1. Come here and take them home yourself.
2. Send sufficient railway fare to enable the two boys to get to Paddington, London, where you must agree to meet them at a certain time to be arranged.

We do not want to lose them, but if they are going to be a nuisance, they had better go back home at once.

(Signed) Headteacher.

Janice Reader *(now Mrs Janice Prentice), having survived her evacuation to Herne Bay, now relates with tremendous detail, her time in South Wales:*

At Easter in 1940 I would be five years old, so brother Billy's teacher at Forge Lane School suggested that it would be a good idea for me to join the evacuation to Wales to begin my education in the peace and quiet of a Welsh valley school. This time I do remember how we travelled – by train, a very long journey, far away, away from the prime target of Chatham Dockyard. I remember the steam train rattling on, me falling from a seat and a very kind Mr Perris picking me up; for the first time in my young life, my mother wasn't there to comfort me. I loved Billy, who was three years older than me, and he was the only familiar face in my whole world at that moment.

When we finally arrived we gathered in a hall in the Rhymney Valley, surrounded by beaming men in dark suits and shiny shoes and ladies with teatrays of orange squash. We stood there clutching our gas masks and, for some strange reason I never knew, a tin of corned beef! Being only four years old I didn't quite know what was happening. Sometime later I was tucked up in bed with Billy in a very high bed in a very quiet house with ticking clocks and the smell of polish, and I was soon fast asleep. During that first night I fell out of bed on to the cold lino floor. The light went on and an apparition in white holding a light, came in to pick me up and put me back into bed. Did I cry? I don't remember – but Billy was there.

Back home in Layfield Road, Gillingham, waking up would be to sounds of my father going to or coming from the gasworks, my mother nursing my baby sister or my maternal grandmother, Nannie French, turning the handle of her Singer sewing machine; she made very neat clothes for us children from pieces of material pulled out of a large bag. The radio would be on and my mother would sing as she busied around.

Before we left home it had been very exciting, because my father had dug an enormous hole in our garden and put in two Anderson shelters joined together. My Aunt Doris and her two children living close by were to share them as Uncle George was away in the Royal Navy, but all that was a long way away.

No such familiar sounds now. Billy and I were in Carn-y-Tylor Terrace, Abertysswg with Mr and Mrs Thompson. I think Mr Thompson was a retired school teacher. We were living with people as old as my grandmother! We bathed in a real bathroom – we only had a bungalow bath in front of the fire back home.

My mother sent us parcels of books and toys, and letters which Mr and Mrs Thompson read to us. Sometimes there were clothes made by Nannie French, then on my fifth birthday I had a doll.

Mr and Mrs Thompson were most kind and gentle foster-parents. Mrs Thompson had a large lump on her neck and Billy told me it was a goitre. The routine must have been genteel – we had tea and cakes in the afternoon. They had a cat that Mr Thompson and I took for walks on a lead, but I never touched it.

We lived in a country lane on the outskirts of the village and there were streams and a field which squelched and frogs leaping about when we walked on it. There were mountains all round and I knew my home was beyond these mountains somewhere. The Welsh voices were strange, but being young I soon understood and then spoke in the same way. Sometimes we would meet other evacuees and I was happy to hear a voice from home. Billy was always out playing with the local boys and one late afternoon Mrs Thompson scolded him as she peeled off his clothes and put him and them in the bath as he tried to explain that it was the Welsh boys who had rolled him in the cow's mess! I was glad it wasn't me – the smell was terrible. He was put into his pyjamas quickly and sent straight to bed.

I can still remember the neat house, with its ornaments and lots of photographs. One morning Billy packed his haversack and told me he was going home with another boy evacuee he'd met. They were going to walk over the mountains, and wouldn't let me go with them. He told me not to tell anyone. I kept the secret until Mrs Thompson became very worried that he hadn't come in for a meal, and then I told her. There was a terrible fuss and Billy and his friend were found and brought back. He said he wasn't unhappy and that they were kind, but he just wanted to go home – he missed his mother!

Then there was school. I'd never seen so many children, and the building seemed enormous. On the first day I ran home five times. Mrs Thompson took me back four times, but gave up on the fifth. No-one seemed to understand that it was because when I went to the toilet across the playground I couldn't find my way back! All the classrooms looked the same, but I did know my house was straight up the lane. Learning was no problem. I liked school and we must have had a lovely summer because I remember the walks in the lane and at the back of Carn-y-Tylor Terrace with Mr Thompson and the cat.

Miss Annett and Miss Lamb were teachers in Abertysswg who had come with the evacuees from Forge Lane School in Gillingham. I recognised them at school and saw them often and at the Thompsons' house. Mrs Thompson had broken a bone in her hand and I had caught chicken pox; the teachers and the Thompsons were talking behind closed doors. It seemed Mrs Thompson could not cope with the plastered hand and chicken pox. There was no washing machine, vacuum cleaner, dishwasher or fast food in those days, and climbing the stairs to my sickroom was taking its toll. My world changed again and Billy and I went into a 'home'. It was like a bad dream; it is one of the clearest memories of my childhood.

I was in a room without Billy. He came and told me 'they' had boiled his woolly underwear and now they would not fit a doll! 'They' were largely unseen, but the other inhabitants were not. There were screaming children, fighting, rough, loud, spotty with shaved heads and smelly clothes. I had porridge with salt on, but I was healthy and the chicken pox got better. Billy caught it and was not able to leave the home for a few weeks, but I could.

I remember a little house with the front door open and a sheep looking in down the hallway, and a pretty little lady in front of a glowing range making tea. I sat on a leather rolled-arm settee – on the end nearest the door. It was the Adams' house, 42 Charles Street, Abertysswg. The road ran straight through the village, on the bus route. I called the lady Auntie Lil, and she was one of the sweetest ladies ever. About four o'clock the kettle and various pans were simmering on the range. Tea was being made again and down the hall came the sound of boots; into the living room came a tall, black person – everything black from the face down. It stared at me for a while and then said, 'By God, Lil, it's nothing but a tup.' I gathered I wasn't what they wanted. I was too small to look after myself. I was sent upstairs. The stairs led straight off the living room which was also the kitchen. I heard a bath clattering through the door from the back yard and water sloshing around. Albert Adams had come from his shift on the coal face and took his bath in front of the fire. Later I was called downstairs and I saw the bath had a crust of coal dust. Albert and Lil were carrying the bath out into the yard to tip it down the drain, and then it was hung on the yard wall until the following day. Black clothes were slung over the line. They must have been washed in the bathwater too.

The Adams were in their late thirties, with no children, and they loved each other very much. Uncle Albert was noisy, opinionated, a joker, fun and soft-centred. A 'tup' he called me and that seemed to be his name for me. When we went out walking, his big hand held mine and I felt safe. Auntie Lil showed me a picture frame on the wall which held Albert's commendation from the RSPCA. He was on the mountain one day with his friend, when his dog fell down a deep fissure in the mountain. The friend stayed by the hole while Albert ran back to the village to get ropes and help. They lowered Albert down to rescue the dog which survived. Even at five years old, I knew that was brave.

Every day after school the routine was at 4pm up the stairs to look out of the window or to read a book. Albert would have his bath and then we would have tea. Life was comfortable for me, but hard for the housewives to keep everything clean. There were no machines to help, no kitchen sink, only a bucket under a cold tap in the larder. There was an outside toilet but no flush; the larder bucket when full served that purpose. There was a front room which was never used.

I had a soft bed in my own little back room, where I lay and listened to the sounds of preparation for the next morning – coal being brought in and wood being chopped and laid in the hearth to be dry for lighting the fire. And finally, I would hear the click of the back door latch and then slept soundly.

I came home from school sometimes to find a huge pile of coal outside the front door which had to be carried in buckets through the house to the yard coal shed.

One late afternoon, Albert was taking his bath downstairs, I was upstairs in the front bedroom as usual, and the rain was pouring down. The mountains were always in a mist when it rained. I looked down the road and saw a grown-up holding the hand of a child. The child had a large, bright coloured sou'wester on and as the figures came closer I recognised the child – it was Billy! I jumped for joy and ran down the stairs crying out that my brother was coming up the street. Albert was standing up in the bath totally naked, and Lil was crossing the room to put a towel across my face. I didn't care. I ran up the hall to find Billy at the door. One of the teachers from Gillingham was with him and she said she was taking him to Auntie Ede's, and Lil said she would take me to see him there after tea. I knew that Auntie Ede had recently taken an evacuee from Layfield Road, a boy called Ralph Dowding, so there were to be two boys staying at 7 McLaren Cottages. Ralph was quiet, always indoors and so different from Billy.

Leaning on the railings after tea was occupational therapy for the miners, as they looked down the valley at the pit head. They had great discussions to set the world right. I heard snippets of their conversation, but one phrase unnerved me. Albert said that, 'If the bloody Nazis came here I'd shoot Lil and the tup before they got to us!' As Albert was in the Home Guard and had a large rifle in the cupboard under the stairs, I often looked hard to the top of the mountain to see if the Nazis were getting any nearer. I knew all about Nazis, Germans, Mussolini and the goose-step and even Lord Haw

Haw from Billy and the boys who acted out scenarios from the newsreels. I didn't mention my worries to Auntie Lil; she was too gentle for me to frighten her about the Nazis.

Once we went to a cinema in New Tredegar where we queued to see *Snow White and the Seven Dwarfs*. We all loved it and the boys used to sing and the girls skipped to the tune of 'Whistle While You Work':

> Whistle while you work,
> Goebbels is a twerp,
> Hitler's barmy, so's his army,
> Whistle while you work.

After a very cold winter, the warmer weather brought the exciting news that my mother and baby sister Brenda were coming. My mother, always bright and sparkling, and my sister had grown so much, but the Tan Sad pram came too. Welsh mothers would stare at the pram; their babies were wrapped close to their bodies with large shawls tied from back to front and over the shoulder. My mother's visit went all too quickly then Mum and Brenda were gone.

Albert took me to Chepstow to stay with his mother and sister, Prina. They lived in a pretty cottage. While we were there Albert and I walked down country lanes picking nuts and blackberries. I watched very carefully the bull in the field that snorted at us and I held Albert's hand very tightly. One of the lanes ended in a great expanse of water and Albert said it was the Bristol Channel. Old Mrs Adams was in a wheelchair and we took her back to Abertysswg with us and I fetched and carried for this smiling old lady. It was the first person I had ever seen in a wheelchair and I have no idea how we managed to travel on the train or from the station.

Two boys evacuated from Gillingham arrived to stay in McLaren Cottages. They were Harry and his younger brother Tony. I had my first crush on Harry. I was always on his side in any fights or disagreements and I was happy when he won.

We played in the snow and never seemed to be cold. We had warm clothes, no synthetic fibres then! Our parcels from home brought us hand-knitted jumpers. Nannie French made trousers and shirts for Billy and skirts and coats for me.

The war across Europe, Africa and Russia was fierce but we knew nothing of it. We saw the Pathé Gazette at the cinema but it had nothing to do with us. Our families sent us parcels and letters so they were obviously alright. Life in Wales was good. Auntie's kitchen produced food like magic – wonderful chips and sausages, eggs from local farmers, Welsh cakes sprinkled with sugar. On Saturday mornings I always took the jug to the milkman's horse and little cart outside the front door. The milkman dipped a huge ladle into the churn and filled the jug. The milk was delicious, like ice-cream.

We would often climb over the mountains to pick whinberries and Auntie would bake delicious whinberry pies for Sunday dessert. We were never allowed to go to the mountains alone, only with a crowd, because of deep and dangerous holes which were covered over and hidden by heathers, ferns and long grass.

Occasionally tap water would be brown and undrinkable, so Albert and I would take some metal containers up to the mountain stream, and my arms would ache carrying back a full billy-can of water.

My mother came alone to stay for a few days. She spoke with Billy's teachers and it was decided that if Billy was to pass a scholarship the following year, he would do better in Gillingham where the classes were smaller. Suddenly Billy and I were packing and we left our very happy daily life to return to the home we hardly knew. When we reached Gillingham, we walked down Layfield Road in the pitch dark and hid behind Mother when we reached the house. There were tears of joy from Nannie French and our father, who didn't know we were coming home – there was no telephone to tell them of the sudden decision.

I didn't consciously think too much of my foster parents in Wales and how they were feeling, but the war took its toll on me. It was out of a warm bed and into a cold air-raid shelter most nights, then we slept in the shelter permanently. I wet the bed. My mother was in despair and took me to a doctor because I never kept still. I fidgeted, tapped my fingers and blinked my eyes. I was a seven year old nervous wreck! One day we walked to Corporation Road after school to see where an aircraft had crashed. We heard that the pilot was hanging in a tree on a farm, but we didn't see that. I saw barrage balloons across the sky and a dog-fight between two aircraft over the River Medway. We collected shrapnel into boxes and swapped it with other children. Auntie Doris worked in the docks and there was an outbreak of scabies, so all of us children had to be stripped bare at the school clinic and painted with a white solution which stung and made us hop about.

By the time I reached eight and a half years of age, my school was again evacuated – back to Wales. It seemed that evacuation was necessary because of the doodlebugs, the unmanned rockets sent by the Germans in a final desperate attempt to frighten England. Brenda, who was five and a half, and I went back to Auntie Lil and Uncle Albert. Brenda shared my little back room and my bed, which was just as I had left it. I was big sister to Brenda, but I couldn't stop her crying at first. She really missed home.

At school Brenda was in the infants and I was in the primary. Miss Biram was my teacher. She had come from Gillingham with the new evacuation. She seemed like a dragon to us children, always pushing me on, making me work hard. One day I was late home from school. I had been playing in the park and by the time I got home, Albert was already bathed. He was cross so I lied and said that Miss Biram had kept me in after school. The next day I was horrified to see Uncle Albert at the school. Miss Biram called me into a room with him and questioned me. I was so ashamed to admit that I had lied, and I had to apologise. Albert had lost an afternoon's work and I had lost face. Miss Biram never held it against me and she became my favourite teacher. Her lessons were so interesting because of her enthusiasm for the subjects. I was eventually top of my year and passed the scholarship.

Evacuees began to drift back home. My mother came to stay for a few days and then took Brenda back home with her. I was lonely. Everyone it seemed had returned home, and I wanted to go home too. I loved Lil and Albert very much, but I was growing older and knew I had a family back home, so back came my mother to take me on the long train journey home. I didn't know for many years after, the pain that Albert and Lil went through as I fell easily into a new routine of school and life in Gillingham.

With Mr Newton, the headmaster at Forge Lane School, and Miss Biram as my teacher, I did well and pleased my parents. My brother Billy was also doing well at Third Avenue Boys' Grammar School. There were piano lessons, Girl Guides and the

Strand for swimming. Then came the street parties to commemorate Victory in Europe, with home-dyed flags strung from house to house, piano-playing in the road, tables with food and games to play. We stayed up until midnight, there was a 'knees up Mother Brown', and my parents were hoarse with singing!

In 1948 we had my foster parents to stay at Layfield Road. It was a wonderful fortnight. They were long summer days and we had walks in the evenings. It was wonderful to be with them again and the house was so quiet when they had gone. There have been many holidays both ways since then. I took my young husband to stay with them, and then my babies, Christopher and Rebecca. Albert said Rebecca was the image of me when I first arrived in Wales. Years later my son Lance was taken to see them – their love for us shone just as brightly.

The funerals have been many over the years. I remember I stood in the front room of a house in McLaren Cottages where Lil and Albert had moved to be close to Ede and Ted, and I cried over Lil's coffin. Albert went into an old people's home and I did not see him again.

There are no dark corners in my memories. I only knew kindness, caring and love. I was comfortable, well-fed and fit. Brother Billy, Auntie Lil and Uncle Albert were my security. My thanks go out to all the families in Abertysswg who, for no reward, took into their homes children from different backgrounds and cared for them. Not every one was a success story, it had to work both ways. But war hasn't any neat edges – it is a ragged jumble of time and events.

Shirley Nokes (*now Mrs Shirley Pritchard*) *comments briefly on her evacuation to South Wales:*

I was evacuated in 1939 at the beginning of the Second World War. I went to Pontypridd in South Wales and celebrated my sixth birthday there. My sister was two years old at the time. I went to school in Pontypridd and have learnt since that Tom Jones later attended the same school. Once the bombs began dropping on Cardiff my parents decided we might as well face the future together in Kent. My memories of my time in South Wales were brief but never to be forgotten; especially the lovely lady, Mrs O'Leary of Bournville Road, who took us in, the visits of my mother and father, our trips to the 'Dragon Stone', the walks up the mountainside and the weekly markets.

Shirley and Patricia Nokes with their father on Dragon's Rock, Pontypridd, during their evacuation

Chapter Six

PRIVATE EVACUATION

NOT ALL PARENTS TOOK ADVANTAGE *of the official Government Evacuation Scheme. There was an obvious reluctance on the part of some parents to let their children go off alone to some unknown destination for an unspecified period. However, as the war progressed, reason prevailed in many households and those who still declined help from the Government Evacuation Scheme made their own private arrangements to evacuate their children. The following examples of private evacuation are given in great detail by the evacuees themselves.*

Colin Fleetney *had managed to escape evacuation until October of 1940, when his parents at last decided that life in the village of Tunstall near Sittingbourne was perhaps not quite as safe as they thought. Private arrangements were then made for Colin to travel to South Wales:*

I was a private evacuee, this is to say that I was not part of a school group; my parents simply made arrangements for me to live with a family in Gorseinon, near Swansea. My cousin, some four years older than me, whose parents had, before the war, established a friendship with this Welsh family, had been evacuated several months before me and would stay on after my return to Kent. However, one lovely September lunch time, with the windows open and the rich scent of the apple orchards filling the house, my father put it to me that I might like to go to Wales 'for a time'. I remember clearly the intense faces of my parents as they searched my face for emotion similar, I suppose, to that which they were experiencing. There was none. As my knowledge of life beyond Tunstall comprised solely of our annual week's holiday in Sheerness, the concept of 'Wales' was meaningless to me.

Thus it came about that I found myself standing on the platform of Sittingbourne station with my mother and father while the October sun of 1940 streamed through the great glass roof covering the platforms and tracks. I was already uneasy – this was not the Sheerness platform. The London train, with a huge engine all green and brass, suggested a fearful importance to this event which certainly was not infused with my parents' usual holiday spirit, a spirit I always associated with the railway station. Porters shouted and doors banged. My father put two huge cases on the rack and then returned to the platform. I had a corner seat. He closed the door and reached for my hand through the window. Never before had I seen my father look so sad. He was about to say something to me when a woman leaned across me, pressed some money into his hand, and asked him to get her a newspaper from the bookstall across the platform. My father looked surprised but joined the queue at the stall. There was shouting. The guard blew his whistle and the engine responded with a shriek. Smoothly the train started to move and the bookstall slid out of view. Suddenly there was my father! He was trotting along frantically thrusting a newspaper and money into the woman's hands. He tried to say something to me but the train was fast gathering speed and as he spoke he fell away out of sight. I was seven years and five months old.

Years later I was told that, at Chatham, I asked if we had arrived in Wales. One can assume that my mother had her problems with a bored child and her luggage as she crossed from Victoria to Paddington and then changed trains again at Swansea for the short journey to Gorseinon. We were met by two young men; one hoisted me on to his shoulders while the other carried our cases, one on his shoulder, one by hand. It was a considerable walk to our destination but these two coal miners never once paused to ease their burdens. We passed along streets in which women leaned in open doorways and children played. All spoke in Welsh, all seemed to stare at us, throwing the occasional remark to our guides, and shaking their heads sadly at the replies. I felt self-conscious perched up on the man's shoulders in my best clothes. In the darkness of that first night I partially awoke to my mother kissing my cheek. I could not understand why. Confused, I sank back into sleep. In the morning I could not find my mother and was told that she had gone home. The following few days were very bad so far as I was concerned.

Children are resilient and I quickly adjusted. As the Welsh language was virtually all that I heard, I learned to speak it fluently, so I am told, within a matter of a few weeks. I had to!

Life in Gorseinon revolved around the coal mine, the steel rolling mill and the tinplate works, all of which were working at full production for the war effort. The community was starting to feel the effects of modest prosperity following the depression. Of my surrogate family Ma was all-powerful. She ran the house and controlled her husband and sons. Dad and the four sons worked in either the mine or the steel mills while a daughter, known as 'Old' to me, in gymslip and broad brimmed beaver hat, went to the high school. The married daughter, with whom my cousin lived, owned a 1930s bow-fronted semi-detached house in the suburbs.

The school, in which I was very quickly enrolled, was a great 1920s pebble-dashed and red brick pile a considerable walk away. I recall a great deal of singing. I remember, too, teachers shouting, not always, but frequently, at me. I took my turn with the rest standing in front of the class to receive a stinging cut of an eighteen-inch ruler across the calf of my leg. Less frequent, but very clearly remembered, was the swish of the headmaster's cane followed by searing pain across the palms of my hands: with good reason, given the attitude of the times. For the majority of the time I was no quiet, lonely, little evacuee. Not a bit of it! I had settled in and, give or take a bit of nationalistic bullying, I was soon integrated into my peer-group, accepted and unexceptional among my Welsh friends.

Apart from my cousin there were, to my knowledge, no other evacuees in Gorseinon. If there were, we had no contact with them. Punishment was generally swift at school as I learned after falling in a stream and arriving late, wet through, and covered in clay. It was instantaneous after I sent my cap, frisbee fashion, across the well of the hall, from the gallery during assembly, while swearing (in Welsh of course) at the officiating Baptist minister. Above all, punishment was harsh for truancy.

Truancy was commonplace. It was almost an art form with my new friends and my cousin was well versed in it, while I quickly and eagerly fell into the system. We were only brought to book when we became careless – or forgot that liars must have good memories.

With truancy and legitimate holidays we had a great deal of time totally unsupervised and we used it to full advantage. The area was a far cry from the orchard-lands of Kent. Here were mine and mill adjacent to heather covered hills. Here too was a network of railway tracks passing along the centres of the streets and on them ran little industrial engines with friendly drivers who would allow you to ride with them. There were acres of huge pieces of machinery stored in the open simply asking to be climbed upon, and behind the mine there were parked a whole fleet of derelict steam lorries submerged in dense undergrowth. Beyond the town we would follow the meandering river towards Pontarddulais, deep and deadly in the winter, sluggish and shallow in the summer when the water and soft brown mud was warm and silky.

Above the river, part way up a great curving hill, amid seas of heather stood 'the old pit' as it was known to us children. Most of the buildings were open to the sky. The pit-head winding gear had long gone and the winding engine house was empty apart from a tangle of rusting weed-grown girders. One could enter the base of the tall brick chimney and gaze up at the tiny disc of sky far above while the wind sighed and tugged at one's clothes. Or we could squeeze and crawl along sinuous brick flues under the rusting boilers. The greatest attraction was, of course, the mine shaft itself which stood open to the sky surrounded by a low brick wall. We found that if one got the aim just right the hum of a brick falling down the centre of the shaft would first increase in volume before fading away before, far, far below, we would hear it strike water. Of course in order to lob the brick into the true centre one had to stand on the narrow wall. More frequently the brick would ricochet from side to side of the shaft in a frenzied clattering before breaking up to fall silently to the water far below.

Sometimes we would meet the shift coming from the working pit. We would wait in the yard while again and again the cages wafted to the surface and the spokes of the huge twin wheels, revolving in opposite, made blurred patterns against the clouds. As signal gongs sounded and gates rasped open group after group of black tired men would walk stiffly to the lamp room and bath house and emerge shiny booted, blackbelted, waistcoated, jacketed and capped, and we would carry their empty snap boxes as we walked home.

The tinplate mill had been built over a stream along which we used to float anything that a child could consider a boat; from electric light bulbs to substantial pieces of timber. The tunnel was several hundred yards long and not straight. We would watch our vessels as the sluggish current carried them into darkness and then cut through the works yard, dodging engines, trucks and cranes with sheets of steel swinging from the jibs, in order to gain the downstream south of the tunnel, from which, given time and luck our vessels would emerge. The voyages were not always successful, especially for tin cans. The stream was of course polluted, carrying all kinds of filth on its surface but, if we thought about it at all, which I doubt, we simply took it as the norm, which it was.

My cousin and the others waded further than I could, some twenty feet, but gave up as the light failed and the roar of the mill thundered through the darkness ahead. We went home with black slug-like creatures clinging to our legs. We called them leaches, perhaps they were; I know that Ma went all to pieces when she found them on me.

My best friend's grandmother died and he very kindly invited me to see her. He said that she had been good to me. Had she? All that I could recall was a little old lady who always wore a black hat tied with a ribbon under her chin as she sat by the kitchen fire. Anyway, in we went. The house was very quiet. He lead me to the parlour door. That his grandmother was in the parlour signified some importance. The door was ajar, my friend eased it open and in a surprisingly polite gesture invited me to enter first. In the centre of the room stood a coffin on trestles. Standing on tiptoe we peered at the peaceful old lady for a moment or two, then stole away.

Sunday was almost a day of rest. Had it not been for the war effort, I am sure that the mine and the mills would have been silent. Even so, Sunday was different: best clothes, chapel in the morning, quiet indoor activities during the afternoon, chapel in the evening. At home in Kent we hardly ever missed matins at Tunstall parish church. Thus on my first Sunday morning as we walked past the gate of Gorseinon parish church I made to enter. It was a bad mistake and I was hauled away with much shaking of heads and clucking. Church, or rather chapel, was a very well maintained corrugated iron building painted cream and brown.

The service was conducted by a rota of lay-preachers who could hold their congregations spellbound. The singing was like nothing I had experienced in Anglican Kent. The chapel also provided most of the social life in the form of teas and picnics (rationing seemed to have no effect whatsoever, food was always plentiful). While the chapel provided most of the social life, dad and his sons were known, on occasions, to come home during weekday evenings from the Working Men's Club a little 'distressed'. The eldest daughter and her husband had 'gone over' to the Anglican Church several years earlier, much to ma's utter disapproval. Thus my cousin had simply exchanged Milton parish church for Gorseinon's.

The cinema in the high street backed on to a piece of waste ground in our street. The ground was used as a dump for the sweepings from the cinema and also as a tip for all the sweepings from the town's several pubs, the floors of which were covered in sawdust. The dump was a wonderland to us. Whenever we could we would carefully search through each fresh delivery of sawdust for money. Of course the sawdust was liberally laced with broken glass, hundreds of metal bottle caps, cigarette ends, spit and so on, and damp with stale beer. We all found money, but such a find was secondary to the pleasure of playing amid this smelly sawdust under the stunted elder bushes.

The cinema was easily entered without money. My cousin would gather up her long straight red hair and jam my cap on. Then we would tinker with an emergency door with a wire device we had made especially for the purpose. There would be a loud clunk and the door would open allowing us to enter the gents. Should a member of the staff have been in that foul smelling area of flaking whitewash, lit by a flickering gas jet, we would have been in trouble. Such an event never occurred. The occasional occupants simply ignored us, perhaps they had followed that route in their childhood! We entered the auditorium well towards the front, hence the necessity to ensure that the film had started and the house-lights were out and that the top half of my cousin looked like a boy.

We spent many hours in the cinema, for with continuous performances from 1.30pm it was a safe haven in bad weather – or when playing truant. We were not discriminating regarding our choice of programme and the classifications of U, A or H were a matter of indifference to us. No one challenged our right to be there as we watched all the horror and violence that Hollywood and, to a lesser extent, Pinewood and Ealing, produced. My cousin gained a tremendous amount of satisfaction by suddenly, no matter where we were, imitating extremely accurately so far as I was concerned many of the creatures that stalked swamp, fog, forest and castle in those films. Occasionally those films are shown on the television today and I watch them in order to recapture those far off days as I huddled in fear close to my cousin in the flickering smoke-filled darkness of that old cinema.

It was in Gorseinon's other cinema, a beautiful building of marble and red plush, that we went to see *The Wizard of Oz*. We were dressed in our Sunday clothes and went upstairs to the best seats in the house. I still find this film difficult to watch; I remember the uncontrollable homesickness that surged over me when I realised that I, like Dorothy, simply wanted to go home. How lucky Dorothy was! I had no ruby slippers to click to transport me back to Kent.

The unsettling caused by *The Wizard of Oz* impelled me to strike out for home late one autumn afternoon. I knew well enough which way – along the railway track! This would take me to Swansea and it could only be a matter of going on past Swansea to Sittingbourne. After perhaps a mile or so the rails started a strange 'ticking' sound, and round the bend came a tank engine without a train. I politely stood back, but the engine wafted to a halt, the warmth of its boiler engulfing me. The driver looked down from the cab and asked me where I thought I was going. I chanted my full postal address, something I always held in my mind and thought about at night. (If I forgot that address I was certain that I would never see Tunstall again.) He gazed down at me for a moment or two and then climbed down and hoisted me into the cab where the fireman poured me a drink of tea into an enamel mug. Then I was taken back to Gorseinon. As we pulled up at the platform the driver said, 'It's a long way to Kent, boyo. We're not even on the Great Western, see! Get along now.'

My mother and father wrote to me regularly and between letters sent me picture postcards. My tenth birthday was marked not only by cards but also by a telegram printed on a very colourful form. The letters and cards were full of positive things; my parents love and concern for me, and so on. They were always very difficult to receive and read, causing great longing as well as great joy. Along with my memorised address they were by far my most treasured possessions and I kept them hidden, frequently looking at them and thereby upsetting myself.

One day I was told that I was going home. It was difficult to believe and I am sure that it was kept from me for as long as possible. On the morning of my departure I was dressed in a new dark blue serge suit and cap. My cousin came down early and was very upset. She said she would miss me! I had not seen this side of her before. There was a great deal of hand shaking and squeezing of my shoulders as this kindly family, into which I had been integrated, said goodbye before ma and I were off to Swansea, London and Sittingbourne. Finally during the late afternoon the brakes squealed while doors slammed and a voice was bellowing 'Sitt-bourne, Sitt-bourne'. Then there was a hurrying through the subway to the booking hall shafted by dusty beams of sunlight, then suddenly I was swept up by my mother. The forgotten but instantly remembered scent surrounded me. Her cheek was wet as she hugged me and my father was touching me and smiling with wet eyes. It was all over. I had been away for sixteen months.

Mildred Hallums *(now Mrs Mildred Colver) and her twin sister **Joyce** were evacuated privately from Rochester to a village in South Wales. Here Mildred sets out her evacuation experiences in great detail:*

Joyce and I were not typical evacuees, as we did not go with our school when they went at the outbreak of the war. Our parents had not wanted us to be evacuated with the school but then they found that the arrangements made for the education of children left behind were not very adequate. One of the teachers not evacuated with our school, called at our house once a week to set us enough work for mornings only and collected the previous week's work for correction.

Several other children joined us at home, and our mother supervised our work. We went for walks in the afternoons. This carried on for nearly a year and, as our parents were not satisfied, they decided to make private arrangements for our evacuation. Mum had an aunt who lived in Rogerstone, near Newport and she was asked if she would help. Aunt Em found us a place to stay with her friend, Mrs Sullivan, who lived close by in The Uplands.

So, on the 2nd June, 1940, Mum, Joyce and I left our home (and Dad) in Rochester and travelled by train to Rogerstone. We hoped that our stay would only be for a few months, but it was to be four and a half years before we returned home.

Mrs Sullivan was a very warm-hearted, jolly person. She and Mum soon became firm friends, and the Sullivans became 'Auntie Rose' and 'Uncle Bill' to Joyce and me. In spite of some food items being in short supply, Auntie Rose still managed to make a lovely cherry cake when Joyce and I celebrated our twelfth birthday on the 10th of June, just days after our arrival in South Wales.

Joyce and I were admitted to Tydu School in Rogerstone and joined the 'scholarship' class, although we were over the normal age, and in due course we sat the entrance

A LAST APPEAL TO REASON
BY
ADOLF HITLER
Speech before the Reichstag, 19th July, 1940

The heading of a German multi-page propaganda leaflet dropped near Rogerstone in 1940 which was picked up and preserved by Mildred Hallums

examination for Bassaleg County School. In the meantime we were taught by Mr Hughes, who also took singing for the whole school, and Miss Marks who was also a talented artist and needlewoman.

We enjoyed singing, doing our best to join in with *Cwm Rhondda* and *Land of my Fathers* – in Welsh! Under Miss Marks' supervision, Joyce and I made several items of embroidery. The headmaster, Mr Moon, was a very kind gentleman. He shocked some people by always wearing an open-necked shirt and white plimsolls to school! Once a week the girls would spend a whole day at the domestic science block, which was well equipped. We did laundry and housework in the morning and cookery in the afternoon. One afternoon a week the girls knitted socks for the miners, in coarse black wool. This was not at all popular and was known as 'black knitting'. It was made more tolerable by Miss Marks reading *Jane Eyre* to us while we knitted.

Joyce and Mildred Hallums with Mum and Dad and Miss Jay outside Gwent Cottage, Caerleon, in August 1942

Joyce and I made friends with another evacuee called June Porter, from London. To help the war effort we produced a 'Red Cross' magazine between us and sold it to our friends at a few pennies per copy. The magazine consisted of puzzles and jokes, etc., and was laboriously copied out by hand. We also joined in with our friends in producing a concert party, held in a back garden in Park Avenue, with all proceeds going to the Red Cross. We all contributed a few pennies a week to National Savings, and there would often be special savings drives such as 'Warship Week' or 'Spitfire Week'.

An unpleasant aspect of life in Rogerstone was the smoke screen. This extended the whole length of the village and was meant to camouflage the large aluminium works at the far end, which was vital to aircraft production. It consisted of contraptions about four feet high, with a base filled with crude oil and a chimney on top. These contraptions were placed every few yards, mostly on the pavements. The smoke and smell were very unpleasant, as well as the obstruction and mess they caused. The army was in charge of them and they were lit every night at dusk. Everyone tried to be indoors before this happened.

One night one of them caught fire in the middle of a field near our house, and the soldiers had difficulty in extinguishing it. Luckily there were no enemy aeroplanes overhead. Strict blackout had to be observed, so it was easy to get lost in the dark and smoke if you ventured out at night.

We soon began to experience air raid warnings at night and had to come downstairs. At first the raids had been more distant, and Mum and Auntie Rose used to watch the

> Dover Girls' County School,
> At the Williams Endowed School,
> Caerleon, Mon.
>
> 10th November, 1941.
>
> Dear Sir,
>
> There is, I understand, a child evacuated from Kent, Mildred Hallam, in attendance at your school. I have been asked by the Director of Education for Monmouthshire and by the Chief Inspector of the Kent Education Committee if I can admit her to this school as there seems to be some difficulty about her transfer either to a Monmouthshire School or to the Technical School to which she would normally have gone. I believe that the child's mother has been staying in the District and that therefore it is advisable that she should remain in Bassaleg or Rogerstone. I am sorry I have not been given her address. The suggestion is that she travels every day to this school and I should think it is possible for her to do so if she can bring sandwiches with her for mid-day. I should be grateful if you could let me know if you think such an arrangement would be satisfactory and, if so, if you could give me the address of the parents so that I could get into touch with them.
>
> Yours truly,
> E. M. Jones (GRUER)
>
> The Headmaster,
> Rogerstone Mxd. Council School.

searchlights and gunfire over Cardiff, about twelve miles away. When the local siren went we all sheltered under the stairs as this was considered to be the safest place in the house. Auntie Rose called this place the 'cooch'.

One terrible night it became much noisier than usual and we were huddled in the cooch when there was a very loud explosion. As soon as the 'all clear' went Auntie Rose went outside to see what had happened. Uncle Bill was working nights at the aluminium factory, so he was not at home. Auntie Rose was told that Park Avenue had been hit, which was a shock to her because her sister lived there. Mum said she would go with her to see if Auntie Lene was alright. Joyce and I couldn't be left alone so we went with them and waited a little distance from the nearby church hall, which was being used as a casualty station. Auntie Lene was not among the casualties and we soon saw her walking towards us, shocked but unhurt. She had scrambled out of the wrecked house where she was working as a housekeeper, with one of the daughters of the house who was home at the time. We all went back home, much relieved.

The next day Auntie Rose somehow managed to give a meal to seventeen people who had been bombed out – plus Auntie Lene's cat! Park Avenue was only a street away from The Uplands, so we were lucky not to have any damage. We heard the next day that twelve people had been killed and many were injured. A girl we knew at school had a serious head injury – and we didn't see her again, I have no idea what happened to her, but I do know that both her parents had been killed.

Mum wrote to Dad straight away to say that we might as well come home if we were going to be bombed in Rogerstone but Dad replied that things were probably worse at home and, besides, the education situation had not improved. Some time later he was proved right as an enemy aeroplane dropped all its bombs in the area before returning home, and our bungalow had all its windows smashed and all the ceilings down, except one. Luckily Dad had just gone to work; he worked long hours as a shipwright in Chatham Dockyard. He was also a member of the Home Guard – and now he had the task of trying to repair our family home. Mum felt torn in two as she felt she ought to be with Dad.

Rumours were rife about the Park Avenue bomb. It was said that it was really a land mine and that it floated down on a green parachute. Another explanation was that it was a sea mine, the pilot having mistaken the smoke screen for the Bristol Channel! After the raid householders were supplied with Morrison shelters. These were strong metal tables which we sheltered underneath. These usually replaced people's dining room tables. Auntie Rose had one put up in her living room, and we tried to sleep under it whenever the siren went, but it wasn't very comfortable. In spite of this we had some happy moments under there, thanks to Auntie Rose's sense of humour.

One morning we heard that an enemy plane had dropped leaflets in a field at Werne Farm. The Sullivans' son, John, happened to be at home on leave from the army, where he was a boy soldier, and John, Joyce and I ran to the field and managed to retrieve a few leaflets before they were all gone. They were Nazi propaganda leaflets, telling the British that they hadn't a hope of winning the war!

We had some pleasant times in 'Rogie' – as Rogerstone was known locally – in spite of the war. We went for walks along the canal, in the woods or down by the river, although the latter was lifeless and jet black, and smelled of coal from the mines in the valley. Sometimes we went with friends, or with Aunt Em, and I remember a happy day we spent with the Sullivans at a local beauty spot, Henlly's Brook. The canal was a favourite walk, and sometimes we went as far as the seventeen locks which went up the hillside. The view across the countryside, outside Newport, which included the locks and the distant hills, was called Allteryn, and was also known as 'Little Switzerland'.

Joyce and Mildred Hallums (left and centre) with Jill Heaver posing in their Girl Guide uniforms in Cwmbran in 1943

The local mountain, Twyn Barllwrn, overlooked Rogerstone. It is a rounded mountain with a large heap of stones on the top, known as the 'tump'.

Joyce and I played with the local children and we enjoyed visits to Werne Farm. The highlight of the year, however, was when Dad came to spend his week's summer holiday with us. Before the war, when Dad was in the building trade, he never had a summer holiday, so we were now able to enjoy a real break for the first time. We went for local walks and climbed Twyn Barllwn, but as Dad was very interested in history, and had just bought a camera, we usually went further afield, visiting places such as Cardiff, Chepstow, Bath, Wells, Tintern, Caerleon and Gloucester. We had some very interesting and happy times together, and it was very sad when he had to go back home to Kent. Mum was always anxious as he had to go through London in the blitz.

Food rationing was beginning to have its effect, at least as far as the children were concerned. When the local shop had a rare delivery of sweets, they had usually sold out before we even got to know about it! Mum joined a women's group called 'Oxford

House', and went to weekly meetings where they learned to make soft toys and various felt items.

We enjoyed trips to Newport, finding the indoor market a novelty, especially seeing lava bread (made from seaweed), salted cod, pease pudding and faggots on sale – we never tried any of these! One day we went to Risca, the next village up the valley, and were surprised to see two ladies waving to us from a seat halfway up Machen Mountain. Then we recognised them as teachers from the junior school we used to attend in Rochester. We later spent an enjoyable day with them and some other people from Rochester.

There were also occasional trips to the 'pictures' in Newport, where we saw films such as *In Which We Serve*, *Target For Tonight* and *Bambi*.

We had a problem when the scholarship results came out, because the Kent Education Committee would not let Kent children attend Bassaleg County School, and insisted that we should attend one of the Kent schools evacuated to Wales. At first they wanted us to go to a school in Merthyr Tydfil but Mum thought it was too far away. There was a term's delay and much correspondence before it was agreed that we could go to the Dover County School for Girls, which had been evacuated to Caerleon, just a few miles the other side of Newport.

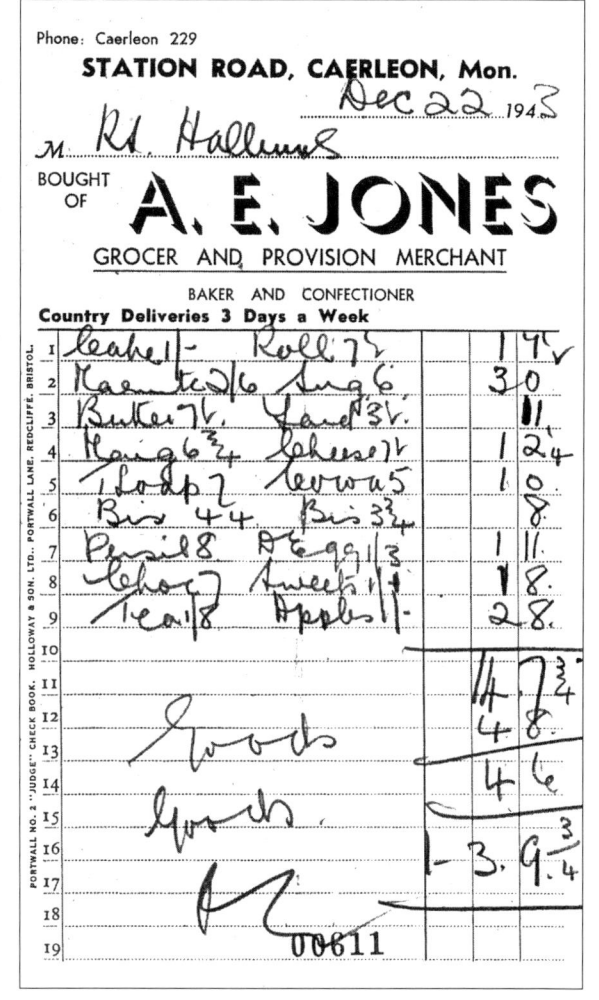

Christmas groceries for under £1.20

In December 1941 we left Rogerstone and travelled by train to Caerleon. We found our way to Gwent Cottage, near the bridge over the River Usk, and were welcomed by Miss Jay together with her cat, dog and parrot. Mum was dismayed to find that Gwent Cottage was sadly lacking in 'mod-cons', having no drainage and an outside 'privy'. The only water source was a tap in our living room wall, and all the waste water had to be tipped on to the garden. Our living room had a beamed ceiling and a range with an oven. However, Miss Jay was very kind, and Mum decided we should stay.

Miss Jay was a very courageous lady, a retired Church Army nursing sister, who was crippled as a result of her work in the slums of Edinburgh, and she had to use crutches.

Joyce and I were starting at the school at the age of 13, so we had a great deal of catching up to do. The headteacher, Miss Gruer, started us on extra lessons in French and Maths as soon as we arrived. We worked very hard and after a few months we were able to skip a form and go up to the Upper Fourth form – but we were still a year older than the other girls in the class.

We were persuaded to join school's Guide Company. This provided us with a much needed break from homework and we thoroughly enjoyed campfires, sing songs and long hikes in the lovely countryside, as well as working for our badges. We extended our knowledge of natural history and we were thrilled when we saw a kingfisher (our patrol emblem) on one of our hikes. On other occasions we saw a little owl and a fox, and once I was startled by a barn owl which suddenly flew out of a gully and over my head. We kept nature diaries each year, recording when we first heard a skylark, or saw a primrose etc.

Miss Rusbridge, the maths teacher, was our Guide captain, and Miss Swain, the geography teacher, was her lieutenant.

Air raids were a little more distant in Caerleon, which was a good thing, as the only shelter when the sirens went off (which was always at night) was under the living room table. We often heard the enemy aeroplanes and heavy gunfire, but there were no actual nearby bombing raids.

School life was quite strict but the staff were fair and friendly to the girls. Miss Gruer was strict about our school uniform in spite of clothes rationing but this was helped out with second hand uniforms, which we accepted as a matter of course. We had to wear school hats, velour in winter, panama in summer, and woe betide any girl seen without hers! We wore the much hated black woollen stockings in winter, which always seemed to need mending, and we had to wear house shoes indoors wherever lessons were held. This was not easy as lessons were held in various places all over Caerleon. Assembly was held in the Baptist church, some lessons were at the local junior school (where desks were too small for us), some at the Methodist church and some at the church hall, which also housed the school library. Gym classes were held at the men's training college. We spent quite a lot of time walking in 'crocodiles' from one building to the next, carrying school satchels, shoe bags, gym clothes and sometimes cookery or needlework items – as well as our gas masks! Things were made a little easier when some 'prefab' huts were erected for our school's use in the playground of the local school and at the training college.

Fraternising with members of the opposite sex was positively discouraged by the headteacher, Miss Gruer. However, one very popular man in Caerleon was Mr Shilston, the postman. He was always besieged by girls on their way to school, asking if he had any letters for them from home.

Caerleon was brought into the war atmosphere, particularly by the American army who were stationed in the area. Convoys of very heavy vehicles, tanks, trailers and armoured cars rumbled through the narrow streets. We avoided crossing the narrow stone bridge near Gwent Cottage when we saw the convoys coming. The parapet of the bridge was damaged several times by the military traffic, and a house in the village had its bay window demolished – several times!

Soon after we arrived in Caerleon, Miss Gruer asked Mum if she would take on the job of welfare worker for the school and she agreed. This involved visiting billets to iron out any difficulties between the hostesses (as the girls' landladies were known) and the girls. Unfortunately, some hostesses expected the girls to do so much housework and other jobs that they did not have time to do their homework. The girls were not all angels, so tact was needed to sort out the difficulties. Mum also had to escort girls to the dentist, optician, hospital clinics etc., usually in Newport.

Most of the unaccompanied Dover girls went home for the school holidays, but this in itself caused some problems. Because of the shelling and bombing in Dover, most of the time had to be spent in the underground shelters. Because of these crowded conditions, some of the girls would return to Caerleon suffering from scabies or head lice. Mum would help to deal with these problems and escort scabies sufferers to an isolation place in Abergavenny for a few days treatment.

Before long Mum was also asked to undertake welfare work for children from a Gillingham council school who were evacuated to Christchurch, about a mile away from where we lived. Some of these children came from large, poor families and Mum often had clothing problems to sort out, by getting the necessary items supplied by the W.V.S. One boy had very flat feet, due to wearing nothing but plimsolls on his feet. Mum had to take him to an orthopaedic clinic in Newport for special shoes and exercises. Another boy was so much happier with his Welsh hostess than he had been at home that he was allowed to stay with her when he left school – and she adopted him!

Dad continued his summer holiday visits and we made the most of these by visiting as many places as possible. In addition to the welfare work, Mum also did a little cleaning work for Miss Gruer and Miss Rusbridge. This helped out the family finances, which were rather stretched with keeping two homes going. However, all this was not considered enough for the war effort because Mum was 'called up', and drafted to do clerical work for the National Fire Service in Caerleon on a part time basis. She was supplied with a uniform and had to learn all about the various fire fighting vehicles.

Tragedy suddenly struck the Dover County School for Girls, as a result of the heavy traffic. Miss Rusbridge and Miss Swain were cycling through a narrow road in Caerleon on their way to a lesson, when Miss Rusbridge was knocked off her cycle by a 60 foot trailer as it swung round a bend. Miss Rusbridge was taken to the Gwent Hospital in Newport, but died during the night. Miss Gruer gave out the sad news at assembly the next morning. We were all stunned at the death of a very popular teacher and Guide Captain. A memorial service was held a few days later at St Cadoc's Church in Caerleon, which the whole school attended. Miss Swain took over as Guide Captain and Mrs Bailey (our only married teacher) arrived to be our maths teacher.

It was not all hard work at school. We had school concerts and the sixth form gave a hilarious prize giving for the staff. Miss Gruer, whose nickname (behind her back) was Cheesey (from Gruyere cheese) was given a piece of cheese, and Miss Mackenzie, a maths teacher, was given an abacus! I can't remember the other prizes, but we all fell about laughing, and the staff took it all good humouredly. We also had trips into Newport to the pictures to see *The Great Mr Handel* and *This Is The Army*.

Back at Gwent Cottage Miss Jay would often invite us to listen to her radio, especially if Mr Churchill was giving a speech. I'm afraid Mum did not always accept, as she was getting rather tired of the war and did not want to listen to bracing speeches!

> **London County Council**
>
> Department and address to which replies should be sent:
> Education Officer's Department,
> The County Hall,
> Westminster Bridge, S.E.1
>
> Telephone: WATerloo 5000 Extension: 6260.
>
> IMPORTANT In any reply please quote N/C.
>
> 10 JUL 1944
>
> Dear Madam,
>
> <u>Evacuation - London Clothing Scheme - Joan Prince - N.C.23407.</u>
>
> With reference to the request for clothing submitted for Joan Prince, I regret that petticoats are not supplied under the London Clothing Scheme. I understand that the shoes and raincoat ordered at the same time as the petticoat have already been supplied by the W.V.S.
>
> Yours faithfully,
>
> E. G. Savage
> Education Officer
>
> Mrs. D. Mallums,
> Gwent Cottage,
> Caerleon,
> Monmouth.

Part of Mrs Hallums' job as Welfare Officer was to help girls with clothing – not always easy!

She had one brother in the RAF, one in the Royal Navy and one in the London Police, and her sister who lived in London was bombed out, so she had them to worry about as well as Dad and her home in Rochester.

We spent our evenings doing homework, knitting, sewing, mending and writing letters to Dad. Food rationing was now very strict and we tried various experiments to make the food more interesting, sometimes with the aid of Ministry of Food leaflets. Peppermint creams, using dried milk powder were the biggest success. Chocolate spread, using cocoa and mashed potato as the main ingredients, was not so popular! The items Joyce and I made at cookery lessons were a welcome addition to our diet. I still remember some of the very tasty lentil soup, carried home in a jug with great difficulty. There was not much fruit, apart from the home-grown sort. The occasional shipment of bananas that got through was reserved for holders of green ration books (the under-fours). We also longed for a boiled egg instead of the dried variety.

One sunny day we saw hundreds of aeroplanes high in the sky, presumably American planes going on one of their daylight bombing raids. The local children soon got to know that the GIs in the convoys that went through Caerleon had sweets to spare and would shout, 'Got any gum chum?', and were usually rewarded. The Dover girls were forbidden to do this, of course!

On the 6th June, 1944, Joyce and I went to school as usual, unaware that it was D-Day, as we had not heard the news on the radio. Our excited friends told us the news, hoping they would soon be able to return to Dover. We wondered what we would do, as we were due to take our General School Certificate examinations the following summer. It was decided that it would be safe for the school to return home in December 1944. A friend offered that we could stay with her in Dover until we left school, but Mum and Dad decided that we had all been away from home for too long, and that we should return to Rochester. Arrangements were made for Joyce and me to be admitted to Rochester Grammar School for our last two terms.

We left our Dover friends and Auntie Jay in December 1944 and returned home at last, after four and half years in Wales. We

Joyce and Mildred Hallums with their mother in Rogerstone in 1944

were sorry to leave our friends and Auntie Jay who had been so kind to us. While in Caerleon we had attended St Cadoc's Church where Joyce and I had been confirmed the day after our 14th birthday. We had happy memories of both 'Rogie' and Caerleon, and had made lifelong friends. We corresponded with Auntie Rose and Auntie Jay, and managed several visits back to Wales until they died many years later.

The first night after our return to Rochester we were woken by one of the last doodlebugs passing overhead and, luckily for us, it kept going! Joyce and I settled in well at Rochester Grammar and took our School Cert (successfully) in due course.

I don't think that Joyce and I fully appreciated the sacrifices that Mum and Dad made for us during the war, until some years afterwards. It was good to be home again and Mum enjoyed spending her hard earned savings in helping to refurnish and renovate our home. Fortunately, all Mum's brothers survived the war, as did the rest of our family, but it is very sad to relate that Mum died in 1952, just when life was getting easier for her.

Joyce Hallums *(now Mrs Joyce Balcombe), Mildred Hallums' twin sister, adds her recollections of their evacuation days:*

My maternal grandmother played a great part in the final decision as to where Mildred and I were to be evacuated to. Grandmother had a sister living in Rogerstone, near Newport in Monmouthshire. She in turn had a nearby friend who could accommodate a mother and two children. This is how, on the 6th June, 1940, Mrs Sullivan, of 100 The Uplands, Rogerstone, entered our lives. Having never left the Medway Towns before in our young lives, the long train journey to South Wales seemed like a huge adventure! Originally we thought that we would only be away for a few weeks until the 'crisis' passed. Those weeks stretched into four and a half long years! Mr and Mrs Sullivan soon became our good friends, and we called them Auntie Rose and Uncle Bill. They had two sons, John the youngest who was serving in the army, and the elder son Brian, who was also a soldier.

In due course Mildred and I sat and passed the scholarship for the local county school at Bassaleg, but the Kent Education Committee refused us admission to a Monmouthshire County School. Instead, we had the choice of two Kent schools – Rochester Grammar School, which had been evacuated to Porthcawl, or Dover County School at Caerleon. As Caerleon was just a few miles away, we opted to go to the Dover School. We managed, through a friend of Auntie Rose, to obtain accommodation with Miss Jay at Gwent Cottage in Caerleon, and started at our new school in December, 1941.

We didn't have any specific buildings for our school, instead classes were held in numerous rendezvous throughout the village. We used Caerleon School, the training college and various church halls. We had no permanent school room or desk so all books had to be carried to and fro. In addition to our books, we also had to carry our 'house shoes' and gym clothes. When we had cookery or needlework, we had even more to carry! To make matters worse, it always seemed to be raining in Caerleon! Still, we coped with all these adversities quite cheerfully.

During the school holidays, the highlight was a trip into Newport, to the cinema. I remember seeing such films as *Fantasia* and *You're In The Army Mr Jones*. I also experienced my first symphony concert and saw Moira Lympany with the London Symphony Orchestra. But best of all was when our father joined us for a week during the summer holidays, when we would go out visiting places. Travelling at that time was quite an adventure, because place names had been removed for security reasons.

We didn't entirely escape the air raids, being on the flightpath to Cardiff and Swansea. On moonlit nights back in Rogerstone, we had to endure the 'smoke screen' – just like smoky paraffin heaters and just as smelly. They were used to obscure the aluminium works in Rogerstone.

We returned home to Rochester in December 1944, but we never forgot Auntie Rose in Rogerstone. We went back to see her in 1959 and later in 1973, to introduce her to our two daughters. Auntie Rose never missed a birthday or a Christmas greeting. We kept in touch with her until her death at the age of 82.

Molly Batey (now Mrs M. Hurford-Jones) had already experienced her first evacuation. Now she was on the move for the second time:

In May 1940, at the time of Dunkirk, the threat of invasion as well as air-raids led to a further evacuation. My school, Chatham County School for Girls, went to Pontypridd in South Wales, but I, for reasons known only to my parents, was sent to relations in Plymouth.

What a beautiful summer it was; long hot days swimming and playing on the Hoe after school – until Plymouth started to experience bad air raids. I was moved on yet again and was definitely not enjoying my school life. Three weeks after I left, my aunt's house had a direct hit. Luckily, they were all down in the air-raid shelter. One of the few things saved from the ruin was my Holy Bible that I still have, covered in water stains from the hoses used to put out the fire.

This time I went with my mother to Maesycwmmer in the Rhymney Valley of South Wales where I had yet more relations – and a much quieter life! Eventually my father joined us and we moved to Barry, where I'm glad to say 'my caravan rested', so I thought, until 2nd January 1941, a date etched in my memory because, after avoiding heavy air raids for many months, this was the day Hitler's bombers caught up with me. My aunt, who was an infant teacher, had also been evacuated with her school, Barnsole Road School, Gillingham, to South Wales. She set off to visit my parents and myself in Barry, but unfortunately picked up the wrong suitcase from the bus in which she was travelling. It belonged to someone in Caerphilly. My mother, my aunt and myself decided to return the suitcase to its owner. We set out from Barry to Cardiff after lunch, thence to Caerphilly. By this time it was getting dusk and snowing. We arrived at the address, exchanged suitcases, but on our return by bus to Cardiff, were appalled to discover we were being taken into the city in the middle of a heavy air raid. There was a red glow over Cardiff that could be seen for miles.

We headed for an air-raid shelter as soon as the bus stopped at the City Hall, stayed for a few hours, then made our way to Cardiff Castle where there were more shelters within the castle walls. Eventually, when the all-clear sounded, we reached the bus stop for Barry. We arrived home in a fleet of buses that had been sent out to pick up people stranded by the air raid, to be received by my frantic father at two o'clock in the morning. All this and I was still only 11 years old! Fortunately, we decided to stay in Barry where I eventually met my future husband.

The Medway Queen *is one of the few ships remaining which took part in the evacuation of school children from Gravesend during 1939 (see next chapter). This fine drawing was produced by K. C. Lockwood of the Medway Queen Preservation Society*

Chapter Seven

GRAVESEND TO WHERE?

At the outbreak of the war some Kent evacuees left for safer areas by ship. Those from Gravesend, for instance, left in convoy as reported in the following newspaper article which appeared in the Gravesend and Dartford Reporter *for 9th September 1939:*

What a thrill for the kiddies as they clambered up the gangway and on to the waiting *Royal Daffodil*. Some explored and some searched the shore for any signs of 'Mum' or 'Dad'. All available space on the roads and banks was lined with sad-eyed parents, ready to wave goodbye to those who might be leaving them for a few days or, on the other hand, a few months or years. Handkerchiefs fluttered afloat and ashore. The trampling of feet went on as more parties arrived and marched to the pier-head.

The pilot jack was hoisted aloft and, shortly after, amid cheers from the children and the waving of hands ashore, the cream and white vessel slid away. Beside me, on a grassy bank in Clifton Marine Parade, women dabbed at their eyes with their handkerchiefs and then, as the ship turned and went downstream, hurried away to hide their emotion.

Other parents took their places and a second ship came alongside and took on a complement of schoolchildren, torn from the happy surroundings, comfort and security of home by the greed for power of one man. In turn, the *Golden Eagle*, *Queen of the Channel*, *Royal Sovereign* and *Medway Queen* embarked with their passengers and departed. Everything went off perfectly and the greatest praise is due to the helpers and marshals controlling the movements of the 3,694 persons from Gravesend who were evacuated in three hours. The children were seen off by the mayor (Councillor Walter C. Fletcher, JP) and several members of the corporation.

The sun shone and the river was calm. Conditions were very good. Aboard the ships every member of the crews, from the captains to the cabin boys, did all they could to make the children and the others comfortable. They distributed chocolates and fruit and soon nearly every child was munching at something; and thereby hangs a tale, for out in the open sea with a following wind, the scene changed and many a little tummy revolted at the combination of lots of sweets and chocolates and the dip and roll of the fast moving craft!

Messages were received on the boats that war was declared between Germany and England but this was kept from the evacuees. At Southend a few minutes later there appeared from out of the mist the grey-clad hulls of British warships, which escorted the convoy the rest of the way. The first boat disembarked at Lowestoft and the remainder at Great Yarmouth. Buses, vans and cars were waiting and the children, women and luggage were soon off the ships and were proceeding to the distribution centres, where they remained for the night. Hotels, cinemas and other large buildings were utilised. Many mothers and children spent the night in the buildings at Yarmouth Racecourse.

'As soon as we got there hundreds of helpers appeared as if by magic,' one helper told me at Gravesend on Wednesday. 'They were all kindness itself and did all they possibly could. They got little baths and hot water for the babies and collapsible chairs were put up on the grass; mothers sat there in the warm sunshine. Older children did not take long to sample the sea bathing.'

Gravesend children aboard the Golden Eagle *as they left for 'somewhere in England'*

On Monday the process of finding billets for the children and mothers commenced. They were transported to towns and villages inland. Some were fortunate enough to find billets on farms. Others were in large country houses and in all sorts of dwellings down to the humblest cottage. Everywhere children and mothers were treated by the East Anglian people in the same way as members of the family.

Phillip Connolly *was one of those schoolchildren evacuated by ship from Gravesend in 1939:*

We assembled at West Court School at 6.35am and then were probably bussed to West Street Pier, Gravesend about two miles away. The day was quite bright as we boarded the ship to the tune of *South of the Border, down Mexico Way* – which I still hate to this day! There were lots of apples and milk in cardboard cups and it wasn't very long before most of the children on board were sick. Going downstream I saw a submarine on the port side and later, a couple of grey ships, possibly destroyers on the starboard side, moving in time with us.

My next memory is of Great Yarmouth and sleeping in what appeared to be a massive hall with an arched ceiling. I think it was the town hall and we were on the floor lying on palliasses. We were awakened in the early hours by the sound of the air-raid warning. After that, the journey to Matlask, five miles south of Sheringham, I cannot remember at all. There, I was billeted with my sister Kathleen with a Mr Shepherd who drove a white van for a Norwich laundry service. He kept pigs which we used to feed twice a day in a sty up the road. I can remember watching the blacksmith shoeing the horses and I used to ride a large grey horse when it was moving cartloads of sugarbeet from the fields.

I didn't like washing in the cold water from the rain water butt, especially in the winter! The drinking and cooking water came from a well in the cobbled yard. There didn't appear to be any electricity in the cottage and it smelt of paraffin, candles and those country smells like fruit. Every time I come across such a smell today, I am immediately transported back to that cottage.

On a couple of occasions I went rabbiting with the local men and boys in what appeared to be a large park close to Matlask. After we had passed through a set of large gates there were several large chestnut trees and the men and boys would use ferrets to bring the rabbits out of the holes.

The men of the village actually built an air-raid shelter. They dug a very large hole down a small track off the main road which they lined with six inch tree trunks. Then they roofed it over with similar tree trunks to support galvanised iron, which was then covered with a thick layer of earth. At about the same time an airfield was being built nearby. I can visualise a large steam-driven machine which had at the front a rotating plate with legs attached to it resembling a table. When it progressed down a hedgerow, the whole hedge was literally torn out by the roots and thrown to one side by this rotating table. This to a boy of my tender years was quite an impressive sight and is implanted in my mind even to this day.

One of my Saturday jobs was to take the two volt accumulators, used in the wireless set, down to the local garage for recharging. Just about all the homes in the village availed themselves of this service, the charge for which was twopence.

The Medway Queen, *reproduced by kind permission of the Medway Queen Preservation Society. Apart from the important role of transporting Gravesend children to East Anglia during 1939, the ship earned herself the title of 'Heroine of Dunkirk' saving 7,000 troops from the beaches in 1940*

We returned with our mother to Gravesend by train just before Easter 1940. On the Southern Region section, between London and Gravesend, I noticed the gun emplacements and barrage balloons at Abbey Wood, in the old abbey there. Later we called in at Woolworth's, which was still open at 7.30 in the evening, and Mum bought us some Easter eggs, one of which was in a milk jug which I kept intact for at least thirty years! This was in spite of being re-evacuated within two months to Dartington Hall in Devon, but that is another story.

The following are extracts from a letter written by an anonymous schoolteacher just after having helped two parties evacuate from Gravesend in 1939:

We had no idea where we were going – all we knew was that we were to be at school at 5am on Sunday, 3rd September, carrying our luggage and with enough food for two days. We also knew that we were to be prepared for a sea journey. Altogether we had a party of 165 children and were being evacuated with some 8,500 other boys and girls, both secondary and elementary, from Gravesend.

We were marched down to the pier escorted by the local police (a distance of a mile

Paddle Steamer Golden Eagle, *built in 1909 and used in 1914 ferrying troops to and from France. The ship was also used in September 1939 to take evacuees from Gravesend to East Anglia and in 1940 she saved 1751 men from the beaches of Dunkirk. (Reproduced by kind permission of Leander Postcards.)*

which was far too long for some of the younger brothers and sisters who were almost as small as their packs) and embarked at 7am upon the *Royal Daffodil* – a very nice pleasure steamer. There were 1200 of us on board – ours was the first of seven boats to sail. It was a glorious day and we set off gaily down the Thames amid greeting sirens from other boats and wavings from the shore. The children were in great spirits and the crew of the *Royal Daffodil* were splendid. Once we were in the North Sea we were intrigued to see that we were being escorted by destroyers – they lay in line between us and the east – it was most reassuring to see them. Unfortunately there was a nasty swell and one by one the kids were seasick. They had been provided with special bags so, on the whole, it wasn't too messy. I should say that 80% were ill – but when you hear that we were on the water seven hours you will not be surprised.

The first officer would not tell us any news so we disembarked blissfully at Lowestoft not knowing that we were at war – we were soon informed by the people on the pier. The swell was so bad off Lowestoft that it was thought we could not be brought in – however we were, but the other six ships had to go to Great Yarmouth.

On our way from the boat to the bus we were regaled with drinks which we took off trays as we went along. I must say that everyone we met was most kind. We were packed into buses and taken to the Odeon Cinema, a very nice modern cinema. Here, the 1,200 of us, were shown into the rows by the manager who directed us from a microphone. We were then informed that we should be spending the night there. We had refreshments (apples, bread, milk) which were passed along most efficiently, and then took the children on to the beach. It was a most glorious day and they all paddled and at least got their feet clean. We then trooped back and had a cinema show. The main film was Deanna Durbin in *Three Smart Girls Grow Up*.

Settling the place down for the night was priceless. We undressed all the eight year olds and under and they slept in the foyer outside the balcony. All those aged 8 – 11 slept on the stage. Most of the boys burrowed into straw in the foyer downstairs and the rest of us lay down in the gangways or sat in the seats. (I must say that the masters settled down right away and fell asleep and snored nearly all night.) It was almost midnight before we got the children settled – they were so excited and we had to keep confiscating electric torches etc.

At last everyone seemed to be asleep when, at 2.50am the siren went. It was a horrid moment – 1,200 children in a cinema on the east coast and the first night of the war. The children were superb throughout. We never heard a grumble or expression of fear, let alone a tear. Most of them woke up, but we just told them to lie down again and go to sleep, which they did like lambs.

The next day we spent on the beach – it was glorious. We expected to be moved but were told we should have to stay for another night (the chief discomfort was that there were only four lavatories and two wash-basins for the girls and presumably the same for the boys – and there were roughly 500 to 600 of each). We went out and had a wash in the town. I cannot emphasise enough how kind everyone was, especially the members of the Women's Voluntary Service and the manager of the cinema who did not take his clothes off for two days and two nights. One of the members of the W.V.S. was so anxious about us, when she heard the air raid warning, that she got up and came to the cinema at 3am to see if she could help.

Anyhow, we were taken away by bus on the Tuesday morning at 10am, having been on the go since Sunday at 4am. We were taken inland to Diss, a dear little market town. It seemed a haven of peace. After a brief week, eight of us were recalled to evacuate a second party. We had been fed up, but not now as we have landed in a very nice spot. We are sharing the high school and also have a house.

The following account is reproduced from the book Children in Retreat *by kind permission of the author, Joy Richardson, and the publishers, Sawd Publications:*

For **John Hopperton** of Gravesend, his evacuation started out happily, but soon deteriorated.

My three brothers and I were evacuated to Norfolk, on the *Medway Queen*. It was nice there and a lovely man and lady met us at Cromer. Initially we all slept in the church hall on straw sacks. But in December, after three months in Norfolk, we had to leave for Cheadle, Staffordshire.

We really suffered there. Both at school, and the house we stayed in, the three 'S's' were more in evidence than the three 'R's'. These were strap, stick and slipper! The second day there it all started. I had kicked a tennis ball with a local lad. He (not I) kicked the ball into the headmaster's garden. I was blamed for this misdemeanour, not him. To add insult to (eventual) injury, I had to get the stick from the headmaster's study. It came from the cupboard covered in cobwebs. He said it was the first time he had used it in four years. He laid it on hard, twice on each hand. I was only seven years old.

My brothers and I found everybody was 'strap happy' wherever we went. It was almost as though they wanted to punish us for going there.

We were shoved around, and from the Midlands to Scotland, all seemed strap-happy. There was a particular man and lady whom we stayed with who were brutal. The strap was four inches wide, with a brass buckle. We had had a three hour journey. For dinner, they gave us six chips and an egg. Like Oliver Twist, I asked for more. The lady replied, 'More of my husband's strap, or slipper, more like!'

In the school in Cheadle they wrote, 'Why don't you go home, you southern pigs!' We wanted to, but there was no way of getting there.

We had gone in 1939. Eventually, we returned home in July 1942. My dad had been a prisoner of war. When he came home he weighed just 6st. 4lb., and had contracted tuberculosis. By comparison, I suppose we were lucky. But we still bear the scars.

My brother goes back periodically. He cannot forget that nearly every day he was strapped by the headmaster. In 1979, he saw an article in a daily newspaper about a school in Blackpool where evacuees has been sent. The placard said, 'DON'T STRAP ME, SIR.' My brother was convinced that the headmaster of that school was the same one we had had in Cheadle. Time passes, but you never forget!

Brenda Gilbert *(now Mrs Brenda Franklin), although evacuated from Essex, has many similarities in her evacuation as those children from Gravesend – and she has other tenuous links with Kent:*

I was evacuated with my mother and my older brother Alfred from Tilbury to Yarmouth by boat on 2nd September 1939. I think the boat we travelled on was a paddle steamer called the *Golden Eagle*. I was just six years of age. After reaching Yarmouth we travelled across country, staying for short periods at Muddesley-on-Sea, Holt and Erpingham until we eventually reached Cheadle in Staffordshire. My mother was put in charge of a children's reception centre where children with various ailments, enuresis, impetigo, scabies and lice, were brought to be healed before being sent on to other billets.

When my brother reached the age of fourteen, my mother took him back home to put him into an apprenticeship – leaving me behind! By this time I was living in Leek. I loved it there. I first went to live with a mother who had three daughters and a son. All of us girls slept together in one bed. The boy, Graham, had a bedroom to himself. Although I didn't know it at the time, the foster mother was divorced – shameful in those days!

I don't know why, but I changed billets several times. The last place was a typical two up, two down mill house, with no electricity. We went to bed with candles. The 'privy' which we had to share with another family was across a cobbled yard.

Food in Staffordshire made a big impression on me. I had never had home-made bread before and several of the regional specialities I found quite delicious, such as potted meats, black pudding and Staffordshire oatcakes.

I distinctly remember some children coming to Staffordshire who had been living in the railway tunnels between Dumpton Park and Ramsgate in Kent. I think it must have been 1940 when they came to Cheadle. Many of these Thanet evacuees were placed in the local 'Cottage Homes'. The only Thanet evacuee I can remember is a girl who came from Ramsgate whose name was Mary Hanrahan. Her parents visited her quite regularly – and always by car.

I stayed in Staffordshire until I returned home in 1945. I have often thought of those happy years I spent as an evacuee, but I have never had the opportunity to return. My late husband, Kenneth Franklin, on the other hand, came from Rochester and was first evacuated in 1939, with his two sisters, to Tankerton in Kent, but returned to Rochester before being re-evacuated with the whole of Sir Joseph Williamson's Mathematical School to Porthcawl in South Wales. I recall him saying that he was not happy there. We went to Porthcawl a few years ago and my husband was surprised at how little the place had changed. We did not visit the address where he had stayed as an evacuee.

*   *   *

The second evacuation of Gravesend school children under the Government Evacuation Scheme was to be to South Devon, although some went to Windsor in Berkshire. On Monday, 10th June 1940, the town clerk of Gravesend announced that the 924 school children that had been registered for evacuation would be evacuated under the Greater London Scheme, Plan IV. (This called for large scale evacuation to be carried out over a longer period, only when heavy bombing became serious, and not including mothers with young children.)

The evacuation would spread over three days:

        Friday 14th June –   199 to Windsor, Berks.
                                  306 to Totnes and Buckfastleigh, Devon.

        Westcourt and Whitehall Schools to Totnes.
        Northcourt and Denton Schools to Buckfastleigh.

Sunday 16th June –   166 to Newton Abbot, Devon.
(Three secondary schools)

Tuesday 18th June –   253 to Newton Abbot, Devon.

In addition to the above figures, 300 children from Northfleet were also to be sent to Newton Abbot on 17th June 1940.

Iris Smith *was one of the evacuees who went from Gravesend to South Devon, and she recalls her own experiences of her time there:*

I remember little of the actual departure and journey to Devon in 1940; my first memories are those of waiting in the village hall at Dartington where we were to learn the meaning of the word 'billeted'. I was lucky to be chosen, along with the Bushell twins, by the lady who lived in Hood Manor, a tiny hamlet a couple of miles from Dartington Village. We were taken off to the manor which was along a tree-lined drive. It was a grand house, with an enormous pond at the front and terraced lawns at the rear of the house.

We were told we must call Mr and Mrs Holder, the owners, Sir and Madam; we were then handed over to the housekeeper and were taken to our room. I think at the time I was more taken up with the pond and the fish it contained than anything else. Life at Hood was very pleasant and I made friends with the daughter of the farmer who rented Hood Barton, the adjoining farm.

I remember the great freedom we had, roaming the fields and copses, walking for miles and miles. Some of the hair-raising games we played on the farm would have horrified my mother had she known about them. They ranged from clambering over rafters in the high barns which contained the threshers and other farm implements which could have been lethal had we fallen on them, hiding in the corn bins and jumping off hayricks. We also played down by the salmon pool in the River Dart, swam like fish in the deep water and crossed the weir which could be running quite fast at certain times of the year.

When I think of the River Dart which wound its way through Dartington, I always think of good and bad, the wonderful daffodils which lined the banks of the river and which always brought to mind Wordsworth's immortal poem. On the other side, the Dart took many lives and earned its reputation of 'Every year the Dart claims a heart'; even one of our own evacuee boys was drowned in that river.

I always remember being so hungry in Devon, it was probably due to all the walking I had to do to go to school, even though we were very well fed. Joan Coaker, the farmer's daughter, and I would gather wild strawberries along the railway track then return to the manor's dairy where we scooped great spoonfuls of cream from the large pans to eat with the strawberries. We also found delight in eating primrose heads, sorrel and lots of other wild flowers and herbs (how we never made a fatal mistake I don't know). Another favourite of mine was cow cake. An old school friend of mine,

Janet Corstorphine from Surrey who was evacuated to Buckfastleigh, never lets me forget to this day how when she used to come to tea at Hood Manor we would all have those lovely strawberry and other home-made jams with lashings of cream after which I would take her to the barn where we consumed cow cake and did handstands on the tiered lawns.

One of my vivid memories was peeping in the wardrobes of Mrs Holder's daughters: there were racks of beautiful ball gowns and grand clothes. I used to think it was like something out of the films I liked to go to at that time. Mrs Holder had two daughters and two sons who were all away in the forces.

Despite the fun and freedom I had there, I was allocated my 'jobs' which included a lot of housework! This probably stood me in good stead as I consider I am a pretty good housewife today!

I remember having to go to church at Dartington two or three times a day on Sundays. Here I was confirmed by the Bishop of Exeter and how proud we were.

Dartington Hall was a delightful spot with magnificent gardens. I still go back to see the 'Twelve Apostles' – handsome conifers which lined the walkway. Apart from the evacuees there were hundreds of American soldiers at Dartington; they were very kind to us children giving us chocolate and gum. It was at this time my mother left Gravesend to come down to Dartington as a housemother to the children there. On reflection I feel the trauma of war and what it involved was worse for her than me. She had been widowed a few years and, having only returned from army life in India just prior to that, to have her little daughter go away and then having to take on the work which was involved, which I understand now was quite intensive, could not have been easy. She had two very bad bouts of pneumonia while at Dartington which left her with a bronchitic chest for the rest of her life. However, she was very fond of her 'boys' and made close friends of Miss King and Miss Jefferson, two of the teachers who were evacuated with us.

Some of the London women used her as a confidante in connection with some of the situations which arose with the American lads! I believe she was a good shoulder to cry on and the women all nicknamed her 'Pru' for Prudence! I remember the strange feeling when the lads all left for what must have been the D-Day landings. Many, many were killed and they must have been very young.

It was at Dartington Hall I began my appreciation of good music; we used to sing while being conducted by the great Gustav Holst's daughter, Imogen. And after I had gone to the Grammar School for Girls at Totnes we had many grand concerts there with Imogen, Leon Goossens, the famous oboe player, and Eric Starling who was often on BBC radio. Imogen would bounce along the road like a ballet dancer humming to herself and, I guess, composing as she went along.

There were lots of 'characters' at Dartington. One of the best I remember was Rex, a mongrel dog, who would regularly jump on the bus from Dartington to Totnes and take himself back when he had had enough of the town. He was adored by us children who treated him as 'one of us'.

The famous Foxhole School was near to Dartington. I never knew very much about this but I remember we all talked in hushed tones about the boys who went swimming in the nude there.

The war was to touch us in several ways while there. I remember one day while at school in Totnes we were machine-gunned by a German fighterplane. We all shot under our desks and I remember how terrified were the girls who had come from Plymouth as they had been through the blitz there when Plymouth was virtually razed to the ground. For myself I felt outraged that they had the temerity to machine gun the bicycle shed where my brand new utility bicycle stood – this I still have today and ride it quite regularly. The German of course had mistaken us for a military establishment.

A young airman was killed at Totnes Station when coming home on leave; this was about the only fatality of this kind there I believe. Whether it was a bomb or a bullet I cannot remember, but we were all so sad.

I remember the day I went for the entrance examination at Totnes Girls' School where I met a girl called Marian Rice and we became firm friends. When we finished and went outside strangely enough our mothers had met each other and we all went off together. Marian has remained one of my oldest, dearest friends and I spent a lot of the school holidays with her and her mother at the village shop in Ugborough.

Although there was much freedom in the early days in Devon, once I started school in Totnes the discipline was much in evidence, but again I think this has stood me in good stead in later life. All in all the girls were well behaved and the naughtiest thing we ever did was to crawl through the hedge in the lunch break to meet the boys from King Edward VI Grammar School, or eat ice cream in the street, for which we were strongly reprimanded. During my whole time there I think we had but one scandal when one of the girls in the Upper Fifth was expelled because she was pregnant. This caused quite a bit of excitement in those days.

How I ever got any exams passed I cannot imagine, for looking at a diary of those years I see I went dancing regularly and to the pictures even more regularly, not to mention the fairs, rugby matches and other events which seem to happen at an alarming pace.

A lot of my friends go back to those years when we were all so young. I consider them my jewels for there is nothing so wonderful as a good friend of long standing. Some married farmers, so I enjoy the annual visit to them. Life has changed a lot for the Devon folk in so many ways for they have a great influx of South East folk today, not necessarilly ex-evacuees. When we were there, holidays were few and far between and to some folk there we might well have come from Mars. I know some children were not as happy as I was. The Bushell girls went home quite soon after we arrived. Being evacuated was not for them.

At school we were prepared for the possibility of 'doing our bit' and I and others enrolled in the Girls' Training Corps. Miss Raffan, our French mistress, was our officer and we learnt to shoot and do things we might need to do in the forces. The war ended before I reached that stage, but many of our girls went on to join one of the women's forces and many became officers. My ambition was to be a WREN, but that was not to be.

Of course, Victory Night in Totnes was quite something. We danced and sang and thoroughly enjoyed ourselves. I often return to Totnes and remember that night in the square. Despite the war and all it involved, they were happy days in so many ways, a different way of life where we children had to make our own fun and there was no television to distract us.

I was lucky to return home eventually, complete with bicycle! My three older brothers all returned from the army, navy and air force respectively. I always remember getting those funny little aerogrammes from them covered with blue pencil by the censor.

Although there were lots of lovely Devon lads I came home to Gravesend and eventually married a Gravesend boy, David Solly, and we have been together ever since. There is really no place like home!

The following contrasting account is given by **Margaret Stevens**, *who was an evacuee LCC teacher at Dartington from 14th June 1940 to August 1945:*

For the second time in nine months, a large group of Southwark mothers with grim faces and stiff upper lips, bade their children goodbye knowing, in contrast to the first evacuation the previous September, the destination to which their children were going. The fall of Belgium and France made the atmosphere an urgent one, that we really were in danger this time after the phoney war and there was every evidence around us of the serious situation. This was especially so as we arrived at Waterloo Station at 8am to board the special train which had come from Gravesend, the children with an age range of 3 to 11 years having walked there from Friar Street School, a thirty minute walk, wearing a name label in their coat lapels, entrusted to the care of their teachers and a few voluntary helpers.

We were met at Totnes Station by Roger Morel, the Billeting Officer, who gave us the choice of being billeted in Totnes homes or together in the Ballet Jooss Dance School. Miss Hunter, our headmistress, conferred with us and our unanimous decision was to remain together in view of the experience of our first evacuation.

On our arrival at Dartington Hall, tired and hungry, we drew strength from the fact that we were at least together and given the quarters of the Ballet Jooss School – most of whom had been interned. Palliasses on the floor and a salad meal greeted us, impressing the teachers, but causing many tears to the children. There are none so conservative as children and especially from deprived areas, as we were to learn. The salad for the most part remained untouched. Such food was unknown to

Margaret Stevens' photo shows her and Jenny Gertz with some of the older children in the courtyard of Dartington Hall in 1940

them and a bed was the most urgent wish. The parents had been given a list of suitable clothing including night attire in preparation for the evacuation. It was with some difficulty, but nevertheless implicit obedience by the children that day and night clothes were exchanged and seemingly the children were soon fast asleep.

From the Jooss Ballet School the teachers were then escorted by K. Hall-Brown (HB) and Mrs Helen Elmhirst to our rooms in the East Wing and to a meal in the White Hart. Although so very exhausted, and by now it was dark, we felt we had come to another planet – the total quiet, the slower pace and total lack of evidence of war was bewildering. Looking up at the moon through the pine tree by the Arts Department and the very beautiful courtyard was truly overwhelming and, although so thankful for the sanctuary, nevertheless we had a sense of guilt in remembering those we had left behind.

But the thought of the children soon snapped us back to reality and with torches we went back to our charges to discover the neatly folded clothes by each pillow had disappeared. Turning back a few covers, we found they had been put on again over the nightclothes. Later we were to learn, 'Tain't decent, miss, to go to bed without clofes on!'

Snatching a few hours sleep, the many problems of adaptation to our new life had to be tackled. For several weeks the great urns of porridge, potatoes and other vegetables, cooked by Miss Hardwick in the White Hart kitchen, had to be carried across the lawns from the kitchen to the school. Once again walking the country lanes, as in the first evacuation, was the main source of our education, for we were without any kind of teaching equipment and, mercifully, the weather befriended us.

During the initial period there was little contact with the courtyard residents. We were so busy, hardly taking time to eat in the White Hart and never indulging in coffee in the Solar. We were bewildered with so much to do and, although teaching in state schools meant being responsible for 48 children in a class, we now looked after their well-being for 24 hours each day, a responsibility *in loco parentis* which seemed to horrify those who were used to the luxury and educational advantage of small classes. The average size of classes at Dartington Hall School was ten to twelve.

It was obvious that we were shy of the specialist exponents of the arts and that they were also going through a traumatic experience of having as their immediate neighbours this large number of people from what is known today as the Educational Priority Areas. There seemed no common ground between us but, over the five years of evacuation from 14th June 1940 until 29 June 1945, great changes were wrought by people and circumstances.

In June 1940, one of the most thrilling early sounds for me while ambling past the junior school to the River Dart late one evening, was the sound of a cello – obviously not being played by a pupil. Later we learnt it was the late Muriel Taylor, a member of the Dartington Hall String Quartet. We looked longingly at the building and its amenities, never dreaming that one day it would be ours for the duration.

The far-seeing British army major, whose troops were billeted in the junior school, suggested that it would be of greater educational satisfaction if the troops and we were to change accommodation. Consultations between the Board of Education, the Local Education Authorities and the Arts Department took place and thus was born the first and only all age State Residential School. The children were two to a room in the

Margaret Stevens' photo of the boot-mending class in Dartington with Mr Jackson in charge in 1941

boarding houses and dormitories were made on the first floor of the main building. Our three and four year old children were given accommodation in the nursery wing of the private apartments by Dorothy Elmhirst, to whom we already owed so much.

By Christmas 1940 the initial problems were beginning to get under way and there was more time for some relaxation and to begin to settle into this new experience of a residential school for which we were totally responsible both educationally and domestically, set in this very beautiful setting. None of us had ever experienced or received any sort of training for this new way of life.

Tragedy soon struck. Availing ourselves of the opportunity to teach the children to swim we roped off a suitable area of the River Dart. The children were delighted in this, but in June 1941 Dennis Morgan aged 8 was drowned. He was an evacuee from Gravesend, an orphan, his grandparents being his guardians. He lies buried in Dartington churchyard.

With the intensity of the war growing, we had been joined by more evacuees from London, Plymouth and other areas. To the late Dorothy Elmhirst so much is owed for the use of the junior school or Evacuation Hostel as it was then known, which became part of the life of Dartington. Her interest in the children, their welfare and discussion of the problems was of paramount importance. So often she dined with those of us who remained in residence in the courtyard, plying us with questions, inviting us to evening coffee, where we met such people as Margot Fonteyn and Robert Helpmann in their early careers.

Imogen Holst was another welder of the evacuees into the community, organising the first children's Christmas carol concert in the Great Hall, bringing together through music the children from Dartington Hall School, the village school and ourselves. Her students were often to be found working with our children. Other notable people who brought their special talents and experience to our community included Jenny Gertz who, on returning from internment and although convalescing, introduced Laban Movement to some of the staff and worked with the children in the open air theatre; Winsome Bartlett who introduced country dancing with her pipe and tabor and George Bennett who entertained us with films.

Some of the boys who began to show an interest in agriculture were given opportunities to assist on local farms at weekends and in the holidays. These and other extra curricular opportunities gave unique experiences to the children and, despite very little equipment, they were given a wider education than most war time evacuees received.

If tears were the measurement of what degree of happiness and security had meant to the children in five years of evacuation, then the amount was immeasurable on the day of departure. Of the extent of the quality of life they had been given no one will ever know, except by realising the tremendous depth of influence Dartington gave to us, the then young teachers. Perhaps the fact that there are today a few men and women living and working in and around Dartington and Totnes who were once those evacuees is an indication of what those halcyon days in the midst of terrible war gave. Dartington was to leave its indelible mark upon all of us.

The following lists (which are not complete) are some of the teachers and evacuees from Gravesend who were sent to Dartington Hall in 1940:

Teachers:
Miss Jefferson (Whitehill School, Gravesend)
Miss King (Westcourt School, Gravesend)
Miss M. A. Mills (Westcourt School, Gravesend)
Miss L. W. Preston (Whitehill School, Gravesend)

Evacuees:
D. Adams, Horace Austin, Pearl Austin, Barbara Austin, Ronald Bardoe, Nin Bardoe, Ken Bardoe, Tom Bardoe, Derek Blackman, Sylvia Blackman, Henry Bradford, Gwen Bradford, Cathleen Bradford, Stan Brown, Gordon BrownMaurice Brown, Michael Brown, George Brooker, Joy Brooker, Betty Bushell, Olive Bushell, Fred Cherry, Godfrey Cherry, Dennis Cherry, Alex Cherry, Ida Colman, Edith Colman, Phillip Connolly, Kathleen Connolly, Kathleen Day, Ted Day, Doreen Day, Margaret Dodds, Joan Eastman, Jenny Finch, Kathleen Finch, Laurence Flurry, Norman Flurry, Violet House, Lionel House, Percy House, Zoe Kennedy, Ken Knowles, Peggy Knowles, Lesley Knowles, Peggy Loft, Lily Loft, Jack Loft, Danny Ludlow, Edith Manktelow, Morris Manktelow, John Martin, Dennis Morgan, Tony Nash, Christine Pearson, Peter Rayfield, Alice Shovelar, Iris Smith, Donald Smith, Alan Smith, Richard Steptoe, Shirley Steptoe, Arthur Stoddart, Bob Stoddart, Bill Whittaker, Doris Whittaker, Joyce Whittaker, Barbara White, Audrey White, Beryl Winch, David Winch.

* * *

Further up the Thames Estuary from Gravesend, just before the town of Erith, lies the village of Slade Green. It was from here in 1939 that 120 school children were evacuated to the village of Hadlow, near Tonbridge. The following article was written by **Norman J. Collins,** *who was a teacher with Slade Green County Primary School:*

Invasion of Hadlow.
A few days after the outbreak of World War II, I was one of some twelve adults and one hundred and twenty children who descended on the good folk of Hadlow to be

billeted as evacuees. We had come from Slade Green Primary School, North Kent. Our first surprise, disturbing to ourselves and doubtless more disturbing to the villagers, was to find that a large contingent of evacuees had already arrived from Charlton, South East London. However, by the end of a tiring day we had all been found accommodation and wondered what life was going to be like. The billeting officer, Mrs Moneypenny (wife of the Vicar), and the headmaster, Mr C. E. Tobyn, must have had a few headaches in finding out who could go where, especially as Hadlow was much smaller in those days – no Hope Avenue Estate, no Great Elms, no Cherry Orchard, no Hadlow Park, no Lonewood Way and no Littlefields. No wonder that some of our children found themselves in Golden Green and Ashes Lane!

I, as a teacher, and my wife as an official helper, (married women were not allowed to teach in those days) found ourselves very much *in loco parentis*. Out of school hours we endeavoured to visit as many homes as possible to check that all was well. Not unexpectedly, all was *not* well. One lady was highly indignant and somewhat affronted because she had provided a roast Sunday lunch complete with runner beans fresh from the garden and Jimmy had refused to eat the runner beans. On being asked why, he had replied, 'I don't eat bloody grass.' Bed-wetting seemed to be fairly rife among our charges. There were difficulties in getting them to visit the loo in the hut at the bottom of the garden – they came from 'posh' houses with indoor sanitation! They brought a surprising number of 'lousy' heads with them and, even more disturbing, an epidemic of scabies soon broke out.

My wife spent every morning for three months in the Memorial Hall (now the Mass Centre) de-lousing, giving sulphur baths and washing and disinfecting clothes. She still shudders at the mention of sulphur.

Two of our lady helpers had set up home with ten children in the previously unoccupied Castle Farm Cottage, furnished with trestle tables, benches and camp beds. After a few weeks, with no bombs falling, the ladies wished to go home to spend a weekend with their husbands. So my wife and I had to move in and become mum and dad for the week-end. Never a dull moment! However, we survived, visitors and villagers, and soon Christmas loomed up. Many children went home for Christmas but some fourteen stayed put. In order to relieve the hostesses and their families we entertained these children on Christmas Day afternoon and evening in the school hall (old one, of course) with the help of a wind-up gramophone. We were originally billeted with Mrs Hervey at 'Faulkners', complete with chauffeur, cook, kitchen maid, parlour maid, etc, but she wanted our room to entertain visitors at Christmas so we were transferred to number 13 The Freehold where widow Mrs Manser ran the house alone and made us very welcome and comfortable.

Scattered School.
The school at this time was full of local children, up to the age of fourteen, so we had to teach as and where we could. Most of the premises have since disappeared or have been modified. I took classes at various times in the concert room of the Castle (shared by two classes), the tin chapel in Court Lane, the Memorial Hall and the upstairs room in Winser House became a canteen for the children. It was run by the WVS, under the leadership of Mrs H. G. Pearson who lived in the castle. There was a large copper cauldron in an outhouse where the washing was done. My wife remembers breaking

the ice before the fire was lit underneath. A hot meal of two courses was provided for 4d, and at the end of term the ladies were embarrassed by the amount of profit made. This was the fore-runner of the School Meals Service.

Integration.
As the new year progressed, still the bombers did not come, more and more children returned to their homes and eventually I was left in charge of the remaining fifteen or so of our evacuees. The folk from Charlton had already gone; they didn't take kindly to rural life. We were integrated into the school and I found myself teaching a class of mainly local children. One of the staff, Mr Ivor Jones, was a member of Hadlow Bowls Club and he introduced me to the game on the green off Court Lane where Appletons is now. I actually made up the team for a match on one occasion. I regret I did not play again until 1977.

During the first winter of the war a village concert was organised to raise money for Comforts for the Troops. The performers were enthusiastic if not professional. I was one of six men who gave a rendering of 'I'm a little Prairie Flower'. We dressed in white plimsolls and socks, short crepe paper skirts, paper bras and wore a flower in our hair. We sang in falsetto and did dance routines between verses – after a few sherries to get us going. We played to a packed house in spite of the blackout and were asked to repeat the show in East Peckham.

Dads' Army.
When the Rt Hon Anthony Eden founded the Local Defence Volunteers (later to become the Home Guard) a Hadlow company was formed under Captain H. G. Pearson at the Castle. We paraded on the castle lawn on Sunday mornings and drilled complete with broomsticks. Later we received denim uniforms and three 1918 rifles between us – no ammunition at first. From dusk to dawn each night a detachment slept on camp beds in the castle concert room and two sentries at a time did look-out duty from the top of the tower. I did first duty on Thursdays with the village postman. I remember that we had just arrived at the top one evening when two hurricanes approached. They were flying very low and they passed, one each side of the tower. We actually looked *down* on them.

In September 1940 I left Hadlow to join the Royal Artillery, taking with me many happy memories of a year spent among the friendly, humorous and often long-suffering inhabitants. I returned to Hadlow School in September 1950 – and stayed till I retired!

Evacuees at Wrens Warren Camp during the war

Chapter Eight

THE NATIONAL CAMPS CORPORATION

SOMETIME PRECEDING THE OUTBREAK of the Second World War the National Camps Corporation was set up under the direction of Sir Edward Howarth, to provide camp schools throughout the country. The camps were regarded as having a two-fold purpose: first, to provide the opportunity for children to experience life in a community, with all the implications this carries in the way of social and disciplinary training, self development and leadership; second, to afford children living in built-up areas, and especially those from the slum areas in big cities, the opportunity for a short stay in beautiful countryside, where, for the first time in the lives of most of them, they could become acquainted with country life and learn a little about farming operations and about the wild life of field and hedgerow, woodland and stream. It was also thought that a third purpose was that the children's residence at a camp would make a definite contribution to their physical fitness and general health by ensuring plenty of fresh air, warmth, a balanced diet, sufficient exercise and adequate sleep.

At its peak, the National Camps Corporation had thirty camps spread throughout the country, situated in rural settings and each providing accommodation for some 240 children. Each camp had a number of specially erected huts, comprising dormitory accommodation, school accommodation, dining room, hall and ablutionary and sanitary provision.

The intention of these camps was to enable local education authorities to send children of school age for short periods into residence in the country.

One of these camps, Wrens Warren Camp, was situated in the countryside of East Sussex and it was to this camp that some of the Medway evacuees were sent to during the war. The City of Rochester Education Committee produced a comprehensive brochure for parents who were unsure about letting their children be evacuated. Overleaf is an extract from that brochure.

John Bell *was one of the Medway evacuees who was sent to Wrens Warren Camp in East Sussex:*

Wrens Warren Elementary School Camp was in East Sussex, about two and a half miles from the village of Hartfield and in the Ashdown Forest on the B2026 road. The fourteen or so buildings were made at Crook in County Durham during 1939, from Canadian Red Cedar. The buildings were assembled on site and handed over to the City of Rochester Education Committee. It was occupied by the first batch of evacuees

> **CITY OF ROCHESTER EDUCATION COMMITTEE**
>
> Chairman: ALDERMAN F. C. A. MATTHEWS, J.P.
>
> Education Secretary:
> EDWARD H. WEBB, F.C.I.S., M.R.S.T.
> Education Office,
> St. Peter's C. E. School, New Road,
>
> ## Wrens Warren Residential School
>
> The problem of what to do for the best with regard to evacuating their children is ever with parents in these days of stress and anxiety. It is the purpose of this Guide to draw attention to a way out of the difficulty which may have been overlooked.
>
> The suggestion put before you is easy to carry into practice. The cost is the same as if your children were evacuated in the usual way, and is paid in exactly the same manner.
>
> There are no tiresome conditions, except that the youngsters must be medically fit, and that there is room for them.
>
> The advantages are worth examination. In brief, they amount to the following:—
>
> 1. The children, boys and girls, go to a quiet, healthy spot miles from any town or city, but only 40 miles from their homes.
> 2. They are educated and cared for by a specially selected staff.
> 3. They receive full-time education, with the fullest opportunities for outdoor work, in addition to the usual school lessons.
> 4. Games, physical training and sport of all kinds are provided in a way which is impossible in towns under war-time conditions.
> 5. Regular medical supervision is afforded free of any extra cost to parents, and there need be no cause for worry on the score of health.
> 6. Once a month parents are able to visit their children, being conveyed at a reasonable charge, to and from the school by buses chartered for the purpose.
> 7. The extraordinary character of the School itself, to a description of which the remainder of this booklet is devoted.
>
> One proviso and one alone is made when admitting a child to the School, namely, that he or she remains there as long as possible whilst the war lasts, and the assistance of parents in not changing their minds without real reason must be insisted upon from the onset.
>
> At the same time, should some serious and unavoidable happening make it necessary to remove a child from the School, permission will not be refused. In such a case the fullest details should be given in writing to the Education Secretary, Education Office, St. Peter's C.E. School.

An extract from the brochure about Wrens Warren Residential School

on the 15th April 1940. I was in the second batch to arrive early in May 1940.

We waved our farewells to our parents at Temple Farm School, Strood, and the single decker bus took us out through Cuxton, West Malling, Tunbridge Wells, Groombridge, Withyam and Hartfield, before turning through the gates of Wrens Warren.

We were greeted by the headmaster, Mr Skerrit and the camp manager, Mr Fenton. Soon we were divided into the dormitories and got unpacked. The girls went to the two dormitories named 'Woodeves' and 'Shailes'. The rest of us lads were put into one of each of the three dormitories named 'Wych Cross', 'Gills Lap' and mine was the last, 'Chuck Hatch'. All were named after places in the local area.

Hidden from the road and protected on three sides by a dense belt of trees, it really was a great place for us youngsters. Although originally planned for 300 school children, I believe only 199 places were ever filled.

In Chuck Hatch there were something between 40 and 50 boys ranging in ages from eight years to fourteen. We slept on bunk beds and two boys each shared a wooden locker. It was all a bit spartan, but very friendly. Mr Frances, the maths and geometry teacher had a small room at one end of the 'dorm' and Mr Keeble, the English and geography teacher, had a similar room at the other end. The camp site was on a slope which lead down to a stream which meandered through the countryside to become the Medway River.

The woodwork hut at Wrens Warren Camp, with John Bell in the foreground

The sick quarters were run by a charming and elegant lady named Nurse Ascombe. One day we were called to the surgery, in alphabetical order to be given a dental inspection. The folding dental chair had a wicker work seat and back. The dentist's drill was operated by a foot treadle.

I had to have one small filling and this was my first encounter with the drill. However, the second visit by this mobile dentist and his awful contraptions was more memorable. There were half a dozen or so of us lads waiting our turn outside – the topic of our conversation, naturally enough, was about dentists and what they did! The air was suddenly filled with a long drawn out scream. Our chat was cut dead and we all stared at the window behind which we could imagine the hapless victim in that chair. I was up and running as fast as my legs would carry me. I could hear footsteps pounding behind me; they may well have belonged to my companions – but I wasn't looking, distance between me and that chair was all that mattered! I ran down the hill and across the stream, up the other side and watched from the safety of Five Hundred Acre Wood till the car and the dentist drove off.

Just inside the tree line, on the edge of our play area known as the 'Dirt Patch' three air raid trenches were dug. Each trench was about 18 feet long, four feet wide and four feet six inches deep. These were covered with corrugated iron sheets to form a roof and earth was piled on top of that.

A telephone call to the headmaster would warn him of an impending air raid. He would then give a long series of blasts on his whistle, this was followed by the teachers

Some of the evacuees learning the skills of boot repairing at Wrens Warren Camp

doing the same. Before you could say 'Jack Robinson' the children were hotfooting it to the 'shelters'. We didn't need to be told twice, but if we were out in the woods and it was too far to the shelters, then we would watch the 'dog fights' going on overhead. The sky would be criss-crossed with vapour trails made by the Spitfire and Hurricane aircraft in combat with 'Jerry'; the faint tut-tut sounds of their guns all made for fearful excitement for us.

There were lots of night raids during the summer. They seemed to come just as we were getting off to sleep. As soon as the whistles went, we would leap out of bed, put on our wellies and rain coats over our pyjamas, grab our gas masks and run hell for leather to the shelters. There were wooden forms end to end and on both sides of the trench, and we would sit knees to knees. Condensation formed on the corrugated iron roof and water would then drip down on our heads – ugh! We would pass the time by cutting little roads in the trench sides and passing Dinky Toy cars and tanks along them.

Those boys needing the 'loo' were not very popular, because they had to clamber over all the knees to get out. I remember one long period in those shelters one night. We passed along mugs of hot pea soup and slices of bread and butter. It all became very musical! When we finally emerged in the morning light we must have looked a sorry, bedraggled sight. 'Go straight to the dining hall,' we were told, where a meal had been prepared for us.

We were just passing the school rooms when we heard the ominous drone of a Jerry plane overhead. We couldn't see it because of low cloud. 'Get down,' yelled a teacher, but we were already down. Some dived under the classrooms, others just fell face down to the ground, then came the terrifying screams of the two bombs as they fell from the plane, only to crump unexploded on the hillside of Gill Lap Clump. To say we were scared would be putting it but mildly! It seems just like yesterday!

It was 1942 when the concrete air raid shelters were finally put up – a bit late, but nevertheless welcome.

Looking back, I believe the eighteen months I spent at Wrens Warren were among my happiest! I was just twelve years old, and my number was 132.

*Another evacuee who remembers Wrens Warren Camp is **Alan Brown**:*

I was a pupil at Troy Town School, Rochester, and I was about ten and a half years old when we were first evacuated on Saturday 2nd September 1939, the day before war was declared. We went from Rochester Railway Station to the village of Saltwood near Hythe, carrying our gasmask, small case – and a carrier bag, given to us at the station, with various food items which were to be given to the lady we were to be billeted with. The only two items I can remember were a tin of corned beef and a packet of cream biscuits. The latter was soon disposed of!

I was billeted with a Mrs Gower who lived in Cylinder Road, Saltwood. She also had the village policeman billeted with her! I made friends with two of the local children, Joey and Phillis Corby. One evening a week a few of us who were interested in the scouting movement would walk down to Hythe to the Life Boat Station where the Sea Scouts met. In the mornings all the children would meet in the village hall for assembly and prayers because the local school buildings were not very large, then we would go to the school afterwards. I was at Saltwood for about three months.

I returned to Rochester but was not there long before I was evacuated again, this time to Wrens Warren Camp in East Sussex. This was a camp of cedar wood huts consisting of dining room, assembly hall, classrooms, five dormitories, two washrooms and one hut divided into two for woodwork and domestic science.

I was there for just over a year and I passed for the Rochester Technical School, so I returned home to attend my new school.

Christmas party at Wrens Warren Camp, 1940

Chapter Nine

EVACUATION – 1944

For some of the Medway and North and West Kent evacuees there was to be a third occasion when they would be sent away from their families and friends. Late in the war Germany developed an unmanned rocket plane, known as the V-1 flying bomb, nicknamed the Doodlebug by British civilians in the south-east of England. This was the first operational guided missile and was designed to fly at 350 miles per hour at an altitude of 3,500 feet. It had a maximum range of 130 miles. Most of these flying bombs were targeted on London and consequently the greater part of Kent was under their flight path. On the 30th June, 1944, the following warning appeared in the Chatham, Rochester & Gillingham News:

FLYING BOMB PRECAUTIONS.
ROCHESTER HOUSEHOLDERS URGED TO OBTAIN SHELTERS.

'Do not run the risk of being caught at the eleventh hour after safely coming through five years of war,' states Councillor T. C. Harwood, the Rochester Sub-Controller of Civil Defence, in a message to the citizens on flying bomb precautions.

Urging all householders without shelters to take the necessary steps of obtaining one at the earliest possible moment. The Councillor points out, 'By sleeping in your shelter, it is possible to have a good night's rest without any unnecessary worry. A large percentage of casualties are caused by glass, therefore do not look out of your windows. When danger threatens, keep sheltered from glass.'

The Sub-Controller also urges citizens to arrange mutual help facilities with their friends, so that if their house is damaged, they will have somewhere to go. Such a precautionary measure taken now, he says, would be of immense assistance to the A.R.P. authorities should any incidents occur.

Applications for shelters by Rochester householders should be made to the A.R.P. Officer at the Civil Defence Headquarters.

* * *

The following article appeared in the national press in 1944:

COUNTRY FOLK ARE IN FRONT LINE AGAIN.
THEY GET THE BOMBS LONDON MISSES.

Southern England, *Friday*. – This is England's new Bomb Alley. This is the open country where flying bombs are shot down on their way to London.

There are the farmhouses, the thatched cottages, the little housing estates under the track of the V.1.

The people living in them would like London to know what is happening here, and London, I think, would like news of the folk who share the southern front line with them.

Mr and Mrs Jamieson went out for their usual walk last evening. They heard a flying bomb coming. Heavy A.A. guns opened up on it, and then went silent. A fighter was on its tail. Mr and Mrs Jamieson took cover in a ditch behind a haystack. The bomb plunged to earth, blew over the haystack and set it alight. Mr and Mrs Jamieson were buried beneath the burning haystack and died. That is the price the people of the villages are paying.

Shells, Bullets.

Of the scores of bombs the people of this village see and hear, only a proportion get through to London. Light and heavy A.A. guns send scores of shells up at them. Fighter pilots pump lead into them. Shell fragments and bullets fall and sometimes kill or wound workers in the quiet cornfields.

The country people get no warning of the approach of bombs. There are no sirens. There are no deep shelters, only the ditches and hedges. There are no steel and concrete blocks of flats – only thatched cottages or, in the market towns, two-storeyed houses.

Some of the bombs sent crashing to earth have fallen on to the little housing estates, and you in London know what that means. Some have fallen on or near isolated farms, and the official communiques say: 'Few cas. Slight dam!' Those abbreviations have already been the epitaph of more than one family of farmers. And they have left behind mourning relatives and friends who knew them as few friends in London ever know their neighbours.

End of 50.

More than 50 bombs have had their 400 mph careers cut short within the sight and hearing of the people who live here – the people who produce their quota of Britain's food in the fruitful gardens and fields.

Here in 1940, during the Battle of Britain, a farmer drove his tractor while 'The Few' fought above his head. Here in 1944, the same farmer drove his tractor while the bombs streaked overhead.

One day recently they brought a bomb down in his fields. He now lies beneath the earth that was his life. The bomb that killed him might have provided another 'Guards Chapel' headline.

The school children take turns at bomb-spotting. They do half-hour watches and blow whistles on the approach of danger, so that the other 160 can take shelter. For them there has not been, nor is there yet, any question of evacuation. The people of Bomb Alley are here to stay.

* * *

There were, however, further evacuations as a direct result of the V-1 flying bombs, as recorded in the Chatham, Rochester & Gillingham News *for Friday, 7th July 1944:*

SCHOOLS' EVACUATION.
RESUMPTION OF OPTIONAL FACILITIES.

As part of the Metropolitan evacuation scheme facilities have been re-opened for the voluntary evacuation of Medway Towns' school children, if their parents feel that in view of recent events such a precaution is advisable.

Schools were open throughout the Towns on Saturday for the registration of children whose parents wished them to be sent away, but the response was not particularly large. Parents who now wish to make use of the facilities may register their children at the schools or at the evacuation offices.

It will be remembered that the Government scheme for the evacuation of school children was closed a year or so ago, although it has still been possible for private evacuation to take place where billets could be found. The re-opening of the scheme now means no more than that parents may now send their children away if they wish. As before, there is no element of compulsion in the scheme.

Up to yesterday less than five hundred children had left the Towns under the official scheme in two parties. The totals are Rochester 121, Chatham 187, Gillingham 160. A number of children with and without parents are being evacuated privately.

Apart from a certain amount of dislocation during this past week due to registration and medical examination of the evacuees, all the schools are and will be open for the children who remain in the area.

* * *

Two weeks later the following appeared in the same newspaper:

700 EVACUEES

About 700 children have left Gillingham under the Government's evacuation scheme, it was stated at the monthly meeting of Gillingham Education Committee on Monday. The Education Secretary (Mr Andrew Johns) said that that number included about 120 mothers in organised parties and those who had arranged to have private billets in safe areas.

* * *

Having first been evacuated to Wales then returned home to spend two years of the war in Chatham, **Roy Utteridge** *was again on the move, this time to Yorkshire:*

When the V-1 rocket planes (known as doodlebugs) started arriving in Kent in 1944, I was again evacuated away from the Medway Towns. This time I travelled with my ten years old sister, Margaret, to the town of Rastrick in Yorkshire.

On arrival we sat in a hall and watched as two people came and took my sister away.

Eventually a man came up to me and said, 'Come on, lad.' The man was Mr Fred Brook and whether I had been allocated to his family or if he just picked me at random I will never know.

His wife Alice and their son Grenville, who was 18 months older then me, were waiting at home in their bungalow at 17 Slade Lane, Rastrick. I learnt later that my sister Margaret was only a few minutes walk away, with a couple named Mr and Mrs Carter.

Not long after settling in at Rastrick, I was in bed one night when there was a strange noise. I looked out of the window and there was a doodlebug chugging across the sky. My foster parents had never seen one before. I thought at the time that it was quite exciting, but they were panicking a bit. How that doodlebug came to be up as far as Yorkshire I don't know, but I can't remember any others while I was there.

It was in Yorkshire that I saw my first trolley buses. The fare from Brighouse to Huddersfield was one penny. We used to use the trolley buses when we went to see a Huddersfield football match. We also used to be taken to see shows in Bradford, Dewsbury and Huddersfield. I remember seeing *The Chocolate Soldier* at one theatre.

After a few months I moved with the Brooks to Mirfield where they had bought a newsagent's shop. I was given a small paper round in the morning before school. After school I used to go with my bag to Mirfield Station, pick up the papers and then deliver them on my way back to the shop. There were no thoughts on age limits in those days. I enjoyed it all.

The shop was next to a farm and we used to go round to the milking shed where the Land Army girls used to turn the cows' teats at us and spray us with milk. We also used to ride the shire horses. I think I often surprised Grenville. He thought that I got away with a lot more than he was ever allowed to.

My mother came to visit me once in Mirfield. As a widow she must have found it quite difficult financially, although she did have a job as a postwoman, the first postwoman to be employed at Chatham Post Office! Anyway, she only managed to stay for the weekend and on Sunday, before she returned to Chatham, my mother was horrified when Mrs Brook served up Yorkshire Pudding on its own with just gravy and a few peas. That is still my idea of the only real way to eat Yorkshire Pudding as a starter!

I returned to Chatham just after V.E. Day in 1945. I still keep in touch with Grenville Brook by letters and Christmas cards.

The following article which appeared in the local press for Friday, 28th July, 1944, mentions the success of the latest evacuation scheme, but what is conspicuous by its absence is the fact that none of the reception areas are mentioned:

EVACUATION SUCCESSFUL

At last night's meeting of Rochester City Council, the Mayor (Councillor C. S. Knight) praised those who had been responsible for carrying through efficiently the recent evacuation arrangements in the City, and in answer to a question stated that as far as was known there had been no difficulty about the reception of the evacuees at the other end of their journey.

Those whom the Mayor thanked for their part in this work were the Town Clerk (Mr J. L. Percival), who had acted as billeting officer for the City and dispersal officer for the district; the Town Clerk's staff, and particularly Miss Day, who had worked long hours to make the scheme a success; the W.V.S. for looking after the issue of emergency clothing to the mothers and children; and the school staffs, teachers and others, who had volunteered to go away with the parties. Fortunately the latter had not been retained in the evacuation area, but they had conducted the parties to their destination and looked after them on the way.

Councillor Wilkinson asked if they could be given an assurance that the experience of some of the evacuees, as reported in the Press, had not been suffered by Rochester evacuees.

The Mayor replied, 'As far as we have knowledge at the moment, the children and mothers we have sent from here have been billeted in very quick time, and as far as we can tell from reports everything in that way has gone very satisfactorily.'

* * *

Shirley Nokes *(now Mrs Shirley Pritchard), having first been evacuated in 1939 to South Wales and who eventually returned home to Kent, also faced the prospect of a further evacuation in 1944:*

In June 1944 when the V-1 rockets (buzz bombs) started dropping in Kent, my parents enrolled my sister and me as evacuees with the local school. We travelled by train from Crayford in Kent to Burnley Banktops in Lancashire. We all stayed the first night at the local 'Rest Centre', sleeping in camp beds, eating at long trestle tables, before lining up in a half circle, adorned with our name labels – waiting to be 'chosen' by local residents.

I remember holding on to my little sister's hand, explaining to anyone who showed interest in her, that we came as a pair! I had been given strict instructions by my mother that I should look after Pat and *not* be separated! Because she was only seven years old she was obviously more acceptable than a scowling ten and a half year old who was beginning to understand and feel humiliated by the 'cattle market' system.

We were some of the last to be chosen. A kind elderly lady who wanted a little boy, chose the little six year old standing next to us, and agreed to take my sister and me to her niece. The niece had her own baby boy and it seemed to me that she only wanted a 'home-help'. Life was bearable but not happy.

We lived in a spotlessly clean little terraced house in Padiham, with a cobbled backyard which backed on to another row of terraced houses, with a cobbled alleyway down the centre. At seven o'clock each morning, these alleyways were crowded with ladies hurrying to work in the mills, and their clogs clipping the flagstones as they walked. Clogs were the footwear our host insisted we wore, so that she could hear us arriving home from school. I remember they were heavy black leather with a side stud fastening. The wooden soles had metal edges nailed to them, like horseshoes! I hated them. Our host was so fastidious that we were only allowed in the back kitchen and never in the front room – except when I went in to dust!

Letters from home were regular and details of the life of my parents, family and friends were eagerly received – as was the wellbeing of my adored Pekingese dog. It was only on my return home that I discovered that my parents had 'given her away', and my faith and trust in my parents faltered. They had lied to me and I couldn't forget it. Years later when I explained how I had felt, they simply said they couldn't cope with a dog in their situation, but couldn't bring themselves to put it in writing to me.

My father was a tool maker with Vickers-Armstrong (Engineers) at Crayford, and was also an air-raid warden during the evenings. Mother travelled once a month to Padiham to visit us. We finally returned home in October 1944, with homesickness probably playing the biggest part in our decision to return.

School life was very erratic during the war years. I remember our local school in Dartford being closed and we had lessons twice a week in the house of a friend nearby. It is quite remarkable that so many of the children at school during this time have done so well in their professional lives.

Elizabeth Brown *(now Mrs Elizabeth James), from Bromley recalls the time the doodlebugs started:*

My brother was born in May 1944, and when the doodlebugs started, my mother arranged to take my brother, my sister of five years and me aged eight away from the bombing. A friend of the family lived in Trealaw, Glamorgan, South Wales, and she arranged for us all to stay with a Mr and Mrs Evans who lived opposite her. I cannot remember the exact dates but I know we were with them for eight months and this took in Christmas 1944. I can remember my mother's worries and frustrations at the fact that my brother's pram, which was filled with our clothes and other essentials, took weeks to arrive at Cardiff Railway Station.

The couple we stayed with, 'Uncle Ned' and 'Auntie Win', were very kind. Uncle Ned was a miner. I remember he had a horrific carbuncle on the back of his neck and my mother putting poultices on it and telling Uncle Ned 'not to be a baby'. I also remember Auntie Win making me and my sister dresses out of a bedspread.

The house was reached from the street by steps to the front door; it was a three up three down terraced house. Outside the back door there was a yard and then you went up more steps to a small garden where Uncle Ned kept chickens, which he killed himself by wringing their necks. From the small garden you could go through a gate on to a rough path at the back of the house, across which you went straight up a mountain.

I know my sister and I went to school during the time we were there, but I cannot remember anything about the school at all.

During this time, my father was in the army, but he did have one short spell of leave and came down to Wales to see us. He brought my younger sister a china doll, which has survived the passing of time and which I still have.

Looking back over the years I feel there is very little I can remember of my time in Wales – and I often wonder why!

Mary Porter *(now Mrs Mary Wagon) remained at home in Maidstone during the war – until the doodlebug raids started in 1944:*

Departure day was not easy as I was 12 years of age, the age where shedding tears in the presence of one's compatriots was to be avoided at all costs. The majority of my travelling companions used the excuse of 'smoke or dust in the eyes from the locomotive' when wiping away tears with the back of the hand. My elder sister Ann and a cousin of the same age were also on the train, as was my younger sister Molly, but we travelled in different compartments because we went to different schools.

The train left Maidstone West Station with hundreds of children, all having a luggage label pinned to the coat lapel, and some accompanying adults with their babies. We each clasped our gas masks cases which contained not only a mask, but a tin of Horlicks or Ovaltine tablets. We must have had some luggage, but I have no recollection of it. People stood on Tovil Railway Bridge to wave to us as we started off on our journey, and I suspect that quite a few tears were shed by them. As all place names had been removed during the war, we had no idea where we were going, but the journey took all day.

Eventually, the train reached its destination of Cardiff in South Wales and we all assembled in Roath Park. Members of the Women's Voluntary Service gave us food and drink while others referred to lists, called out children's names and gradually the children dispersed, being shepherded into a variety of charabancs. I began to feel very uneasy when my younger sister and I were still in the park after the majority of people had left.

Eventually it was our turn to board a vehicle and we were taken to a village near Cardiff, called Rhiwbina. My elder sister and cousin had already gone to their new home in Whitchurch. Molly and I were handed over to our hostess, who, I thought, was a funny old dear, but thinking back, she was probably only in her mid-forties! Her house was posh by our standards as it had electric lights – our house in Maidstone only had gas! Our billet also had a bathroom and an *indoor toilet*!

My sister was a placid child of about seven and was no problem, but I have always had a contrary nature and the hostess soon decided that she couldn't cope with two children. I distinctly remember the 'breakfast battles' we had. I have never liked hot milk, or sugar on cornflakes and happily ate cereals at home with cold milk and no sugar – a good thing in view of the rationing. So when I was given cornflakes with hot milk I would take a spoonful and refused to eat any more. I never liked eggs either, so this lady's kindness of acquiring new-laid eggs which were given to us, soft-boiled, at tea time, was also not appreciated by me.

After a couple of weeks I was moved to a house a few doors away, which was even more posh than the first one. It had a flame-shaped electric lamp on the lower and upper bannister uprights, a fluffy mat in the bathroom (we had no bathroom in Maidstone) – and hot water on tap in both the bathroom and the kitchen. My bedroom had a deep-rose coloured satin bedspread and matching eiderdown and for the first time in my life, I had a room to myself. My hosts were Mr and Mrs Fisher and they thoroughly spoilt me.

They both went out a lot in the evenings, wearing evening dress, and they didn't return until late. I used to sit in a terrified state stupidly listening to Valentine Dyall in *The Man in Black* on the wireless, with only a snuffling pekingese dog for company who yapped at the slightest noise. I always thought that the dog was barking at prowlers, but I realised later that the noises were the wind and rain blowing at the side of the house. I was often too scared to go to bed and sometimes I waited until the car came up the road, when I would dash up to the bathroom, then hop into bed to feign sleep when Mrs Fisher looked in to make sure I was still there! In her eyes I could do no wrong and she always stood up for me, to the extent that when the evacuees were issued with wellingtons and I was the only one who did not have shiny ones (I had such large feet and needed an adult size), she refused to accept them, insisting that a shiny pair be found for me. A few days later, I was the proud possessor of a pair of shiny boots to wear to school

I went to school in Whitchurch and walked there, following a stream, so with our new boots we could actually walk to school *in* the stream – which was more fun! The only lessons I remember were Welsh Language. None of us 'foreigners' could see the point of learning Welsh but our less than serious attitude was soon corrected by the remarkable aim that the teacher had. She could direct the blackboard pointer to a chosen pupil with great accuracy and not many of the class escaped sore, bruised knuckles or the occasional lump on the head when the unfortunate soul sitting in front of the teacher's target didn't duck in time.

School dinners have been dismissed from my memory, except for the dessert which was always rice pudding. On Monday it was white; Tuesday pink; Wednesday green; Thursday white with a blob of jam; Friday pink again! I haven't eaten rice as a dessert since! We endeavoured to opt out of school dinners by going to the nearby fish and chip shop when it was open but the headmaster decided to keep the playground gate closed. However, never daunted, the girls helped the boys to scale the six foot fence and they went off to buy the fish and chips for us as well as themselves. Returning from school, we let off steam by skylarking and splashing our way home through the stream, often arriving soaked to the skin.

Most of my friends in Rhiwbina were locals but I became friendly with a girl named Sylvia, who had been sent from Tottenham to stay at her aunt's house nearby. We spent most of our non-academic time together. We kept in touch for a while after the war. During our stay in Wales, my sister and I went to Pontypridd once to visit the family of a chap who was in my father's regiment. It was the first time that we had been close to a coal mine and it seemed a very depressing place.

After some months we returned home to Maidstone and, on the day we left for home, we were taken by car to Cardiff to catch the train. Mrs Fisher gave me a brooch in the shape of a butterfly, which I still have. I wrote to her for a few years, but then she stopped replying. I have often wondered what happened to them. I have never been back to Cardiff or Rhiwbina.

Molly Porter (*now Mrs Molly O'Brien), younger sister of Mrs Mary Wagon, now tells her evacuation story:*

We lived near Maidstone West Railway Station during the last war. My father was serving in the army and my mother was desperately trying to keep his job open (school caretaker) so that we wouldn't lose our house. The final straw so far as she was concerned was when a flying bomb hit the railway line quite near to my school. We scrambled under our desks fortunately, because all the tall windows fell in on top of us. The school had to be closed anyway for repairs, so she decided to agree to the evacuation of my two older sisters and me.

On the day of evacuation I remember getting on the train clutching my doll. I was just six and a half years old. My sisters cried but I was quite matter of fact about it all. It seemed a very long journey and I remember going through the Severn Tunnel. My next memory is being deposited at 1 Groes Lon, Rhiwbina with my sister Mary, and being introduced to Mr and Mrs Brown. They were an older couple and I don't think they had any children of their own. Mr Brown was a very stern gentleman but his wife was a gentle kindly soul and had cooked us a large roast dinner on our arrival. We were served marrow which we hadn't eaten before and I was really worried – my sister was more outspoken! They really didn't believe the stories coming out of London about the flying bombs, which made us rather cross.

Unfortunately, I was a bed-wetter, not helped by being removed from home, and poor Mrs Brown couldn't cope with both me and my sister so after a few days Mary was moved in with my other sister at nearby Whitchurch. I remember a woman coming to see me (presumably in charge of placements) and really telling me off about the bed-wetting. When I cried she said, 'They're only crocodile tears, we take no notice of them here!' Mrs Brown though was really very understanding and gave me a calendar so that I could mark off the nights I had been 'good'. Mr and Mrs Brown were 'posher' people than I was used to. The house was very comfortable but very quiet. I got another telling off when I idly lay in bed one day filling in the gaps on the flowery wall paper with crayons! My poor foster parents must have wondered what they had let themselves in for.

I don't remember much about school, except that all the children and teachers spoke Welsh, so how I learnt anything I don't know. After about five or six months I was suddenly told that we were going home. The timing coincided with three family birthdays and the fact that my father was coming home on leave, so back we went. In that short time I had acquired a Welsh accent and I was teased unmercifully when I got home.

My mother kept in touch with the Browns for a while, but Mrs Brown died quite young – she never appeared to be very strong. I have never been back to Rhiwbina but I can still picture the road and the house near the corner with a crab apple tree in the garden.

In 1995 I watched a television documentary showing some of the appalling experiences some of the evacuees of the last war had lived through. I consider myself to be one of the fortunate ones.

Ann Porter (now Mrs Ann Hayes), elder sister of Molly and Mary, now recalls her memories of being evacuated in 1944:

I was about 14 years old when I was evacuated with my two sisters and a cousin. My cousin and I were lucky enough to be billeted together at the home of a former Mayor of Cardiff, a Mr and Mrs Jenkins. They lived in a large house in Whitchurch; it was very much 'upstairs, downstairs', as after the first day, we evacuees had all our meals in the servants' dining room.

I can remember that as we were Technical High School girls, we were expected to be almost perfect – which I'm afraid we weren't! We always seemed to be caught when doing something we shouldn't be doing. On one occasion one of the boys threw my hat up a lamp post and I was caught straddling the bar at the top trying to retrieve it. My cousin made an acquaintance with a young lad and they used to leave 'love letters' in the hedge outside the house, again we were caught in the act and were confined to the house after school. The only way we were allowed out was in the company of our teacher, who took us off to chamber music concerts in Cardiff – very boring!

One day we made the excuse of visiting my youngest sister who lived in the nearby village of Rhiwbina. Instead of visiting my sister, we went to a large tin hut to see the film *Gone With The Wind*. We thought we were very grown up going to see that film. Unfortunately for us our host phoned to ask what time we would be home – so yet another ban!

School meals were atrocious. Luckily for us my sister was table monitor and gave large helpings to all the little ones – and just a scraping on the plate for us. My mother used to send us food parcels, which I hid in the wardrobe, and we had midnight feasts, which all seemed great fun.

One of the daughters of the house used to take us out from time to time. We used to go to Penarth and Bargoed which we thoroughly enjoyed because the scenery was very pretty.

When we arrived at our new school to start our commercial studies, the headmaster raked out some really old typewriters and when the covers were removed, mice ran in all directions so you can imagine the screaming that went on among us girls. Our lady host at the billet served on several committees and wasn't always home, so we were given our own front door key. Her absences gave us the opportunity to flirt with the convalescent soldiers in a nearby park. Yet again we were in trouble. We didn't get back before the family and Mr Jenkins had to force open a window to get in. As he used a stick, it must have been very difficult for him to climb over the window sill. I wonder what they must have thought of us!

We didn't stay in Wales for very long, as my father was given embarkation leave and Mum wanted us all to be together for his leave. It was a great adventure travelling home on our own. Amazingly, it had been reasonably quiet at Maidstone while we were in Wales, but once we were back home we had to contend with the flying bombs.

Looking back to the time of our evacuation, I view it as a great experience – but I often wondered what Mr and Mrs Jenkins thought about having us. I should think they were quite relieved when we returned home.

The following article typifies many such reports on the dangers of flying-bomb activity. This appeared in the Chatham, Rochester & Gillingham News *for 11th August, 1944:*

FLY-BOMB CRASHES ON VILLAGE
POLICE-SERGEANT & CHILDREN AMONG THE CASUALTIES.

Eleven people were killed and others injured when a flying bomb slid silently out of the evening sky on Saturday and crashed on houses in the main road of a large South of England village.

Three houses were completely demolished and others badly damaged, including that of a Czech refugee doctor, who was holding his surgery at the time and was badly cut about the face by splinters of glass. Although bleeding heavily, he did what he could

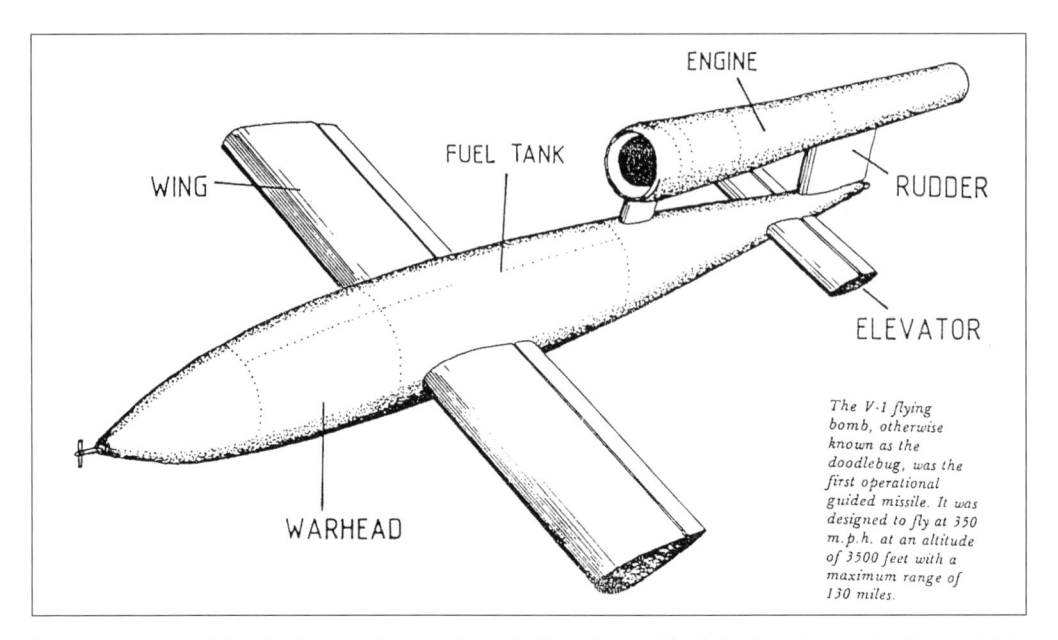

The V-1 flying bomb, otherwise known as the doodlebug, was the first operational guided missile. It was designed to fly at 350 m.p.h. at an altitude of 3500 feet with a maximum range of 130 miles.

for other casualties before going to hospital to have his injuries dressed. One of his patients, nine-years-old Narcissa Gladdish, was killed.

Police-sergeant W. Braddick, his wife and two little girls, Annie Orpin and Bernice Stokes, both aged fourteen, who were staying with them, were all killed, as were some neighbours, Mr Leonard H. Brooker, his wife and his 28-year-old daughter Alice, together with two unidentified women who were staying with them for the weekend. The other fatal casualty was Mr Horace Wells, aged 70, who lived by himself in one of the wrecked houses.

In one of the badly damaged houses Mr and Mrs W. Wimsett were celebrating the fifth anniversary of their wedding, with four friends. They all escaped with only minor injuries, but Mrs Wimsett's mother and father, Mrs Eileen Saunders, aged 77, and Mr Hayden Saunders, aged 79, who were in other parts of the house, were seriously injured, and Mr Saunders died in hospital subsequently.

The first aid services, encountering the biggest incident and number of casualties they had yet to deal with, worked well into the next day.

On Tuesday morning another flying bomb landed in a field some mile or two away, causing slight damage to buildings and crops, but no casualties.

* * *

Edna Eacott *(now Mrs Edna Everitt), who had first been evacuated to Wales in 1940 and had eventually returned home to Chatham, was off again in 1944:*

My father was working in the Naval Dockyard in Chatham on very secret work which involved working most nights. My mother was at home looking after us all, which included twin boys just 10 months old, my younger sister not yet five years old, twin girls aged six and a half, my other sister, ten and a half, and myself, the oldest at twelve and a half years old. With father working most nights, it was impossible for my mother to get us all to the air raid shelter during the night raids. When the flying bombs started arriving in 1944 it was decided to evacuate us again. We went through the same procedure as before – met at the school, got checked over by the school doctor and nurse and assembled in groups.

We had a problem with my young sister who was still under school age because the authorities said she couldn't go, so my mother said, 'Right, if she can't go, none of them are going,' and started gathering our cases to go home. In the end the authorities relented on the proviso that I would be responsible for her throughout the journey. So in July 1944 we were off by train to Yorkshire, although we didn't know our destination at the time, just that it was 'somewhere north'.

We finally arrived late in the day at Harrogate. Others went to different places, but we were taken to a hall where we had a nice meal on long tables. Later we were allocated camp beds and spent the night there. The next morning we were taken to buses and I ended up in Sowerby Bridge near Halifax. I had my little sister with me and I guarded her with my life! My next sister was billeted on her own as they wouldn't let her go with the twins, but she ended up with a lovely widowed lady who had a grown up son and daughter, and they were all very nice to her. The twins didn't fair so well and they were treated badly! My 'auntie' let them come over for tea every weekend, and when she saw me crying over them, she said that if she had had another room she would have taken them in.

I suppose we were lucky in that we all went to the same school – infants, juniors and seniors, just across the playground. So we were all together most of the time. The surrounding area was lovely and we took many picnics to Triangle Woods, which were so safe in those days. The streams and brooks were so clean that we could drink the water without fear of it being polluted.

Although the Yorkshire people we saw were very poor, they were happy, friendly and very kind to us. We met many London evacuees in Yorkshire and became friends with some of them from Canning Town to the extent that we wrote and visited each other when we returned home and the war was over.

We learned to make bread in Yorkshire and in needlework classes we made lovely skirts and dresses. We were never reminded of the war in that lovely place – except when it was time for shopping and we had to use our ration books! It was very quiet there and I can't remember us ever having any air raids.

When the war was finally coming to an end we all returned home to Chatham and were able to live as a complete family again after years of disruption and separation – but I enjoyed my time in Yorkshire!

The following short article which appeared in the Chatham, Rochester & Gillingham News *for the 8th September, 1944, indicates the extent to which Kent was subjected to the flying bomb attacks:*

KENT AND THE BOMBS

In the eighty days of the major flying bomb attack on this country 2,400 of them fell in Kent, 100 more than fell in London. There were 1,388 shot down on Kentish soil, and

1,000 or more shot into the sea off the Kent coast. During the first week 101 were shot down over the county. The price paid by Kent was 152 dead, 1,716 injured, and considerable material damage.

The Medway Towns and district were among the many places to suffer. These figures are in addition to the other areas of Kent – Erith, Crayford, Bexley, Chislehurst, Sidcup, Orpington, Bromley, Beckenham and Penge – where 294 bombs fell, killing 310 people and injuring 2,392.

* * *

The final comment on this chapter is in the form of a poem written in 1944 by a seventeen-year old young lady who once resided at 28 Forge Lane, Gillingham. The poem was printed in the Chatham, Rochester & Gillingham News *for 22nd September, 1944:*

Fly Bombs over Kent

The fly-bombs they have shattered
The scenes of dear old Kent,
But not for half-a-second
Have we let our hopes be bent.

We are not frightened by these things,
They are only a bomb with a pair of wings,
But yet 'tis very sad to say
They have taken many lives away.

Each night and at the break of day
I look up to the Lord and pray
That we the people here in Kent
Will be given faith, courage and hopes unbent.

We will stand up to the air-raids,
The fly-bombs, shells and pain,
And one day when the world is stilled
Our Kent will rise again!

M. D. Gibson.

Chapter Ten

THE SCHOOLS' PERSPECTIVE.

School magazines are a mine of information, and can be the source of many interesting facts and figures. The following report is a good example of the problem most schools had to cope with in securing suitable premises in which to teach in the reception areas:

HEADMISTRESS'S REPORT, DECEMBER, 1939
FIRST TERM OF EVACUATION.

The County School for Girls, Chatham, re-assembled on Saturday, August 26th, and has been in session ever since. During the week preceding evacuation the girls were at school all day and were given informal lessons, sing-songs, etc.

After a practice evacuation on Monday, August 28th, the real evacuation took place on Friday, September 1st, the party consisting of 198 County School Girls, 65 brothers and sisters from other schools, and the staff.

The party was transferred to Faversham and billeting took place quickly and efficiently. There were, of course, misfits and the process of adjustment has given and still gives hours of work to the staff.

Since the original party reached Faversham 65 children have left and 85 girls have joined. The finding of billets for these extra girls has been done entirely by the County School Staff.

The number of girls at present attending the school is 228.

Our headquarters is the William Gibbs' School, where we are in possession on Tuesdays, Thursdays and Saturdays. On these days too we are allowed 30 girls on the premises of the Boys' Grammar School. Morning school for the seniors is from 8.35am to 12.35pm. and afternoon school for the middle school is from 1.20pm to 4.40pm.

On Mondays, Wednesdays and Fridays, the Gibbs' School pupils leave at 3.35pm, so our School Certificate classes and the Sixth Form attend for an hour from 3.40pm to 4.40pm.

During the first week of evacuation I was offered the use of the Preston Parish Hall, and the Upper Third Forms attend there alternate mornings and other classes attend for singing in the afternoon.

I then had the offer of the Queen's Hall (belonging to the Faversham Parish Church) and the L Vth and U Vth Forms are taught there on Monday, Wednesday and Friday mornings.

Owing to the kindness of Mr J. Neame, the Preparatory Form under Miss Kerr has

*The day of departure – a drawing by Ione Bates of Lower V.A. for the
school magazine depicting the evacuation of her school,
Chatham County School for Girls*

been allowed the use of a room in his house, and they consequently get full-time teaching in pleasant conditions.

In order to get yet more school for some of the classes I got the use of two rooms in the District Elementary School for Saturday morning and afternoon.

The playing field, which is about a mile from the school, has been well patronised on Monday, Wednesday and Friday and the organised games have helped very considerably in keeping the girls fit and healthy.

* * *

The following is an extract from what was probably the first attempt at producing a school magazine in South Wales by the pupils and staff of Chatham County School for Girls:

EDITORIAL.

For the second time in the history of our school, our country is at war with Germany. People were glad when the Great War, with all its hardships, came to an end. It had been a war to end wars, and yet in 1939 we found ourselves caught up in the same infernal machine.

The older part of Chatham Grammar School for Girls, photographed by the author in 1998, as it might have looked at the outbreak of war

We were rushed off to Faversham before war was declared, as Chatham was not considered a safe place. For many of us it was the first time away from home, but we settled down and were soon no longer strangers in a strange place. We were within easy reach of home and could see our parents quite often. Although perhaps we did not appreciate the stuffiness of Queen's Hall or the 'below-zero' atmosphere of Solomon's Lane, we spent a fairly happy nine months in Faversham, and many of us were sorry to leave when we were hastily re-evacuated in May (1940) to Wales.

However, now we find ourselves in a country with the most tongue-twisting names and an incomprehensible language of its own, hundreds of miles away from home, with not much prospect of getting back to England for a year or two – but, are we downhearted? No indeed! The Welsh people have been very kind and hospitable and some of us have become so attached to the place that we shall hardly want to go back when the war ends.

As regards the magazine itself – it has not been possible to have printed copies this year, but the one copy that has been made will be passed round for everyone to see. We wish to extend our thanks to Miss Simmons and V1 Sec. who have kindly typed the magazine for us. It is hoped that we shall be able to reprint some of the articles on evacuation and our activities in Wales, when the war is over and normal publication begins again.

*   *   *

The following poem also appeared in the same Welsh issue of the Chatham County School for Girls magazine:

Evacuation Alphabet

A for the apples we ate on the way.
B for the boys who were quite good that day.
C for the cap which fell out of the train.
D for the dust which gave our eyes pain.
E for the engine which took us along.
F for the fun when we each sang a song.
G for the girls of our County School.
H for the hats we wear as a rule.
I for the illness which some people had.
J for the jelly which perhaps made them bad.
K for the kit which we all had to take.
L for the letters for our parents' sake.
M for the money, we had quite a lot.
N for the nuisance when we got so hot.
O for the oranges kindly supplied.
P for the people who to help us all tried.
Q for the quest on which we were bound.
R for the row when lost gasmasks were found.
S for the songs as I've said before.

T for the long time which was rather a bore.
U for the umbrella which sadly got lost.
V for the vexed one whose tomatoes were squashed.
W for the weariness which we survived.
X for the 'xcitement when we arrived.
Y for the young ones who came in September.
Z for the zeal we shall always remember!

SARAH CULLEN and RUTH BARDEN (Upper VA)

One school which appears to have managed production of their magazine no matter what their circumstances, was the Sir Joseph Williamson Mathematical School from Rochester. The very informative article which is reproduced below appeared in the Summer Term, 1940, edition of the school magazine and highlights the almost impossible tasks teachers had to contend with in keeping the school together as a viable unit:

A SHORT HISTORY OF THE SCHOOL, SEPTEMBER, 1939 TO AUGUST, 1940

When we broke up for the summer holidays in July 1939, there was still a faint hope that a European war might be averted. Nevertheless, the outlook was already so menacing that we were warned we might at any time be recalled to school in order to carry into effect an evacuation scheme long prepared. That recall came on Friday, August 25th. The next day the school reassembled, though not in full strength, for parents whose children were in holiday resorts were asked not to send them back. A somewhat weary time ensued; every day the staff and boys met in the school, awaiting news of evacuation. Meanwhile final arrangements for the event were being pressed forward. At last, on August 31st, came the order to assemble early the next morning, with such baggage as could be carried by hand, in order to proceed by train to Canterbury.

Some may have looked forward with pleasure to this new adventure, but for most of us the day on which we left our homes for an indefinite period was a heavy one. Yet there was no sign of melancholy visible on the faces of the party that entrained at Rochester Station at 11.15am. Including the staff, their families, and a few sisters and younger brothers of some of the boys, our contingent numbered two hundred and sixty-three persons. The headmaster saw us off, but did not himself come to Canterbury until some days later; so that we were under the charge of Mr Pattenden.

The journey to Canterbury was soon over. On arrival, we were marshalled in the yard of the East Station, where, as we waited, we heard the fateful news that Poland had that morning been invaded. That news weighed more heavily upon us than our evacuation. Indeed, the kindness of the welcome accorded us at Canterbury did much to alleviate the sadness of exile. We were presently conducted to Simon Langton School, where Mr Pattenden, an old boy of that school, at least felt at ease, and where some of the staff renewed friendship with men they already knew, especially with Mr Humphreys, once a master at our school and now a member of the staff of Simon Langton, Mr H. L. Sharman, an old boy, and with Mr H. J. Hines, another old boy – of whom more hereafter.

At the school we were given light refreshments; then we were taken to the billets allotted to us. The majority of the boys and some of the staff found themselves in the Wincheap area, but others were housed in the finest residential roads. Everywhere, however, true hospitality and sympathy were evidenced.

For several days there was no possibility of beginning lessons. The boys had previously been divided into groups, each under the supervision of one of the staff; in order to keep them together and check their movements, meetings were arranged every day in such places as the Dane John and the playground of Simon Langton School. Soon the halls of the Presbyterian and the Baptist churches were generously offered us for indoor recreation, and this concession proved a great boon. Other activities in which several of our boys engaged were filling sand bags and helping to pile them against the outer walls of the new hospital, and hop picking, an occupation which provided a little pocket money for those who took part in it.

At the end of September, the Sixth and Upper Fifth Forms began lessons at St Augustine's College, while the other forms had two periods of schooling a week at St John's School. At last, through the generous co-operation of Mr H. J. Hines, principal of the Technical School, Canterbury, Mr Pattenden was able to make a most satisfactory arrangement, which was heartily endorsed by the headmaster. Mr Hines had managed to acquire the use of the Old Hospital, in Longport Street, as the site of his expanding school. Rooms were being refitted and redecorated for that purpose. But as the classes of the Technical School were to be held in the evenings, the rooms would obviously be unused during the mornings and afternoons. It was therefore decided to allow our school and the Rochester Girls' Grammar School, from which a large number of girls had been evacuated at the same time as our boys, to furnish a number of rooms with their own desks, and to open school on October 11th in this ample and pleasant building. The few boys of the Erith Technical School who had come to Canterbury also held classes there.

By arranging shifts, the schools were thus enabled to work to a time-table that provided a good number of teaching periods, especially for the upper forms. Every alternate week we had to begin at 8.40am, but we soon became used to early hours. We rather liked them, for it meant an early end of the morning session, to make room for the girls. Another concession of great value was the permission granted us by St Augustine's College to use their field on certain afternoons for rugby. Their field! How lovely it looked in the sunshine from the windows of the old hospital, with the spacious ruins of the old abbey on our side of it, and the handsome college buildings flanking it on another side. Indeed, our memories of the Old Hospital are very pleasant. There, in addition to bright and spacious class-rooms, even to large and well-equipped laboratories and a little workshop, we were provided with an excellent shelter in the basement to safeguard our bodies during hours of peril – but we had no raid in Canterbury! – and, to sustain them during working hours, with excellent meals (for those who came from a distance) cooked in the fine kitchen on the premises, and with milk, tea or coffee.

To Mr Hines and his committee, and to the Warden of St Augustine's College, we owe the deepest gratitude.

Naturally, difficulties occasionally arose in connection with the billets, but these were overcome without much delay, the local billeting officers being most helpful and sympathetic. As Canterbury is only twenty-five miles from Rochester, boys and parents frequently saw one another; and as, after the three air raid warnings that closely followed England's declaration of war, Kent was rarely disturbed by the screech of a siren, there developed a gradual drift back to the Medway towns, a movement encouraged by the decision to reopen classes in Rochester for the many pupils who had not been registered for evacuation.

Soon after we had been moved into the Old Hospital, Messrs. Morriss, Cheeseman, Stone, MacDonald and Pearce returned to Rochester to conduct lessons at the Mathematical School and at Hoo and Cobham vicarages, in each of which a room was provided – and a roaring fire in the severe winter weather – so that boys living in or near these villages could assemble on three mornings a week for instruction. To the Vicar of Hoo St Werburgh (Revd L. J. Walters) and the Vicar of Cobham (Revd J. Butler), we owe a deep debt of gratitude. The masters at Rochester had no easy task. They had no headmaster to consult, no office, no secretary, no porter, nor anything very helpful. Mr Morriss was in charge from October until his recall to Canterbury at the end of February. By February (1940) nearly 200 boys were attending school at Rochester, Hoo or Cobham, though receiving only six hours' instruction a week. When Mr Morriss returned to Canterbury, Mr Fearnley joined the staff at Rochester, where Mr Cheeseman was now put in charge.

A little before Christmas, the Mayor of Canterbury, Councillor Mrs Williamson, at her own expense gave each evacuated boy and girl a ticket in exchange for which could be obtained at any of certain shops a present worth one shilling. For this magnanimous generosity we and other recipients feel the sincerest gratitude.

At Christmas (1939) a week's holiday was granted. Most of the boys spent the time at their homes. For those who remained in Canterbury a fine Christmas dinner was provided. Miss Butterfield, Mr Clark and Mr Newth, the headmaster of Erith County School, presided at this function. Cinema shows, concerts, lectures and games further enlivened the festive season for the evacuees. Funds for these activities were generously provided by friends of the school and by the Rochester City Council and the Gillingham Borough Council.

Our numbers remained more or less constant during the hard winter that followed. Some boys left us, but new arrivals came. Work proceeded smoothly, while outdoor enjoyment was found in rugby, in snowballing and tobogganing. When spring approached, organised bicycle rides began.

On February 25th the members of our staff who were at Rochester, co-operating with several of the mistresses of the Girls' Grammar School, began to conduct classes at that school. Girls attended in the mornings and boys in the afternoons. We of the Mathematical School are greatly indebted to the staff of our sister school, who worked so harmoniously with our staff and made their stay at the Girls' Grammar School most pleasant. Mr Cheeseman, now in charge, had already, from November 6th, been teaching mathematics during two and a half days a week at the school. From February 25th to May 24th the Upper Fifth and Fifth Forms had lessons at the Mathematical School; there was not sufficient accommodation in shelters at the Girls' Grammar School for all the boys and girls attending school in Rochester.

At Easter there was again a short holiday and then came a big slump in our numbers. Our apparent immunity from air raids was doubtless largely responsible for the return of so many. In order to cope with the increase of pupils in the Medway towns a proposal was made to provide greater educational facilities in that district as soon as adequate shelters could be completed. Our scholars were to attend at both the Mathematical School and the Fort Pitt Technical School. It was hoped to begin the new scheme on May 27th. All the members of the staff except six were to return to Rochester, as it seemed likely that comparatively few boys would remain in Canterbury.

Arrangements were made for cricket on the ground beside the Sturry Road, and everything seemed set for the summer term. But alas for human plans! On May 10th, Holland and Belgium were suddenly invaded by Hitler's forces. Within a few days the resistance of the Low Countries collapsed and it became obvious that Kent, especially East Kent, had already ceased to be a safe refuge for children. Canterbury was declared to be no longer a reception area. Boys who had not returned home for the week's holiday granted at Whitsun were ordered to attend daily at the Old Hospital. Their parents and the parents of those who had returned were advised of a possible second evacuation. On Friday, May 17th, the headmaster told the boys that all whose parents consented were to be sent to South Wales, and that there would no longer be any schooling for them in Canterbury. To many the news came like a bombshell, rending ties of friendship and scattering hopes and visions; but to others the sudden change brought merely fresh excitement.

The next day was filled with hurry and bustle; postcards and labels had to be written, ration cards and library books given in, school books and bags and bicycles collected, lists made, groups arranged, telegrams and telephone calls answered, anxious parents interviewed and, at the billets, packing and provisioning effected.

At eight o'clock on Sunday, May 19th, the majority of our pupils who were still at Canterbury, together with others who had hastened from the Medway towns, met for the last time at the Old Hospital. Thence they walked to Canterbury West Station, where a special train was waiting to convey them, and girls of the Rochester Grammar School and the few boys of the Erith Technical School and some boys and girls attached to one or other of these groups, to Pontypridd in Glamorgan. To their surprise the mayor and town clerk of Rochester met them at the station. There too, were parents, hostesses, friends and members of the staff who were not accompanying the party, masters' wives and children, station officials, policemen, onlookers – in fact, quite a company, including a press photographer – anxious to wave farewell and wish good luck to one of the first parties of English evacuees rendered both pathetic and romantic by a second exile from their homes.

Accompanying our boys to Pontypridd were Messrs. Pattenden, Rigg and Thornhill, Mrs Rigg and Mrs Thornhill. Mr and Mrs Williams had decided to motor to Cardiff where Mr Williams has relatives, and to meet our party at Pontypridd Station.

At half-past nine the train steamed slowly out of the station to commence a seven hours' journey whose monotony was relieved by sunny glimpses of exquisite English scenery in Kent, Surrey and the Thames Valley, and by the lovely Welsh hills encountered soon after we had left Cardiff. Mild excitement was caused by the passage through the Severn Tunnel but, by the time Pontypridd was reached, most of the boys and girls who had become weary and hungry and thirsty – for only at a few halts was water available for them – were glad the journey was completed.

Cover of the 'Maths' School magazine, summer term 1940

Their reception at Pontypridd roused their flagging spirits. The education and billeting authorities of this town, having within a couple of days selected billets, organised helpers, prepared receiving centres and found educational facilities for the newcomers, arranged a truly generous welcome. The evacuees, who arrived a little after four o'clock, were met on the platform by the chairman of the Urban District Council (Mr J. Powderhill, J.P.), several of his councillors, the clerk of the council, one of His Majesty's inspectors, the chairman of the Local Education Committee, the education officer, and many others representing the teaching profession, including Mr E. R. Thomas, M.A., headmaster of the Pontypridd Intermediate School for Boys. Mr Williams was also there. But what drew their immediate attention was the great crowd that could be seen from the high platform and the strains of a band. It was the Salvation Army band, which had come to give them musical honours. The crowd, with difficulty held back by the police, had assembled not only to gaze, but also to enhance the official welcome. Through a section of this dense mass of people we were conducted to the Graig School, where refreshments were served and the boys medically examined. There some of us first met the headmaster of the Boys' Intermediate School and Miss Jenkins, the headmistriss of the Girls' Intermediate School, to which seminaries our boys and the girls of the Rochester Girls' Grammar School and of the Chatham Girls' County School were to be attached for an indefinite period.

The next morning we of the Mathematical School, in number ninety-eight – including some 'attachments' but not including the masters – met in the great hall of the Intermediate School in order to be divided into classes and into groups to be assigned to the care of the masters. On this day we had our first opportunity of inspecting and admiring the splendid new school buildings.

On Tuesday we were invited by Mr Thomas to sit in the hall with the boys of the Intermediate School in order to hear a lecture on the British and Foreign Bible Society, by Revd Cowys Williams, the Archdruid of Wales and a Welsh poet of great distinction. The lecturer's wit and cheerfulness made his talk a thing of pleasure. Mr Thomas took the opportunity formally to welcome, in gracious words, the boys of our school who henceforth would become attached to the Pontypridd Intermediate School. Mr Pattenden thanked Mr Thomas warmly; and thus began an association that has proved to us most encouraging and agreeable. While we have our own forms, our own timetable and our own games periods, yet we are under the general care of Mr Thomas, by whom we are allotted rooms for work; and our staff has the privilege of the use of the masters' common room.

To Mr Thomas and his staff we owe and feel the deepest gratitude for their genuine kindness and sympathy. We can assure them that they have made us happy in our exile.

On May 24th, the members of our staff who were at Rochester severed their co-operation with the Girls' Grammar School. The number of our boys attending school at Rochester had gradually risen to 270, and the number of the girls attending had also increased. It had therefore been decided to separate the boys and girls and give them full-time education, the younger boys at Fort Pitt and the seniors at the Mathematical School. But the news from Europe frustrated all such plans. Registration for further evacuation from Rochester was undertaken on May 27th, 28th and 29th. Again the headmaster was busy interviewing parents. Finally 123 boys were registered and with them were to travel twenty-three 'attachments' – younger brothers, sisters and so forth.

Late on Friday, May 31st, (1940) this second contingent of re-evacuees learnt that they were going to South Wales – but to Porthcawl, not to Pontypridd. So on Sunday, June 2nd – exactly a fortnight after the departure of the party from Canterbury – they left Rochester Station at eleven o'clock. On the same train were a number of girls of the Rochester Girls' Grammar School, bound for the same destination.

The day was full of sunshine; and the journey, through Clapham Junction, Woking, Basingstoke, Salisbury, Westbury, Bath, Bristol, the Severn Tunnel, Newport, Cardiff, Llantrisant – where some schools detrained – and Bridgend – where yet other schools alighted – proved most interesting. At Salisbury – the first stop – drinking water was provided, as also at Westbury and Cardiff. A little disappointment seems to have been felt that the passage through the Severn Tunnel did not last longer!

Our evacuees arrived at Porthcawl at half-past seven. As had happened at Pontypridd, a great welcome was given the newcomers. They were met by the chairman of the Urban District Council (Dr R. D. Chalke, J.P.), the clerk to the council, Messrs. Prys Jones and Powell (HM inspectors), prominent officials of the Welsh Board of Health, and many others, including one of whom the school owes a great deal – Mr L. S. Higgins, M.A., headmaster of the Porthcawl Senior School. Revd D. Hubert Thomas (Congregational Minister), who had been a good friend to the school, was also present. All the boys were taken, together with their luggage, by bus and car to Coney Beach Cafe, where a huge spread awaited them and where a medical examination was held. All were billeted by half-past ten that night.

As a result of intensive work it became possible to begin school at 1.15pm on Tuesday, June 4th. Accommodation was arranged at the Porthcawl Senior School, which our boys shared with the Rochester girls. This school was built in 1933 and is an exceptionally fine modern building including a wonderful gymnasium.

Here our boys worked a 36-period week, attending school in the afternoons from Monday to Friday and on Saturday mornings. On the mornings of Monday to Friday they could enjoy swimming under the supervision of Messrs. Pattison, Hook, Stone and Pearce, and cricket under Mr Hadlow. For this latter privilege we owe our best thanks to the headmaster of St John's Preparatory School at Newton, who very generously placed his cricket field at our disposal. At Porthcawl, Mr Cheeseman has acted as second master.

On June 12th, Messrs. Morriss, Meade and Stott left Porthcawl for Pontypridd. Until their arrival some of the work of the junior forms at Pontypridd had been taken by Mr W. N. Tallis, of Erith Technical School, who is a native of Pontypridd. With the arrival of Mr Morriss, cricket gear began to arrive also.

At Porthcawl the evacuees received an invitation to attend the pavilion on the evening of Sunday, June 16th, for community singing and a concert. The whole school was present, sitting in the gallery. Mr Fearnley acted as conductor. The boys' singing of 'Immortal, Invisible, God only Wise' to a Welsh tune was greatly appreciated by the Welsh audience, themselves no mean vocalists. The chairman on this occasion was County Councillor W. Howell, who gave the scholars a very warm welcome.

On June 21st a lecture for both boys and girls from Rochester was given in Porthcawl Senior School hall by Dr R. D. Chalke. His subject was 'Porthcawl and the surrounding district'. Dr Chalke, who is the author of the official guide to Porthcawl, gave a most interesting talk, which was thoroughly appreciated by his audience. He had been introduced by Miss Butterfield, headmistress of the Rochester Girls' Grammar School and, in the unavoidable absence of Mr Clark in Rochester, was thanked by Mr Cheeseman.

On Tuesday, June 25th, more boys arrived at Porthcawl from Rochester. They were escorted by Mr Taylor, who had been delayed in Canterbury and Rochester by the sad illness and subsequent decease of Mrs Taylor.

On July 6th, the traditional Founder's Day Service was held both in Porthcawl and Pontypridd, by the kind permission of the Vicars of All Saints' Church, Porthcawl, and St Catherine's Church, Pontypridd. At Porthcawl an inspiring address on faith and tradition was given by Revd Fenton Morley. The usual prayers were offered – the bidding prayer, the prayers for the school and the Old Boys – and the customary lesson from Ecclesiasticus, in praise of famous men, was read by the headmaster. The service began at ten o'clock and ended in time for the headmaster to travel in Mr Williams' car to attend the twelve o'clock service in Pontypridd. Here the vicar, Revd Shilton Evans, conducted the service and gave the address.

He exhorted the boys, following the example of Christ, the greatest pioneer in the world, and of another pioneer, Sir Joseph Williamson, to embrace the desire to push beyond the mass in the sort of things they think and say and do.

From the last week in June until after Founder's Day the Upper Fifth Forms at both Pontypridd and Porthcawl, and the Sixth at Pontypridd, were taking the London General School and the London Higher School Certificate examinations respectively. Except on two occasions at Pontypridd and one at Porthcawl the candidates were not disturbed by sirens. Those remaining at Rochester sat for their examination at Maidstone Grammar School, where Mr Taylor assisted with the supervision.

On July 9th, boys of the Mathematical School and of the Gillingham County School began to attend at the Chatham County School for Girls, under the headmastership of Mr I. Keen. Assisting him have been Messrs. Taylor and MacDonald of our staff and three members of the staff of Gillingham County School.

On July 16th, many of our staff and older boys at Porthcawl attended a packed meeting at the pavilion to hear Sir Paul Dukes, of the British Secret Service, give a fine and most encouraging address entitled 'Behind the scenes in Germany'. The lecturer held the attention of the audience for over an hour.

From July 26th to August 19th the boys enjoyed a short holiday, though they were expected to report five mornings a week. Swimming and cricket were arranged for their benefit.

Boys and staff of Rochester Mathematical School pictured in Pontypridd in 1940

It was expected that the Porthcawl section would join the Pontypridd section in September, but the scheme was vetoed by the Welsh Board of Health. So for an indefinite period one section of the Mathematical School will remain at Porthcawl – where, in addition to accommodation at the senior school, they have now the use of three rooms at the Congregational Church – and another section at Pontypridd. Which section is more fortunate is not easy to determine; Porthcawl is a beautiful seaside resort, with magnificent sands and sand dunes; Pontypridd lies within a circle of lovely and lofty hills, and among its amenities is an extensive park bordering the River Taff and containing facilities for various kinds of sport, and a splendid open-air swimming bath. Both places are exceptionally healthy; and in both not only is nature stimulating, but the inhabitants are generous and helpful.

* * *

The following extract appeared in the summer term, 1941, issue of The Williamsonian, *the magazine of the Rochester Mathematical School:*

On Saturday, July 19th (1941), we were told by the headmaster that after protracted negotiation it had been arranged that the Porthcawl section of the school would be joining the other part of our school in Wales at Pontypridd at the beginning of September. Some of the boys received this news with the enthusiasm that a new adventure always brings to the young, but others quite naturally had somewhat mixed feelings. We have heard of the many amenities which Pontypridd has that Porthcawl has not, and we know that educationally the move will be a definite improvement, as we shall now have accommodation in a very fine secondary school which is situated in the best part of the town. We shall miss our many friends in Porthcawl, but we are glad to know that our lads at Pontypridd have been quite as happy as we have been, and we shall join them with the confidence that we too shall find happiness there.

* * *

The following is another extract from The Williamsonian *school magazine, this time from the autumn 1942 issue:*

On July 7th (1942), towards the end of the London General School Certificate examination, and before our unique examination form was disolved, a farewell celebration in honour of the seven girls of that form was held in the dining room of the Pontypridd School. This took the form of a high tea – marvellously generous and varied in spite of war time restrictions (thanks to the contributions of individuals) – and of speeches. The headmaster and Mrs Clark, and the headmaster of the Pontypridd County School were present, as well as our staff at Pontypridd and Miss Featherstone. After the tea the headmaster called upon R. Hurley and A. Whaley to speak. We were entertained with two graceful speeches, in which tactful reference was made to the fair members of the form. Then topical verses, composed by themselves, were read by Jean Aldridge and Margaret Cullen. These were so much appreciated that a general desire was afterwards expressed that they should appear in this magazine. They are therefore given in full, first Jean's rhymed alphabetical list of boys of the form, and then Margaret's description of the staff:

ODE TO THE UPPER FIFTH
M.S.R., 1942.

A is for Arthrell, a diligent worker;
Also for Ashby, who's hardly a shirker.
B stands for Banfield and also for Bell;
What pranks they are up to you never can tell.
Brockwell's a bowler with not much renown,
While Capell's a fellow you'll seldom see frown.
At lessons, I fear, Crouch is not very hot,
But he's good on the sports field – believe it or not.
Daffey and Denney – their names go together;
We know that they're friendly in all kinds of weather.
Eames is a boy that you'll never hear groan,
While Ellen, we all know, is one on his own.
Now Howard is keen on a seat by the wall,
And Hurley's a fellow who's grown very tall.
Jones is a scout, and he's terribly keen,
And you'll always find Latin where Maurice Kidd's been.
Lamb is the linguist of our form, you know,
While Laming's a boy who has never a foe.
Do you think Llewellyn sounds like a Welsh name?
Because George is an Englishman, proud of the same.
Friend Sealey, you'll find, is a very nice fellow,
And fire-watcher Spencer's not what you'd call yellow.
Weatherhogg used to go out fishing daily,
While maths is the joy of statistical Whaley.
Wheeler's a cyclist – a cricketer too;
And Wright, with the Vicar, gets scripture to do.
(With all due apologies to the above named.)
J. K. Aldridge.

SCHOOL PERSONALITIES

Our Head, like a policeman, is awesome sometimes,
  But his bite's not as bad as his bark,
And although they may call him the Head of the School,
  In fact he is really a Clark.

To have made Mr Cheeseman a master of maths,
  In a school seems to me rather silly,
A 'cheese-man' should certainly be with his cheese
  In Stilton or Cheddar – or Caerphilly.

A school, like a ship, must be always in trim,
  Be it small, be it ever so big,
And a sailor will tell you a seaworthy craft
  Depends very much on its Rigg.

A master named Pearce had an old grey mare
  Whom he taught to quote Racine – and Moliere,
She said, given potatoes, 'Ah! pommes de terre!'
  They had 'French without tears' down at Widdicombe Fair.

We like reading Tennyson, Wordsworth and Blake,
  We also read Shakespeare sometimes,
But we like Latin poetry equally well
  Because of its metres and Rimes.

Now dear Mr Thornhill has missed his vocation -
  He should be commissioned to cheer up the nation;
I think he's the most interesting of 'blokes'
  With his history, geography, German and jokes.

Whatso'er you find to do
  Do it then with all your might.
Tasks there are like stone so heavy,
  Tasks there be like feathers light,
Heavy burdens lightly borne
Signify Miss Featherstone.

A certain young fellow one very wet day
  At the top of his voice he was singing,
Now why do you think Master Bell was his name?
  And the answer is 'cause he was ringing.

Now 'Hank' is a brilliant historian and should
  Be promoted next year to form seven,
When asked what he knew about 1066
  He said 'twas six minutes past 'leven.

And now to conclude I would just like to say
  How much we've enjoyed classes here,
And though very soon we'll be all gone away,
  We wish you good luck through the year.
                            Margaret Cullen.

Also in the same issue appeared this tribute to Pontypridd County School written by one of the masters of the Rochester Mathematical School:

To the Pontypridd County School

(First published in The Pontypriddian, *July 1942)*

Two years and more have passed since first we strayed
Within your hospitable halls, and heard
Your words of welcome; straight our hearts were stirred;
For here was peace, while Terror sought to invade
The homes that we had left. Here, unafraid,
We could relume the lamp of learning, gird
Our limbs for sport, be mirthful – in a word,
Live as strong youth should live, free, undismayed.
'Twas you who gave us thus our chance to grow
Nearer to English manhood day by day;
You gave us fellowship in work and play.
Now, in the war-scarred towns to which we go,
We shall remember, eager to repay
With love and gratitude the debt we owe.

R. E. Rigg

* * *

The following short extract is taken from information contained in the Holcombe (now the Chatham Grammar School for Boys) log book for the early years of World War II and was compiled by Mr W. T. Killen, who was a staff member of the school from 1930 until his retirement in 1989:

By 1938 the shadow of World War II was deepening. In 1939 evacuation forms were filled up and air-raid shelters were constructed. By September (1939) the shadow became a grim reality. The school was closed and 200 boys and 27 staff sought safety in Faversham.
  The school log-book records:
  Sept. 3rd, First air raid siren;
  Sept. 6th, Sand-bag filling.
  By November the first panic had subsided and the school re-opened with a few die-hard non-evacuees and two teachers. In February 1940 they left to amalgamate with Rochester Technical School.
  The grim turn of events in Europe resulted in the Faversham contingent being transferred to Pontypridd in South Wales. The following month the Chatham die-hards went to Swaun-Cal-Gurwen. The A.R.P. reigned supreme at Holcombe and another chapter in the school's history was closed.
  In 1941, after 28 years as headmaster, Mr Keen retired. His last log book entry seems both pathetic and triumphant. It lists the names of five Holcombeians decorated for bravery – and six killed on active service.

* * *

The following lists of Medway evacuees have been extracted from the admissions registers of some of the Welsh schools. The lists are by no means complete:

MAENDY SCHOOL, COWBRIDGE, SOUTH WALES:
Those from the Woodland Road Schools, Gillingham:
Margaret Andrews, Eric Billngham, Barbara Billingham, Patricia Blackman, Donald Blackman, Peggy Cowin, Lionel Dench, John Dench, Ronald Dench, Brian Else, Ian Frazer, Hilda Harding, Margaret Haywood, Anne Haywood, Daphne Lingham, Molly Lingham, Harold Lloyd, Jean Messenger, Maureen Messenger, Brenda McLean, Patricia Maltby, Peter Noake, Evelyn Oliver, William Packer, Hugh Powell, Kenneth Powell, Peter Savage, Gloria Shepherd, Ronald Smith, Douglas Stanley, Alitza Syrop, Patricia Spenceley, Jean Spenceley, Ruth Spenceley, Derek Tong, Ann Terry, June Wells, Audrey Wells, Shirley Walker, Geoffrey Tendell.

Those from Rainham School:
Diana Brookman, Jean Gale, Pamela Gale, Gwen Hayward, Pamela Hayward, Peter Hayward.

Those from Barnsole Road School, Gillingham:
Barbara Blackman.

Those from Twydall Lane School:
Patricia Noake.

RHOOSE SCHOOL, PENARTH DISTRICT, GLAMORGANSHIRE:
Those from St John's School, Chatham:
Sydney Barker, Brian Barnes, Jack Climpson, Gerald Elmore, George Fowle, Fred Green, David Horne, Margaret Johnson, Alan Johnson, Charles Pluthero, Anthony Sangwine, Marcus Sangwine, Gordon Sangwine, Michael Sangwine, Leanard Smith, John Stokes, Charles Stanfield, Raymond Waters, Stanley Waters, Ramon Wimble, Peter Wimble, Patricia Wimble, Arthur Wood, Leslie Wood, Maurice Whitlock.

Teachers accompanying the St John's School pupils:
S. G. Edney and R. W. Stubbs.

WHITCHURCH SCHOOL, GLAMORGANSHIRE, SOUTH WALES:
Those from Hempstead Junior School, Gillingham:
Robert Foster.

Those from Richmond Road School, Gillingham:
William Pugh.

Those from Byron Road School, Gillingham:
Brian Rogers.

Those from James Street, Gillingham:
Gordon Mottram.

Those from Gillingham (school unknown):
James Filmer.

Those from St George's School, Chatham:
Reggie Cobb.

Those from St Paul's School, Chatham:
Michael Terenzy.

Those from St Michael's School, Chatham:
Eric Sinfield.

Those from Chatham (school unknown):
James Smith.

Those from a private school, Chatham:
Ronald Staines.

Chapter Eleven

EPILOGUE

In the preceding chapters we have followed the journeys and shared in the emotions of those children who, so many years ago, were separated from their families and sent to strange places. We have seen how these children have coped with not one unknown location, but several, not one strange billet, but many. We have seen the bulk of them separated from parents, from sisters and brothers and friends. We have also seen how unhappy and homesick some of them were to become, and how a proportion of evacuees were abused, mis-treated and neglected. But we have also seen the love of many foster parents towards the evacuees, which has resulted in many of the children remaining in contact with their foster parents right into adult life.

We have seen how schools had to cope with inadequate school premises and how the teachers themselves took on duties far beyond what was required of them in looking

8th May 1945 – the war in Europe is officially over

VE Day street party in Chatham, 1945 (Photo by Don Phillips)

after the evacuated children – to become *in loco parentis*!

As Christmas 1944 approached, the time came for most of the Kent schools to return home, but this in itself brought more problems. Many homes had been destroyed by enemy action, some schools were still occupied by the armed forces – and the war was still going on!

Changes in family life had also occurred. It is hard to imagine the depths of emotion that must have engulfed the mothers on the days their children were evacuated. It must have been a heart-breaking decision, taken after much soul-searching, to sign the papers that allowed their children to be taken away, their destinations unknown and their future uncertain.

Added to this wrench, many women were separated from their husbands because of the war and thrust into the most challenging of occupations. Today we can't imagine making such sacrifices. But at the time, there was little choice. For many Kent women, the role of wife, mother and domestic worker was totally transformed into an independent, temporarily childless, government worker. And all this while the family home was under threat of destruction by enemy action.

These changes, that women had to endure for many years during the last war, made the resumption of 'normal' family life very difficult when the war finally came to an end. Men returned to find that their wives had learned to manage without them – to become independent! And that their youngest children hardly knew them. I was evacuated at the age of three years four months and when our family was reunited at the end of the war, I asked my mother who the strange man in the house was. My mother replied, 'He is your father!'

Mothers were reunited with children who had either bonded to wonderful foster parents, or resented their own parents for sending them away. It is little wonder that family life became strained for many and that divorce rates soared. A whole generation of children had been robbed of their right to a normal family life with their natural parents and siblings, and we can only guess how this would go on to affect their own parenting skills in later life.

Many look back now and realise that evacuation and separation from their families has had a long-term detrimental effect. For others being evacuated was to be the most exciting time of their lives.

The Government Evacuation Scheme during the last war was a unique experience, an experience unlikely to happen ever again, and I hope my book will provide a permanent record of events that happened to those children from the Medway Towns and North-West Kent who were part of the greatest exodus this country has ever known.

I cannot finish without mentioning those hundreds of thousands of kind-hearted volunteers, the unsung heroes and heroines, who, during wartime, helped in so many different ways to make life more bearable for the evacuees: the Women's Voluntary Service (later to become the Women's Royal Voluntary Service) who did sterling work in the organisation, transportation and reception of the evacuees; the St John Ambulance Service; the Red Cross organisation; the Civil Defence; the British Legion; the Scouts and Guides movement – even the brass bands who welcomed many of the evacuees when they arrived at some destinations! And then there are many of the mothers of evacuees who accompanied their children, and who would go on to become welfare officers and helpers, looking after the welfare of the evacuees, dealing with billeting problems, escorting sick children to medical appointments, running evacuee hostels. The list of these unsung heroes and heroines is seemingly endless – and should not be forgotten!

One such 'unsung heroine' was a young lady from Pontardawe named **Ailsa Evans** *who came to know many of the evacuees and who eventually made her home in the Medway town of Chatham. The following passages are Ailsa's own memories of the war years – and beyond.*

At the time of the outbreak of the war in September 1939, many smaller towns and villages in designated reception areas of Britain experienced an influx of evacuees. Pontardawe, situated in the valleys near Swansea, South Wales, was one such community expected to find homes for evacuees. The Billeting Officer and Civil Defence Unit had three months to arrange billets and other accommodation for evacuees from a variety of locations, including London, Liverpool, Birmingham – and the Medway area! It was a daunting task for any group of people to arrange satisfactorily. It is doubtful if parents volunteering to allow their children to be evacuated realised that billeting in Reception Areas was compulsory. Anyone with room to spare was forced to accept an evacuee into their home.

The main employment in the Pontardawe area was at the Gilbertson Steel Works. When the Gilbertson family moved from their old home to a more modern one they presented Ynisderw House in Swansea Road, Pontardawe, known in the village as The Big House, to the local council. Once under the control of the council, some adaptation of its interior went ahead to accommodate various organisations, although it was never adapted for any one specific purpose.

All Saints Church held Sunday School classes on the premises and the brass band held band practices there. The house was the natural choice as a hostel for evacuees, thus reducing the demand for billets in private houses. Pontardawe was fortunate in that in the early days of evacuation the compulsory nature of billeting was not applied. 'The Hostel', as the house became known, had sufficient room to provide dormitories and living accommodation for short or long term occupancy. (Ynisderw House was eventually demolished sometime after the war and was replaced by new flats.)

Ailsa Evans became involved in all these activities as a member of the Civil Nursing Reserve. At that time, apart from her nursing work, she was captain of the 2nd Pontardawe Girl Guides who held their meetings at The Hostel. Mrs Gilbertson was the District Commissioner for Girl Guides, thus retaining a link with her old home. It is from Ailsa Evans' own story that it is possible to learn a little about how evacuee children from the Medway Towns were received and absorbed into the local life in June 1940. The arrival of the children and the teaching staff was to have a profound effect on her own life.

Ailsa Evans spent much of her early life at the Cross Hotel, Pontardawe, where her family lived and ran the hotel. After leaving school she studied nursing in London before returning to Pontardawe to work locally. Her mother died shortly before the outbreak of war and the family was no longer living at the Cross Hotel. Her sister, who was teaching, moved away, leaving Ailsa to keep house for her father. It was a time of compulsory employment but, because of her father's situation, Ailsa was exempt. She wanted to make use of her nursing knowledge so she joined the Civil Nursing Reserve and volunteered for work in the local Civil Defence.

The Civil Nursing Reserve was an organisation consisting of nurses who had retired from nursing for personal reasons. They were then 'on call' to go wherever they were needed. Through this organisation Ailsa volunteered for local work. Recruits attended refresher courses, in her case at the Penrhwtyn General Hospital at Neath. As part of the course she also learned about the treatment for gas warfare cases. Once the refresher course was over she became involved in the work at the The Hostel.

In May 1940, the war situation in Europe was grim as German forces invaded the Low Countries and France. On 29th May 1940 the local medical officer of health called a meeting of groups involved in civil defence in Pontardawe. He warned them to expect the arrival of school children from Chatham on the afternoon of Sunday 2nd June. That left less than three days to organise accommodation for the evacuees.

Everything did not go according to plan. Camp beds were delivered but insufficient bedding to use with them. It was necessary to beg for blankets and pillows among friends and relatives to help with the shortfall in supplies. The Women's Section from the local British Legion worked day and night. They scrubbed and cleaned the dormitories and did a wonderful job in the short time allotted to them.

Glencoe Road, Ordnance Street and Walderslade Schools arrived from Chatham on Sunday 2nd June. It was a very hot afternoon when they arrived at the GWR station at Neath. They continued the rest of the journey to Pontardawe by coach. When the school groups arrived, some of the teachers were unhappy with aspects of the arrangements, but had no idea of the amount of work that had been accomplished on their behalf. The teachers, weary after travelling for hours, were worried about the welfare of their charges. The children had spent far too long with little food and no drink. To add to the misery, many of the trains used in the evacuation were without corridors and, consequently, no access to lavatories.

Once in Pontardawe the children were taken to local schools for medical examinations and provided with food and drink before delivery to their billets. The medical separated the healthy children from those with a variety of problems. The latter group was destined for The Hostel. One little girl arrived smothered in spots – she had chicken pox! A day or two later her sister was covered in similar spots, to be followed shortly by others who had shared the same compartment on the train. Other problems were cases of children found to have head lice and/or fleas. These had to be quarantined until cleared of their unwelcome lodgers.

The boys and girls from the three Medway schools covered age ranges from infants only five years of age to teenagers of fourteen on the verge of leaving school. The five year olds went to Brynamman, some older children to Godregraig, Ystalyfera and Clydach, all within a three mile area and administered by Pontardawe Council. The senior pupils travelled to Pontardawe to attend the grammar and technical schools.

Ailsa remembers many of her young patients and charges with affection. As well as cases of measles, warmer weather brought with it outbreaks of impetigo and scabies. One little girl was ill for a long time. She needed a great deal of care as she was recovering from an appendix operation followed by complications. Another girl she remembers very well and with great sadness, because the poor girl developed tuberculosis and spent some time in Graig-y-nos Sanatorium. At that time tuberculosis was a dreaded disease with little hope of recovery. To the dismay of everyone associated with her, the little girl died. Another, nearly old enough to leave school, was so homesick that she ran away and became lost in the countryside. The police found her and returned her to the hostel. For some the homesickness was very hard to bear. Others settled well and enjoyed their time among the mountains, so very different from the countryside they knew back home. Some of the children, having little knowledge of the locality, asked how much they needed to pay to walk or play on the mountains.

The children at The Hostel were cared for by the nursing staff, helped by volunteers who came daily to do any work needed. They bathed and put the children to bed before the night staff arrived on duty at 8pm. Running the hostel was full time work catering for the sick children and those for whom private accommodation was considered unsuitable. There were children moving between billets and others who just happened to be sent there, rather than to homes with local families. The cook, who came in each day was a Mrs Strange. Her other work was as the family cook at the home of Mrs Gilbertson. The only paid member of the staff was the matron.

The local people made a great effort to show the children that they were welcome in the village. The Sunday following the arrival of the evacuees, people with private transport took the children staying at The Hostel on an outing to Swansea and the Gower Coast for the day.

Among the teachers who accompanied the children to Wales, was a Scotsman, Frank Semple, who was the science and games teacher at Glencoe Road School for Boys. With him in Pontardawe were his wife and two children, Jean and Douglas. As Jean was only five years old she was sent to Brynamman on arrival. However, she was retrieved before nightfall and reunited with her parents. They all stayed at the Dynevor

Hotel for a time. It was from there that Frank Semple wrote a letter home via the *Kent Messenger* dated 22nd June 1940, as spokesman for the other teaching staff. The letter reads:

'I have been asked by the Chatham teachers to this area to write on their behalf assuring readers of the *Kent Messenger Observer* of the excellent welcome that has been accorded to all the children that came here from Chatham two weeks ago.

'No effort has been spared by the householders to make their pleasure at the presence of the Chatham children evident.

'The children themselves are extremely happy and have found new pursuits in the different countryside in which they find themselves. Parents and friends have no need to worry about their distant charges for their health and happiness are as sure as anything can be in these times.

'But only one point needs attention, and this is the matter of luggage. Only hand luggage could be brought and weighty spare boots were often neglected. Might I suggest to parents that as children are more active than ever on rather rough country roads there will soon be need for new boots or for repairs. Arrangements between parents and foster parents on this matter will be desirable.'

Mrs Semple was a diabetic and, tragically, in November she died. As a teacher, Frank Semple was committed to staying with the children from his school, so he and his two young children continued to live at Pontardawe. A year later, in 1941, Ailsa Evans married Frank Semple and they set up home in the village with the two children.

In 1942 Frank Semple was ordered to return home to Chatham. Ailsa elected to return with him and keep the family together. Her relatives and friends were horrified that she should be going into a danger area. She was certain that it made little difference. After Swansea was so badly bombed, she realised that no place could be considered safe.

Once back in Chatham, Frank Semple became involved with secret war work. He used his scientific knowledge to instruct soldiers into the mysteries of radar at the Maidstone Technical School, from where, after passing necessary examinations, they went on to what were known as 'hush-hush' courses.

In 1943 Ailsa and Frank Semple added a daughter, Norah, to the family. As the years went by Frank Semple became involved in the political life of the town and was elected to serve as a councillor for Chatham. In 1958 he and Ailsa became mayor and mayoress of Chatham, positions they held until 1960.

Ailsa Semple, now an octogenarian, still lives in Chatham where she arrived in the grim days of the war. She has not lost her strong Welsh accent but considers herself to be as much at home in Chatham as in Pontardawe. Unfortunately, Frank Semple died some years ago but is well remembered by his old pupils. Ailsa keeps in touch with some of 'her evacuees' and has many memories of those days. She takes great pride in the silver badge of the Civil Nursing Reserve, as do many of her friends who served with her.

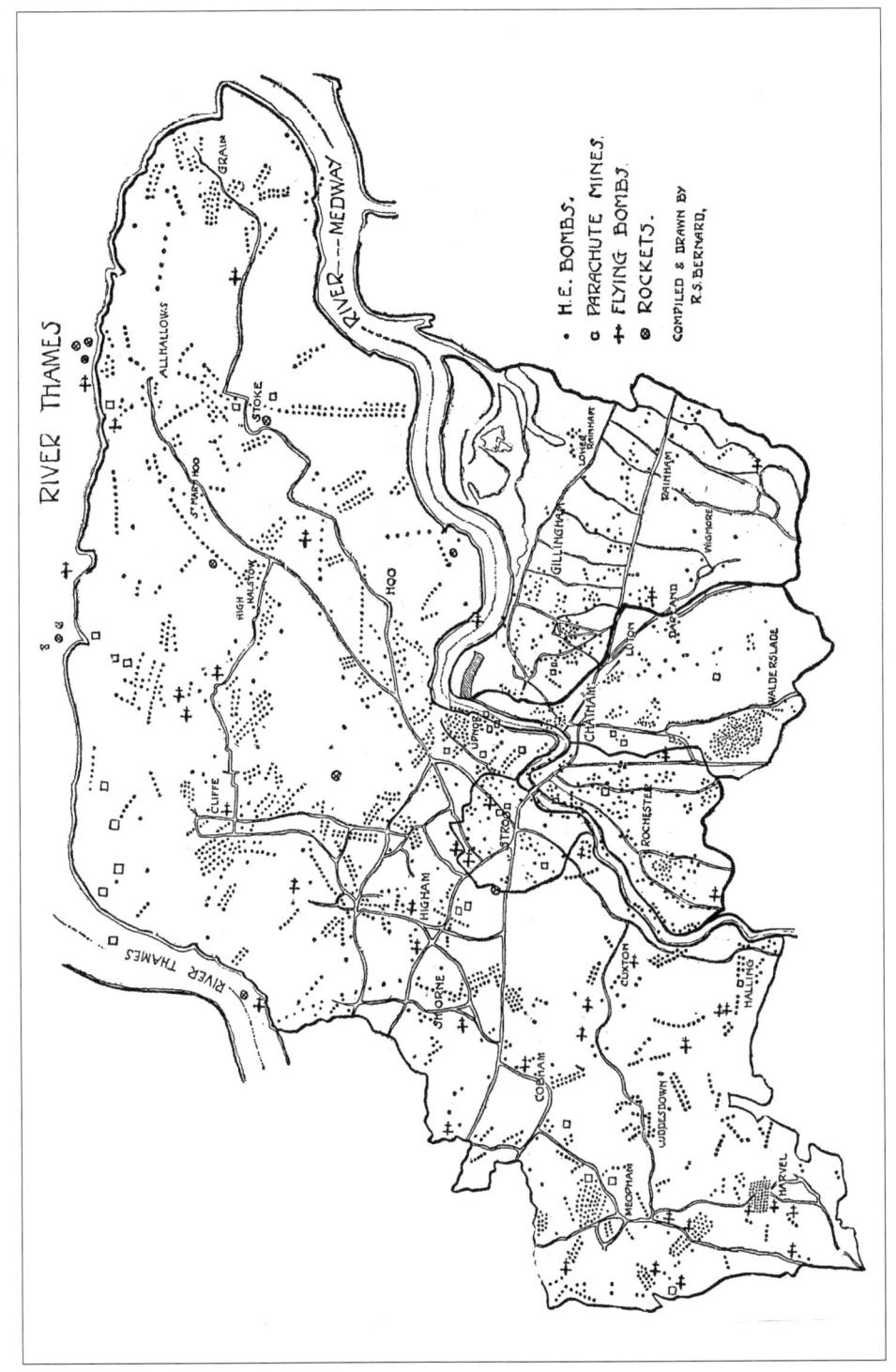

During the war, the Medway towns, happily, did not suffer a sever blitz. However, nearly 3,000 high explosive bombs were dropped and this map shows where they fell. In addition, nearly 30,000 incendiary bombs rained on the area.

ACKNOWLEDGEMENTS

My warmest thanks go to all those ex-evacuees and other contributors, mentioned by name in this book, who were kind enough to share their evacuation memories with me and without whose help this book would not exist. My special thanks go to Mrs Winifred Rolfe who, through her own research and continual support throughout this project, was able to provide me with a great deal of information on the Medway evacuees. My thanks also go to Phillip Connolly for providing me with information and photographs of those who were evacuated to Dartington, Devon.

Others, whose help has been invaluable, include the editors of the following newspapers for allowing me to quote from many articles on the evacuees:

Gravesend Reporter
Medway News
Herne Bay Gazette
South Wales Argus

And to the *Kent Messenger Group* and the Imperial War Museum for allowing me to reproduce certain evacuee photographs.

I am also grateful to the staff of the following libraries, heritage centres and record offices: Canterbury Reference Library; Gillingham Reference Library; Strood Heritage centre; Glamorgan Record Office; County Record Office, Cwmbran.

My thanks also go to the headteachers of the following schools for the help they have given me during my research:

Chatham Grammar School for Boys; Chatham Grammar School for Girls; Sir Joseph Williamson's Mathematical School, Rochester.

I am grateful to Sawd Publications and to Joy Richardson, author of *Children in Retreat*, for allowing me to quote an evacuee account from that book. Also, my thanks go to the secretary of the Evacuees' Reunion Association, to BBC Radio Kent and to the secretary of the Medway Queen Preservation Society for helping me in my search for material.

Finally, my most grateful thanks go to my wife, Deborah, whose continued patience, understanding and constant help and encouragement have made this book possible.

Every effort has been made to trace the copyright holders of certain photographic material in this book but we apologise if any copyright has inadvertently been breached.

8th June, 1946

To-day, as we celebrate victory, I send this personal message to you and all other boys and girls at school. For you have shared in the hardships and dangers of a total war and you have shared no less in the triumph of the Allied Nations.

I know you will always feel proud to belong to a country which was capable of such supreme effort; proud, too, of parents and elder brothers and sisters who by their courage, endurance and enterprise brought victory. May these qualities be yours as you grow up and join in the common effort to establish among the nations of the world unity and peace.

George R.I.

The King's message which was sent to all British schoolchildren in recognition of the hardships they had to endure during World War II

INDEX OF CONTRIBUTORS AND EVACUEES

Aldridge, J. K.: 226
Austen, Pamela: 37
Austin, Gladys: 26, 80
Bassett, Winnie: 26, 110
Bates, Ione: 47, 125, 214
Batey, Molly: 42, 176
Bell, John: 195
Bradley, Daphne: 46, 123
Brooker, Eugene: 105
Brown, Alan: 199
Brown, Audrey: 150
Brown, Elizabeth: 205
Bubb, Emily: 114
Chew, Pamela: 36
Churchman, Bill: 55, 136
Clark, John: 30, 81
Collins, Norman: 191
Connolly, Phillip: 179
Costen, Pamela: 36, 90
Coultrop, Maurice: 154
Cross, Helen: 49, 129
Cullen, Margaret: 227
Eacott, Edna: 126, 210
Evans, Ailsa: 233
Fleetney, Colin: 162
Gilbert, Brenda: 183
Godden, Roy: 119
Hallums, Mildred: 167
Hallums, Joyce: 175
Hoad, Peter: 51, 130
Hopperton, John: 183
Hughes, Patricia: 46, 121
Hussey, Mr and Mrs: 57
Johnson, Arthur: 40
Jones, Jean: 114
Killen, W. T.: 9, 137, 228

Kingsnorth, Freda: 123
Lyons, Jean: 44, 148
Macey, Rosemary: 147
Manley, Colin: 133
Moller, Karen: 117
Mortley, Pat: 48, 128
Murray, David: 138
Nokes, Shirley: 161, 204
Ostler, Margaret: 154
Phillips, Don: 27, 82
Phillips, John (Jack); 28, 82, 91
Porter, Ann: 208
Porter, Mary: 205
Porter, Molly: 207
Prager, George: 56, 151
Prentice, Janice: 38
Prosser, Joan: 45
Quarrington, Joan: 22, 103
Reader, Janice: 155
Rickard, Freddie: 133
Rigg, R. E.: 228
Rusted, Sheila: 140
Semple, Frank: 236
Shilling, Dorothy: 39, 145
Silver, Fred: 61, 135
Smith, Iris: 185
Smoker, Albert John: 24, 152
Stevens, Margaret: 188
Ticker-Fry, Nora: 43, 101
Towlson, E.: 24, 75
Townsend, Roy: 60
Tudman, Miss: 42
Turner, Frank: 49, 129
Utteridge, Derek: 41, 75
Utteridge, Roy: 202
Whale, Mrs E.: 53, 132